AF084478

Guru, Maṇḍala, *and* Guru Maṇḍala

Guru, Maṇḍala, *and* Guru Maṇḍala

Yagyaman Pati Bajracharya

Translated from the Newar by
Samuel M. Grimes *and*
Alexander James O'Neill

VAJRA
Publications Inc.Pvt.Ltd.

Published and Distributed 2025 by
Vajra Publications Inc.Pvt.Ltd.
Jyatha, Thamel, P.O. Box 21779, Kathmandu, Nepal
Tel.: 977-1-5320562
e-mail: vajrabooksktm@gmail.com
www.vajrabookshop.com

© Authors, 2025. All rights reserved.
No part of this book may be reproduced in any form or by any means electronic or mechanical, including photography, recording, or by any information storage or retrieval system or technologies now known or later developed, without permission in writing from the publisher.

ISBN 978-9937-624-53-4

Printed in Nepal

Table of Contents

Translators' Preface VII

Abbreviations IX

Introduction XI

1. Guru: Meaning, Definition, and Importance 3
2. The Guru's Importance: Sphere and Demarcation | *guruyā mahatva kṣetra va sīmā bandī* 27
3. Selecting a Guru | *guru varaṇa* 57
4. Examination of the Disciple | *śiṣya parīkṣaṇa* 71
5. The Guru-Disciple Tradition | *guru-śiṣya paramparā* 85
6. The Meaning, Importance, and Boundaries of the Maṇḍala | *maṇḍalayā artha mahatva va sīmitatā* 101
7. Maṇḍala Generation | *maṇḍala sṛjanā* 113
8. The Guru Maṇḍala | *gurumaṇḍala* 121

9. The Occasion to Undertake the Guru Maṇḍala | *Guru Maṇḍala chyalegu avasarat* 155

10. The History and Importance of the Guru Maṇḍala | *Guru Maṇḍalayā aitihāsik pakṣa va viśeṣatā* 169

Appendix A: The Guru Maṇḍala Procedure in the *Kriyāsamuccaya* 187

Appendix B: The Offering of the Ratna Maṇḍala | *ratnamaṇḍala dohalapegu* 193

Appendix C: 15 Steps for Summoning and Propitiating a Deity in Guru Maṇḍala 203

Glossary 209

Index 213

Translators' Preface

All Sanskrit passages in the original are retained in the translation in Roman transliteration following IAST standards. In the cases where Yagygaman Pati translates the Sanskrit into Newar, we copied his Newar translation to English but did not translate the original Sanskrit. Often, Yagyaman Pati leaves the Sanskrit untranslated to Newar; in these cases, we have provided an English translation of the Sanskrit. There are several instances where an explanatory gloss was given of the Sanskrit rather than a Newar translation. For clarity, we have sometimes added an English translation of the Sanskrit and an English translation of Yagyaman Pati's Newar gloss. However, often the gloss is enough for an English reader to understand the Sanskrit without belaboring the explanation with a redundant translation. In those cases, we have not added our translation to the gloss.

Sometimes, we place a word in Yagyaman Pati's original in parenthesis to display the heavy incorporation of a Sanskrit lexicon into Tibeto-Burman Newar writing on Buddhism. This is for the benefit of readers familiar with Sanskrit but perhaps unfamiliar with Newar so that those readers may get a sense of the heavy incorporation of Sanskrit into the Newar literary lexicon. We also elide the final -a in our transliteration of several Sanskrit terms so that the terminology is closer to contemporary conventions in spoken Newar, e.g. recording *vrat* rather than *vrata*, or *kalaś* rather than *kalaśa*, or *samskār* rather than *samskāra*, etc.). The original, written in Devanāgarī script, does not mark whether a word is pronounced a final -a or not, so such necessity of clarity was unnecessary in the original.

We retain Yagyaman Pati's notes, which appear at the end of each chapter as they did in the original. These are marked with Roman numerals. The translators' footnotes are marked with numbers and appear at the bottom of the page containing the relevant text.

We wish to express our thanks to Bidur and Lokesh Dangol. We are grateful to Bidur for agreeing to publish our book the moment he was asked. We thank Lokesh for his hard work on the proofs and swift turnaround. We thank Eric Huntington for commenting on a section about creating the Ratna Maṇḍala. Most of all, we thank Yagyaman Pati for trusting us to make his work available in English.

Samuel M. Grimes
and
Alexander James O'Neill

Abbreviations

New.	Newar
N.	Nepali
S.	Sanskrit
P.	Pāli

Introduction

In December 2016, my guru, Yagyaman Pati Bajracharya, instructed me to translate his 2004 book *Guru, Maṇḍal va Gurumaṇḍal* from Newar to English. I protested that my Newar was not sufficient enough to accomplish this. "You will manage," he replied. But shortly after leaving Nepal at the close of 2016 I began my Ph.D. studies at the University of Virginia, and the prospect of completing this translation became more remote. Every time I saw the book on my shelf I was ashamed of my failure to have translated it.

In 2022 I saw a Facebook post celebrating a reissue of this book distributed among Yagyaman Pati's close disciples in Kathmandu. Now I was done with my Ph.D. and could undertake the project. Still, if my Newar was insufficient in 2016, it was certainly insufficient in 2022. I hesitatingly asked my colleague Alexander O'Neill if he would be interested in co-translating the book with me. Although he had previously translated several Mahāyāna sutras from Classical Chinese or Sanskrit to English, and was presently engaged in a project at SOAS to train machines to read handwritten Newar manuscripts, I expected that such an out-of-the-blue request would turn him off. Instead, Alexander enthusiastically responded that he would be very interested in collaborating on the translation.

We translated the short book from June of 2023 to January of 2024, on alternating chapters. Serendipitously, Alexander was part of an ongoing project to create an online Newar-English dictionary, and we utilized the lexicography from this work for our translation. We also utilized OmegaT software, a legacy language-learning program, that allowed for an exceptionally efficient translation project.

We are delighted to offer a modern Newar Buddhist exegetical text translated into English for the first time. Newar Buddhism has a reputation for being the most difficult form of Buddhism for outsiders to access, with those interested in the tradition limited to exploring texts or anthropological fieldwork but with no teachings from actual living Buddhists. Here, readers will find the position of one of the most prominent Newar Buddhist teachers of the 21st century.

The original work is in Newar, but features heavy inclusion of Sanskrit, and a bit of Pali. The academic style of Newar, in which it is written, incorporates several archaic features and occasionally includes terminology that does not appear in modern Newar vernaculars. For these reasons, the work would be exceedingly difficult for the average Newar speaker to read. The book's intended audience is *vajrācārya* priests already steeped in their Buddhist tradition. While the esoteric tenor of the book would alienate many Newar speakers, it is this very aspect that will appeal to the translation's intended audience of serious practitioners and academics. By removing the linguistic barriers, we hope to make this formerly inaccessible book easily approached by the informed reader.

Yagyaman Pati's work offers discourses supported by arguments from several sources. He draws from the Pali Canon, tantric songs in vernacular languages, English-language works of secondary scholarship and philosophical and religious texts in Sanskrit. In his exposition, one detects a hint of the *paṇḍita* style indicative of the Sanskrit Buddhist commentarial tradition. His personal library consists of dozens of issues of the rare Buddhist text journal *Dhīḥ*, translations to English and studies of Buddhist tantras, scholarship on Tibetan writings of translators and *mahāsiddhas*, and his own, personal library containing hundreds of handwritten, medieval Sanskrit manuscripts. These sources are woven throughout his writings, quoted as they are relevant, so that Yagyaman Pati can incorporate the whole of the Buddhist tradition in his writings on tantra.

Cover to the 2004 original—*Guru, Maṇḍal va Gurumaṇḍal*

Biography of Yagyaman Pati Bajracharya

Yagyaman Pati Bajracharya was born during a bright fortnight in 1941 during the auspicious month of Guñlā. He grew up in the joint family home overlooking Basantapur (New. Maru Tole),

Kathmandu's royal square. The family home encompasses the southern wing of Lāyku Bahī (New. for "Palace Bahī"), a *vihāra* that contains as its saṃgha only the four sub-lineages of the Buddhist *rāj* guru (New. *rāj gubhāju*, royal preceptor) lineage. His is, therefore, a lineage from which Buddhist *rāj* gurus were once drawn—although he does not consider himself to bear a blood relation to either Pushpa Ratna Bajracharya or Majushri Bajracharya, the two most recent respective *rāj* gurus and members of another of the four sub-lineages. He emphasizes that his most recent blood relative to function as the *rāj* guru lived about a century ago. Yagyaman Pati's family's primary saṃgha membership is that of Śikamū Bāhāḥ, and the family traces their ancestry to Līlāvajra, who is credited in the Kathmandu tradition with founding that *vihāra*, as well as Kathmandu's namesake Kasthamandap, a stone's throw away. Until the construction of the kumārī ghar during the reign (1750-1768) of Jaya Prakash Malla, the ancestors of the family resided directly adjacent to Śikamū Bāhā, but relocated across the royal square to Lāyku Bahī following that building's demolition in the mid-18th century.[1]

Despite his ancient pedigree, Yagyaman Pati grew up in a middle-class home and the family occasionally struggled financially. His father was Bhojmanpati, and his mother Astamaya. He had an older brother, Gangamanpati, an older sister, two younger brothers, Gyanmanpati and Shyammanpati, and two younger sisters, Ratna Devi and Nilam. His father worked a number of jobs, including occasionally as a *vaidya*, a traditional Newar Buddhist tantric physician, but never as a *purohita* (professional ritual priest) due to the financial instability such a profession afforded. Nevertheless, his father possessed clout as a ritualist, for as a young man Bhojmanpati served as the

[1] Tree, Isabella. *The Living Goddess: A Journey Into The Heart Of Kathmandu*. New Delhi: Penguin Books, 2014. pp. 301.

karmācārya (ritual master) during the 1918 renovation of the Svayambhū mahācaitya, meaning he was one of the three leading *vajrācārya* priests in the event.[2] Bhojmanpati advocated on behalf of the *vajrācārya* caste and the Newar people and their language in the political and public spheres, and as a result, was thrown in jail a number of times when Yagyaman Pati was a youth.

Yagyman Pati's father Bhojman as a young man.
Photo courtesy of Shailendra Bajracharya.

[2] Shakya, Hem Raj. *Śrī Svayambhū Mahācaitya: The Self-Arisen Great Caitya of Nepal.* Translated by Min Bahadur Shakya. Kathmandu: Svayambhu Vikash Mandal, 2004. pp. 321. The other two leading priests are the *upādhyāya* (preceptor) and the *mūlācārya* (chief priest).

Yagyaman Pati with his brothers and parents in front of the main shrine at Jamal Bāhāḥ. Undated. Estimated ~1970. From left, Yagyaman Pati, Gangaman Pati, Bhojman Pati, Astamaya, Gyanman Pati, Shyamman Pati. Photo courtesy of Shailendra Bajrachayra.

The *pañcabuddha* at the base of the Goṣṛṅga Hill during a *saptavidhānottar pūjā* performed during the 1918 Svayambhū *mahācaitya* renovation. Yagyaman Pati's father, Bhojman Pati, is in the center of the *pañcabuddha*. Photo courtesy of Yagyman Pati Bajracharya.

Yagyaman Pati was a feisty child, so much so that he changed his birth name, which was Upendraman. Unhappy with the name's phonetic resemblance to the Newar word for flea (New. *upiyāñ*), Yagyaman Pati would not respond when his name was called at the start of primary school, leading to his father being informed that his son was chronically truant. When the cause of the problem was uncovered, the young Upendraman was asked his name, to which he replied: "Yagyaman. My name is Yagyaman."[3]

Although his father was not himself a professional ritualist, the young Yagyaman Pati was steeped in the Newar Buddhist tradition from an early age. As is customary, he received *cūḍā karma* around six years of age. Bhojmanpati trained him in several rituals, and he has practiced Buddhist rituals daily for over 75 years. But his father adamantly discouraged Yagyman Pati and his brothers from pursuing any kind of ritual training with the goal of becoming a *purohita*. He encouraged them to seek professional positions that would pay well and ensure their security.

Following his father's advice, Yagyaman Pati enrolled, tuition-free, at Durbar College in Kathmandu to study economics, and following completion there he studied at the newly-established Tribhuvan University. After a year-and-a-half working at Rastra Bank, he resigned to study for his Master's of Commerce examinations, which he passed. He was called by the Finance Minister personally to be offered the position of Section Officer in the Department of Finance. He traveled, mostly by foot due to the lack of paved roads, all around Nepal, accompanying the

[3] "*Yajñamān. Mero nām Yajñamān.*" Aji's Podcast. August 13, 2021. I thank Birat Raj Bajracharya for his invaluable help in the transcription and translation of this podcast interview.

accountant general and completing audit work. Yagyaman Pati reflects that those days "were a lot of fun."[4]

Then, in the early 1960s, the Land Reform and Management initiative was started, and Yagyaman Pati was appointed to head it. He found himself working six days a week, from 8 in the morning to 9 in the evening. As a reward for his diligence, in 1965, at age 23, the king awarded him the Gorkha Dakshina Bahu medal, the second highest award given under the Kingdom of Nepal. He wore his medal proudly to work and was given significant authority for a civil servant, including the rights to arrest someone and have them jailed, and even the right to shoot someone![5] He performed well, eventually reaching the position of Chief Auditor General for Nepal. At such a high rank, he initiated several progressive reforms for the civil service to attract people to government jobs and away from the more lucrative private sector. He implemented a policy wherein one's pension increased commensurate with a salary increase, and he expanded pension opportunities available to the police, the military, and teachers. He also introduced a policy that allowed a widow to collect 50% of her late husband's pension income. After 28 years of government service, Yagyman Pati retired.

Becoming a Teacher, Leader and Master

As he settled into retired life, like so many pensioners, Yagyaman Pati became increasingly interested in his heritage. Not only had he received extensive ritual training from childhood and received *dīkṣā* alongside his wife, but he possessed an extensive, inherited manuscript collection. Perusing these manuscripts, he developed increasing curiosity regarding the intertextuality and development of those rituals he had practiced all his life. He also grew

4 "*Majjāko thiyo*," ibid.

5 Ibid.

frustrated over what he perceived to be an excess of ritual impropriety among Newar Buddhist practitioners, ranging from the man doing his own daily morning *pūjā* in private to the *purohita* in the temple undertaking large rituals like the fire ritual (*hotra*). He sought to address these shortcomings and correct them.

Around the beginning of the millennium Yagyaman Pati launched his movement, which has largely taken the form of educating practitioners on the meaning behind rituals and *caryānṛtya* (tantric dance). This movement started with lectures aimed at lay practitioners to educate them on the meaning behind the rituals performed for them by *vajrācārya purohitas*, who may or may not have had this knowledge. He also lectured on general topics in Mahāyāna, such as emptiness and compassion. These lectures could be considered introductory, intended to give Newar Buddhists a basic literacy in the philosophical and ideological foundation of their religion.

Yagyaman Pati encountered resistance as he began teaching to lay practitioners. Professional *vajrācārya* ritualists, frequently suspicious of change and ever-wary of competition, did not immediately accept him. After all, here was a career civil servant suddenly giving instruction to their patrons. Teaching Dharma to lay practitioners, especially in the form of storytelling from *avadānas* and *jātakas*, is a common practice undertaken by many *vajrācāryas* educated in the subject.[6] It was not the teaching itself that was the issue, but rather the sudden popularity of someone whom they perceived might become a potential competitor. From their point of view, he was nothing but a bored retiree, moving in on their territory. The Newar community, like any tightly-knit

---

[6] For a summary of the tradition of storytelling see Lewis, Todd & Naresh Man Bajracharya. "The Tradition of Vajrācārya Storytellers," In *Dharma and Puṇya: Buddhist Ritual Art of Nepal*. Edited by Kim, Jinah & Todd Lewis. Leiden & Boston: Hotei Publishing, 2019. pp. 156-161.

group, is no stranger to gossip and disagreement, but this resistance was not enough to dissuade Yagyaman Pati. On the contrary, it motivated him to continue his education initiative and confirmed for him that the community was in need of reform.

Perhaps as a direct result of this initial drama, Yagyaman Pati has largely conducted his activities at *vihāra*s that receive little traffic and ritual activity. He began teaching biweekly classes in Kathmandu around 2004,[7] in a private home at Iku Bāhāḥ, a Newar Buddhist temple site.[8] These informal gatherings quickly took on a more formal identity with the foundation of Yagyaman Pati's teaching organization, Bauddha Darshan Adhyaya Pucha (Buddhism Study Group).

He also intentionally taught female students from the start of these classes, most prominent among them *gurumā*s, the wives of *vajrācārya*s, *vajrācārya*s who are themselves always referred to as *guruju*s in the context of ritual performance. This was done to expand awareness of the Dharma among Newar Buddhists beyond the limited confines of the male priesthood, and reflects Yagyaman Pati's position that Buddhist practice and teachings are meant for all, not only a select few. After six months of training these women, he organized an event in 2005 at Jana Bāhāḥ in Kathmandu where 108 *gurumā*s chanted the *Pañcarakṣā*, a Vajrayāna text invoking five protector goddesses, as part of the elaborate and apotropaic *saptavidhānottara* ("seven element")

---

[7] Lewis, Todd, and Naresh Man Bajracharya. "Vajrayāna Traditions in Nepal." In *Tantric Traditions in Transmission and Translation*, edited by David B. Gray and Ryan Richard Overbey, 87–198. New York: Oxford University Press, 2016. pp. 170.

[8] Rospatt, Alexander von. ""Past Continuity and Recent Changes in the Ritual Practice of Newar Buddhism. Reflections on the Impact of Tibetan Buddhism and the Advent of Modernity." In *Revisiting Rituals in an Changing Tibetan World*, 209–40. Leiden & Boston: Brill, 2012. pp. 236..

ritual.[9] Such a public recitation is "traditionally restricted to *vajrācārya* (and *śākya*) males" and "signifies a marked departure from established practice by putting females in public, in charge of the ritual use of a sacred tantric scripture."[10] Yagyaman Pati has included female practitioners in several major rituals, mostly through their chanting of scriptures throughout a ritual performance, such as the *Nāmasaṃgītī*.

To date, there are around 350 women involved in such public recitations, and Yagyaman Pati has reflected that the prominent Theravāda nun Dhammawati has supported him in this endeavor.[11] However, his instruction of non-traditional students, whether females, foreigners, or Hindus, has met with criticism from conservatives. He has been "scolded" frequently, and for his inclusion of women, has been labeled a "destroyer of the family" (New. *kulāṅgār*) and "destroyer of the lineage" (Nep. *kulako nāśa*). To this he replied, "let them say anything they want."[12]

---

[9] von Rospatt 2012: 224. "This 'seven Element Ritual' is a very popular Newar householder practice, one that conjoins meditation and ritual offerings. It is performed for any Buddhist deity, but is most popularly directed to *caitya*s, and bodhisattva images such as Avalokiteśvara or Tārā. [...] The central ritual focuses on the water jar (*kalaśa*) surrounded by eight auspicious symbols (*aṣṭamaṅgala*) that symbolize the eight bodhisattvas. The purpose of this *pujā* [sic.] is to take refuge in Triple gems [sic.], offer sensory objects, confess misdeeds with vows not to commit them again, rejoicing in the good deeds of the śrāvakas, bodhisattvas, and Buddhas, and finally, requesting that the latter not enter *nirvāṇa* [italics added], but remain in *saṃsāra* for the welfare of living beings. Those doing the ritual then take a bodhisattva vow to seek Buddhahood in the future; the *Saptavidhanuttara pūjā* reaching completion after all are given the bodhisattva initiation (*abhiṣeka*)." Lewis & Bajracharya 2016: 146-147.

[10] von Rospatt 2012: 224.

[11] Aji's Podcast. August 13, 2021.

[12] Ibid.

Younger female students, ranging in age from as young as ten up to the mid-30s, have sought Yagyaman Pati out for instruction in *caryānṛtya*, tantric song and dance. Such instruction has resulted in over one hundred women receiving Padmanartyeśvar *dīkṣā*, the necessary consecration for performing *caryānṛtya* independently and publicly, named for the "Lotus Lord of the Dance" (Skt. Padmanṛteśvara, New. Nāsadyaḥ). A group of his female students (all Newars, none of whom are *vajrācārya*s or *śākya*s) opened the studio Nepa Dance Academy in the early 2010s to teach *caryānṛtya* to girls in the kind of environment where one would typically encounter types of modern dance. The studio integrates traditional tantric dance into a contemporary

Yagyaman Pati Bajracharya, in full ritual garb as Vairocana, in the courtyard of Śikamū *Bāhāḥ* on the day of Kasthamandap's 2016 consecration. Photograph by Samuel M. Grimes.

setting, one which is ubiquitous for dance studios worldwide. Groups of the teenaged students of Nepa Dance Academy regularly receive Padmanartyeśvar *dīkṣā* from Yagyaman Pati. The tradition, however, can only be made so flexible—to my knowledge, none of these women may themselves confer Padmanartyeśvar *dīkṣā*, and in the public recitation of tantric texts, the leader of the ritual is always a male.

A Critical Leader

In July 2008, the fifteenth renovation of the Svayambhū *mahācaitya*, the most important *stūpa* in Nepal, began. Sponsored by the Tibetan Nyingma *lama* Tharkung Tulku, who is based at his Nyingma Institute in Berkeley, California, this was a grand affair involving hundreds of artisans, priests, devotees, organizers, and municipal workers that opened with a deconsecration rite in 2008 and a reinstallation ritual in 2010. Many of the major rituals were performed in tandem, with the Newar camp on the Western side of the *stūpa* and facing Amitābha, while the Tibetans sat on the Eastern side and faced Akṣobhya. Both sides claimed the site.

Yagyaman Pati was one of the three Newar priests leading the rituals. He functioned as the *karmācārya* (ritual master) alongside *upādhyāya* (preceptor) Badri Ratna Bajracharya and *mūlācārya* (chief master) Satvara Bajracharya, who was subsequently replaced by Min Bilash Bajracharya, while the elders (New. *thakāli*) from the caretakers of the stupa and site, the *śākya* Buddhācāryas, functioned as the *jajmāns* (patrons).[13] As

[13] Shakya, Manik Ratna. "Pujas Performed." In *Light of the Valley: Renewing the Sacred Art and Traditions of Svayambhu*, edited by Tsering Palmo Gellek and Padma Dorje Maitland, 120–23. Cazadero, California: Dharma Publishing, 2011. pp. 120. Shakya refers to Yagyaman Pati as "a scion of the lineage of royal Buddhist priests serving the king and kingdom."

karmācārya, Yagyaman Pati performed the same role his father had undertaken 90 years previously. He co-led the deconsecration in 2008 wherein the life-force (Skt. *nyāsa*, lit. "deposit") of the *stūpa* was removed and placed for storage in a water pot (Skt. *kalaśa*) to remain for the duration of the ritual, before the final consecration in 2010 when it was placed back into the *stūpa*, a ritual also co-led by Yagyaman Pati. Alongside the other two leading *vajrācāryas* and dozens of other *vajrācārya* and *śākya* priests, he performed rituals throughout the two-year period that the *nyāsa* stayed in the water pot waiting to return home, firmly establishing his position as a leader in the Newar Buddhist community through his involvement in this monumental event.

During this interim period, in 2009, Yagyaman Pati traveled to Portland, Oregon to lead the *pratiṣṭhā* rituals[14] for the establishment of Nritya Mandala Mahavihara. This center, established and managed by *caryānṛtya* master Prajwal Ratna Bajracharya, is the first officially-sanctioned Newar Buddhist temple outside of Asia. The decision to involve Yagyaman Pati in its creation was due to his position at the intersection of erudition and respect within the tradition on the one hand and a willingness to engage in innovation and expand the possibilities of that tradition on the other. While it received a traditional *pratiṣṭhā* at its establishment, the lack of any *guthis*, a hereditary Saṃgha, or any fully-consecrated practitioner beyond Prajwal Ratna leaves the official status of Nritya Mandala Mahavihara unclear when viewed in light of the tradition in Nepal. This situation notwithstanding, Yagyaman Pati's leadership in the center's consecration cemented his status as one of the very few *vajrācārya* priests with an international platform.

---

[14] *Pratiṣṭhā* are installation rituals. There are *pratiṣṭhā* rites ranging from installing deities in statues, to installing deities and power into a building.

Starting in 2014, perhaps as a direct result of his experiences participating in the Svayambhū *mahācaitya* renovation, Yagymanpati expanded his outreach to include interested Buddhācārya priests at Svayambhū. For two years, until the course was complete, he traveled to Svayambhū twice a week and lectured to those priests who chose to attend the classes in the building across from the Ratnasambhava shrine on the southern side of the *stūpa*. This outreach was motivated by an intention to increase the erudition of the *śākya* Buddhācāryas concerning the meaning behind the rituals they perform daily. Long marginalized by *vajrācārya*s, who have tended to treat the Buddhācāryas as assistants to be told what to do, Yagyaman Pati maintains that the Buddhācāryas, as caretakers of Nepal's most sacred Buddhist site, are taken for granted and deserve to be given more respect and consideration than they have historically received. To ensure ritual propriety atop the Gośṛṅga Hill (the hill upon which the *mahācaitya* sits), those performing the ritual must understand what they are doing and why. That is to say, this need for propriety includes not only the stūpa but also the shrine of Śāntipūr, which is also atop the Gośṛṅga Hill and to the northwest of the *stūpa*.

During the mid-2010s Yagyaman Pati began teaching foreign students. At first, this teaching exclusively took the form of instruction in *caryānṛtya*, tantric dance and singing. He trained a Japanese woman, a Belarussian woman, and an American man (not me), the last of whom was sent to Yagyaman Pati by Prajwal Bajracharya in Oregon. In all these cases, Yagyaman Pati enlisted his students to instruct these individuals in "courses" that he had designed and to regularly report the students' progress to him. In 2014 the Belarussian woman and the American man gave a public performance to an of mostly elderly Newars at Jamal Bāhāḥ.

In 2016 Yagyaman Pati performed a *caryā* dance to renew and aid in the twelve-year restoration of the Bijeśvarī/Ākāś Yoginī temple overlooking the western side of the Bishnumati River about halfway between Svayambhū and Thamel. He was particularly pleased to participate in this ceremony, as his father had participated in renovations at both Svayambhū and Bijeśvarī as well.[15] Also in 2016, he accepted an American, me, as his first foreign student for ritual training. Several of Yagyaman Pati's devoted students selflessly instructed me in the practice of the gurumaṇḍala ritual, and I was subsequently given initiation (Skt. *dīkṣā*, New. *dekhā*) into the Vajrayāna and worship of Amoghapāśa at Jamal Bāhāḥ.

Productivity as a Response to Crisis

The vitality of traditional Newar Buddhism has waned since the establishment of an official Hindu kingdom, and the rate of decline seems to have increased exponentially with each new Hinduizing regime. These political shifts, combined with the loss of land and patronage as well as competition from Theravāda practitioners in the form of new teachings and rituals, all contributed to the reduction in status and influence of the Newar Buddhist institution. As if the challenge was not already great enough, this reduced status directly influences how the institution is perceived by young Newars, who are, as a result of the state of their traditional institutions, far less likely to engage in ritual practice and religious learning than their ancestors a few generations back. They instead pursue vocations and paths they believe are better suited for the globalized world, of which Nepal is now a part. It is, therefore, already a critical situation that revivalists like Yagyaman Pati find themselves operating within. This situation was made even more dire by the occurrence of two disasters: the 2015 earthquake and the COVID-19 pandemic that dramatically impacted Nepal throughout 2020 and 2021.

15 Aji's Podcast. August 13, 2021.

Rather than allow these crises to deal a further blow to Newar Buddhist institutions, Yagyaman Pati turned each into an opportunity, which, in combination, arguably placed his religious tradition in a better position than it was prior to the earthquake. A casualty in the 2015 nationwide devastation was the medieval building Kasthamandap.[16] This structure is where the name for Kathmandu was drawn, and the impressive open-air temple is revered by Nepalese of all religions. He was a leader in the Rebuild Kasthamandap Project, involved at every step of the way, beginning with consecrating the ground where Kasthamandap[17] would be constructed. This massive ceremony, involving hundreds of participants performing rituals, reciting sutras, and

---

[16] Kasthamandap is traditionally said to date to the 7th century, during the Licchavi period. Indeed, inscriptions that date to that period were found in excavations following the structure's collapse in 2015. However, this only establishes that a structure, possibly named Kāṣṭhamaṇḍapa as well, was located on the site. Considering the many earthquakes in the region, it would be unlikely for a structure of such antiquity to have survived so long. Further complicating the 7th century dating is that every other structure around Kasthamandap in Basantapur (most of which fell in the earthquake) would then postdate Kathmandu's namesake by nearly 1,000 years, as all of those structures date from no earlier than the 15th century, and most are from after 1600. Furthermore, the Sultan Shams ud-dīn raid of the Valley in 1349 is said to have left no wooden structure intact. This does not seem to be hyperbole, as the Maheśvara Temple in Panauti is the only major wooden structure antedating this event. Even if the claim of leaving no wooden structure left intact is hyperbole, it would nevertheless be strange indeed if such a prominent building as Kāṣṭhamaṇḍapa was left alone during this raid.

[17] Maru, the Newar name for Kathmandu's royal square, Basantapur, is, itself, derived from the Sanskrit "*maṇḍapa*," The *maṇḍapa* namesake is certainly Kasthamandap, meaning "Maru Sattal" is a redundant name, since with the Newar name derived from the Sanskrit for a rest house, functioning adjectively to modify the Newar word for the same structure, "*sattal/sataḥ*," Maru Sattal could therefore be translated as "The rest-house rest house."

2016 Kasthamandap *pratiṣṭhā*. Photograph by Samuel M. Grimes.

Yagyaman Pati leading the procession of priests-as-the-five-buddhas for the *Saptavidhānottar pūjā* at the 2016 Kasthamandap consecration. Photograph by Samuel M. Grimes.

singing and dancing, was televised and brought significant attention to both the restoration of the site and Yagyaman Pati's movement. Once the structure was complete, with only aesthetic additions remaining, Yagyaman Pati led several major rituals inside the nearly-reconstructed Kasthamandap. Most of these were held in 2021 and featured a variety of rituals, all of which involved coordinated *caryā* dances performed by up to 15 participants at a time. When the golden plinth was placed atop the completed Kasthamandap in September 2021, it was Yagyaman Pati who ritually installed it.

Yagyaman Pati installing the final finial atop Kasthamandap in 2021. Photograph courtesy of Binita Magaiya.

Near the end of March 2020, Nepal entered a nationwide lockdown in response to the COVID-19 pandemic. Due to the state of the national infrastructure and a lack of knowledge worldwide concerning the epidemiology of the virus, the government felt they were left with little choice but to undertake drastic measures. The government's implementation of a lockdown was sprung on the population with no official warning, and lasted until July. People were suddenly stuck in their homes, and temple courtyards and major intersections, usually a frenetic bustle of humanity, were deserted.

One might think that such a situation would significantly hamper Yagyaman Pati's teaching efforts. On the contrary, he adapted swiftly and moved his entire operation online, holding all of his regular classes over Zoom.[18] Bauddha Darshan Adhyaya Pucha, his Buddhist Study Group formed in the early 2000s at Iku Bāhāḥ, moved from the temple teaching rooms to the Zoom room. The shortcomings of being separate and only able to meet online are apparent, but the predicament had an immediate, productive aspect. Yagyaman Pati had already utilized Facebook as an organizing tool and regularly instructed his students to make Facebook posts explaining particular Buddhist teachings. While this provided a public interface unprecedented for traditionally insular Newar Vajrayāna, the other side of the interface, Yagyaman Pati, was not the one giving the teachings directly; rather, teachings were read or listened to after they were posted and, therefore, not live. When he began teaching on Zoom in April 2020, links were publicly shared on Facebook without the need for registration or a password, effectively making the rooms open to all.

[18] I have written elsewhere on this. See Grimes, Samuel M. "Online Rituals in Newar Buddhism." *Tricycle*, July 28, 2020. https://tricycle.org/trikedaily/newar-buddhists/.

As his stature increased, Yagyaman Pati grew his ecumenical outreach to Buddhists outside the Newar tradition. This primarily includes Newar Theravāda practitioners and those in Tibetan lineages, those in the shared space of the Kathmandu Valley. He has especially advocated to the Newar Buddhist community for Shree Dhar Rana Rinpoche, for whom he feels a particular affinity. In 2018, Yagyaman Pati took over as president of the Dharmodaya Sabha, the Buddhist organization founded in the 1940s by the Theravāda monks expelled by the Rana prime minister (an uncle of Shree Dhar Rana). As chief of this organization he has striven to involve all Buddhists in Nepal in events he maintains are crucial for all Buddhists, which most frequently took the form of practices in the reconstruction of Kasthamandap.

Following the completion of the rebuilt Kasthmandap in 2021, Yagyaman Pati scaled back his involvement with Valley-wide heritage endeavors and focused primarily on teaching to his direct disciples at Jamal Bāhāḥ. Here a group of young *vajrācārya*s began to undertake many ritual and teaching responsibilities, thereby allowing Yagyaman Pati to further reduce his activities as he passed his 80th birthday. At Jamal, regular group *pūjā*s now occur, with monthly *saptavidhānottara*, *aṣṭamī vrat*, and fire *pūjā*s. The teaching room of Bauddha Darshan Adhyaya Puca is bedecked in framed portraits of Yagyaman Pati, and teaching here is undertaken by students such as Anand Muni Bajracharya and Binita Magaiya. In an adjacent room, his disciple Rajeev Bajracharya meets with clients for tantric healing sessions and astrological readings. In the upper rooms, ritual is regularly practiced as an increasing number of young *vajrācārya*s from across the Valley come to learn from Yagyaman Pati's students, rather than Yagyaman Pati himself, cementing the continuation of his lineage and the impact of his life's work.

Organization of the Book

Alexander and I had several brainstorming conversations regarding how to structure the format of our translation and how heavily we should annotate the text. We settled on presenting the book in an approachable way to both serious practitioners and academics. At times, it was difficult to resist the urge to make extensive arguments in the notes referring to secondary scholarship on Newar Buddhism. We followed the annotation style of Todd T. Lewis and Subarna Man Tuladhar's translation of Chittadhar Hṛdaya's poem *Sugata Saurabha*, entitled *The Epic of the Buddha*. Like *Guru, Maṇḍal, va Gurumaṇḍal*, this poem heavily utilizes Sanskrit terminology and makes frequent references to culturally specific Newar rituals. Rather than write lengthy endnotes detailing this terminology and this ritual, like Lewis and Tuladhar we try to make our notes as simple and digestible as possible to not distract from the body of the text itself. After all, here we present Yagyaman Pati's scholarship, not our own.

We made slight rearrangements to the organization of chapters to improve the reader's encounter with the text. Chapter 9 was originally Chapter 2. The original text's Chapter 11, on the *Kriyāsamuccaya*, is now an appendix. We have also split the book into two thematic sections. Part One: Guru includes Chapters 1-5, and Part Two: Maṇḍala includes Chapters 6-10. The result of this rearrangement may be seen below.

Original	Translation
	Part One: Guru
1. Guru: Meaning, Definition, and Importance	1. Guru: Meaning, Definition, and Importance
2. The Occasion to Undertake the Guru Maṇḍala	2. The Guru's Importance: Field and Demarcation
3. The Guru's Importance: Field and Demarcation	3. Selecting a Guru
	4. Examination of the Disciple
4. Selecting a Guru	5. The Guru-Disciple Lineage
5. Examination of the Disciple	*Part Two: Maṇḍala*
6. The Guru-Disciple Lineage	6. The Meaning, Importance, and Boundaries of the Maṇḍala
7. The Meaning, Importance, and Boundaries of the Maṇḍala	7. Maṇḍala Generation
8. Maṇḍala Generation	8. The Guru Maṇḍala
9. The Offering of the Ratna Maṇḍala	9. The Occasion to Undertake the Guru Maṇḍala
10. The Guru Maṇḍala	10. The History and Importance of the Guru Maṇḍala
11. The Guru Maṇḍala Procedure in the Kriyāsamuccaya	Appendix A: The Guru Maṇḍala Procedure in the Kriyāsamuccaya
12. The History and Importance of the Guru Maṇḍala	Appendix B: The Offering of the Ratna Maṇḍala
	Appendix C: 15 Offering Steps

Chapter 1, "Guru: Meaning, Definition, and Importance" presents Yagyaman Pati's views regarding major Buddhist concepts such as guru, wisdom (*prajñā*) and the Three Jewels. The chapter begins with an etymology of the term "guru," which utilizes both Newar and Sanskrit. Yagyaman Pati lays out the case for the critical need to have a guru to gain liberating *prajñā*. He also details the connection between the tantric Buddhist master (*vajrācārya*) and the role of the guru without referring to the Newar Buddhist caste (*jāt*) of *vajrācārya*, demonstrating his position that one becomes a *vajrācāra* not through birth but through merit and accomplishment. The Buddha, Dharma, and Saṃgha are each explained respectively from a Mahāyāna position, and all three are linked to liberating *prajñā*. This chapter closes with a brief discussion on Vajrasattva, the ideal *vajrācārya* and practitioner of the Vajrayāna.

Chapter 2, "The Guru's Importance: Field and Demarcation," examines the role of the guru across a range of Buddhist traditions. The concept of guru is subdivided into several categories to demonstrate the wide range of potential guru types and to illustrate that the propriety of each type corresponds to the needs of the prospective disciple. Yagyaman Pati quotes from a wide range of Buddhist scriptures and commentaries to illustrate the different kinds of gurus. Pali texts are referred to when examining the gurus of Śākyamuni Buddha and when discussing the purpose of a guru in the Theravāda. Tantric thinkers such as Advayavajra (Maitrīpā) and Āryadeva are referenced, as are texts such as the *Advayasiddhi* and *Jñānasiddhi*. Tantric songs in a Middle Indic language are also referenced when lyrics attributed to Līlāvajra are cited. Here we see the full range of Yagyaman Pati's learning as he details the figure of the guru across the whole Buddhist tradition.

Chapter 3, "Selecting a Guru," provides several criteria that a prospective guru must adhere to before being accepted as a teacher. Yagyaman Pati states that this topic may be a "surprise" to his Newar audience, who may believe that "testing" a guru is disrespectful. To argue his case, Yagyaman Pati cites a wide breadth of Buddhist scripture from the *Milindapañha* to Maitrīpā to eventually make the point that a guru should be benevolent, wise and caring. But this caring may sometimes take a stern form, as he illustrates with the relationship of Tilopā and Nāropā.

Chapter 4, "Examination of the Disciple," follows directly from the previous chapter to lay out the criteria that the guru should use to inspect a potential disciple. Woven throughout descriptions regarding how to sufficiently scrutinize a student are examples taken from tantric Buddhist lore (Indrabhūti), songs (Līlāvajra), and a text attributed to the *mahāsiddha* Anaṅgapāda. Continuing his *paṇḍita* style, Yagyaman Pati synthesizes several texts across a range of tantric Buddhist positions to showcase the universality of his position within the Vajrayāna.

Chapter 5, "The Guru-Disciple Lineage," provides a short exposition on the importance of *paramparā* (lineage or tradition) in transmitting the Dharma. Following this, several lineages corresponding to various tantric traditions are given. Some of these are associated with particular tantras (the *Guhyasamājatantra* and *Cakrasamvaratantra*), while others are local to Nepal (the lineages of the *Kriyāsamuccaya* and Līlāvajra). Lineages given in modern English scholarship (the lineages in David Snellgrove's *Indo-Tibetan Buddhism* and Roerich's translation *The Blue Annals*) are also given. The point here is to demonstrate that both the Vajrayāna and Buddhism writ large are only passed along from teacher to student.

Chapter 6, "The Meaning, Importance, and Boundaries of the Maṇḍala," launches the discussion of maṇḍalas and maṇḍala worship, which is the subject of the remainder of the book. An etymology of "maṇḍala" is given before a range of textual traditions within Buddhism are referenced to give various interpretations of the meaning and importance of the maṇḍala. This chapter closes with a list of 15 different maṇḍalas and the Newar Buddhist rites they are constructed for.

Chapter 7, "Maṇḍala Generation," describes the various means through which a maṇḍala may be created. First, Yagyaman Pati details the visualized form of the maṇḍala. He explains that this is the best maṇḍala form since, being non-physical, it is more purified than a physical maṇḍala. He briefly provides the steps one undertakes in the mental generation of a maṇḍala and states that the Guhyasamāja maṇḍala serves as an ideal template for considering maṇḍala visualization. He then describes the construction of a physical maṇḍala from various media, such as painting, stone powder, uncooked rice or wheat *stūpas* (New. *gvaja* (pronounced "goza"), Tib. *tsa tsa*). The chapter closes with a brief mention of the need for *mudrās* and mantras to install and stabilize a maṇḍala, whether it is mentally generated or made in gross, physical form.

Chapter 8, "The Guru Maṇḍala," includes all the mantras recited during the Guru Maṇḍala *pūjā*, with descriptions and occasionally translations of each. In the original, Yagymanpati divided longer recitations into smaller pieces to make them more approachable to the audience. This chapter was written for a *vajrācārya* audience who were familiar with the performance of the Guru Maṇḍala rite to inform them of the meaning of the recitations throughout the *pūjā*. For this reason the description of the acts undertaken during the ritual is not included in the original. Rather than insert these descriptions directly into the translation and muddy it up, I have included a description of the Guru Maṇḍala ritual practice as taught by Yagyaman Pati at the end of the chapter to supplement this lack of description in the original work.

Chapter 9, "The Occasion to Undertake the Guru Maṇḍala," comprehensively details all Newar Buddhist rituals in which performance of the Guru Maṇḍala rite is compulsory. Not only are those rites performed by *vajrācāryas* listed, but so too are all instances in which the ritual client (*jajmān*) is required to perform the Guru Maṇḍala under the guidance of the precepting *vajrācārya*. This was originally the second chapter of the book, but given its thematic relationship with the chapter on the Guru

Maṇḍala, we have shifted it to immediately follow that chapter to improve the overall flow of the book.

In Chapter 10, "The History and Importance of the Guru Maṇḍala," Yagyaman Pati argues against the position that there is some pure, unchanged Ur-Guru Maṇḍala ritual (the traditional Newar Buddhist position) to demonstrate that the ritual formed through a process of centuries of historical development. He does this, especially, by relating various forms of the rite performed today and mentioning textual parallels to the contemporary ritual that, while similar, are not perfect matches. That the form of a ritual is a product of historical development may seem obvious, but for the conservative community to whom Yagyaman Pati began his preaching, this was a scandalous position. This chapter, which closes the book, best showcases Yagyaman Pati's prerogative to bring scholarship into conversation with his ritual tradition in a productive way. That is to say, for Yagyaman Pati, obsessing over the organizational structure of a ritual is missing the point entirely. A ritual is performed to help the practitioner gain awakening, not to assert entrenched, culturally-specific models.

We have included three appendices after the body of the translation. Two of these appendices were stand-alone chapters in the Newar original; one appendix is our addition. Appendix A, "The Guru Maṇḍala Procedure in the *Kriyāsamuccaya*," was its own chapter in the original that served as a point of comparison for the chapter that immediately preceded it, "The Guru Maṇḍala." We moved this chapter to an appendix since it does not form part of Yagyaman Pati's overall exegesis and is almost entirely made up of quotations from the *Kriyāsamuccaya*. For a similar reason, Appendix B, "The Ratna Maṇḍala," was moved from the body of the main work. This appendix largely takes the form of Yagyaman Pati's transcription and translation of a description of the Ratna Maṇḍala located in a manuscript in his personal collection. Since, like the chapter on the *Kriyāsamuccaya*, this section does not feature Yagyaman Pati's own work or interpretation, we moved it to an appendix. Appendix C, "15 Offering Steps," includes images from my personal Guru Maṇḍala ritual manual, that was compiled by Yagyaman Pati. This is because in the Guru Maṇḍala, on two separate occasions, a deity (or deities) are summoned to and enthroned upon a maṇḍala. After their arrival they are worshiped, and at the end of the rite they are dismissed in the *visarjana* (which is included in the chapter on the Guru Maṇḍala). Rather than insert these lengthy recitations into Chapter 8, we have noted the two points in the ritual where a deity is propitiated, with a note directing the reader to the appendix to see the recitations used at that point in the ritual.

Guru, Maṇḍala, and Guru Maṇḍala is a discourse on two of the most critical aspects of Vajrayāna practice: the guru and the maṇḍala. In the Guru Maṇḍala, these two coalesce to form a physically enacted ritual that incorporates the whole of Buddhist theory. For *gurubhā* Yagyaman Pati, the topics in this book are integral for a practitioner to reach awakening in this very life. The teaching of the guru is paramount and, as Yagyaman Pati once told me, "Guru is greater than god. There is no god, but if there was, guru would be greater."

Samuel M. Grimes
Berkeley, California
2024

Part One
Guru

I.

Guru: Meaning, Definition, and Importance | *guru: artha tathā paribhāṣā va mahimā*

Guru: Meaning | *guru artha*

It is easy to explain the meaning of guru. This is a matter which everyone knows. All know its meaning: children, the elderly, youths, and women. Everyone must know what a guru is, whether in the village or the city—everywhere. These days, they are called master, teacher, instructor, principal teacher, and so forth. The meaning of guru is general. Therefore, everyone, everywhere, knows it. A guru is a teacher on matters of knowledge, an instructor in reading letters, and someone who instructs. If this general account of the meaning of a guru is accurate, and one views them as necessary, then, they are still regarded pleasantly.[1]

---

[1] *ajha nhyaïpu tāi jui*—literally, up until now, one will still be happy. But it seems that the guru might be the implied referent.

The Meaning of the Letters | *akṣarasa artha*

Let's look at the word "guru." The word "guru" is comprised of the two letters "gu" and "ru." There is a meaning in guru's syllable "gu." There is also a meaning in the syllable "ru." Now, if we take a look at the meaning of its two syllables, the meaning of the word guru will come from the syllables.

First, we will look at the meaning of "gu." The meaning of "gu" is a dark place. It is also said to be "*guṁ*," which means a jungle. That is a place where "might makes right." That is called "ignorance." The meaning of "gu" is darkness. According to the dictionary,[i] "gu" and "guṃ" are the same. In English, the meaning is "strung together, woven." That is like how a thread is seen as a ball. That is a jungle. Therefore, "gu" is also said as "*guṁ*." When we use the word jungle to mean "*guṁ*" in this refined and developed form, it is not the jungle of the contemporary definition. Jungle means "entanglement," which is the state where you cannot say, "this is alright," and "that is not alright." It is the forested jungle of primordial time. In such a state, the residents of that forested jungle are equally beasts. How will they go on living a life in that "might makes right" place? Their mutual adversaries will always oppress the evil. The good also will always go on living after having oppressed their adversaries. There was no importance placed upon the matter of beheading and killing to get revenge. One lived such that whatever was done, there would be the oppression of one's adversaries. There, there was indeed no matter of law as we know it. Therefore, everything there was frightful. This is the law of the jungle. It is also called the "law of the fish." To eat, having seen the meek, the mighty consumed them. To eat, other mighty ones, having seen those very mighty ones, would also swallow them. The world before was just like that of these fish that dwell in the ocean. In Buddhist terms, such a state is called "ignorance" (*ajñāna*).[2] That means "not knowing" or "not known." Not knowing, or not being known, is equivalent to the eyes of a blind man. Even though he has eyes, you cannot show him anything. How much more [than the blind man] can we see in a dark place?

Internally, such a state is one where there is no fullness in knowledge; one will awaken to such a state. This means a state of ignorance. The Buddha designated it as "delusion" (*avidyā*). Ignorance, or delusion, is the foundational snare of suffering in this world (or is a snare that is the root of all suffering in this world). This is the supporting root, or underlying foundation, of Buddhism. Ignorance means that this world is greatly confused in the entanglement of delusion. The foundation of Buddhist teachings about the world, based on the foundation of such ignorance or delusion, is causality. The letter "gu" is a reflection of this state.

Because of this "*guṁ*," here, in this world, at various times and occasions, various incidents of chaos and panic have occurred. Various countries have fought and gone to war. Many men have gone to their deaths at war. Many women have become widows. Many children have become orphans. This world bore two world wars, and it cannot bear another one. If it faces a third world war again, it will undoubtedly be finished.

Even within the nation, surrounded by ignorance, the government is needlessly prone to corruption, problems have arisen, and the peace has been disturbed. Now, in such a state, civil war has been brought, and there are bandits, terrorists, violence, rape, looting, and corruption. If some day such news is

---

[2] We have elected to translate *ajñāna* as ignorance, rather than nescience, and *avidyā* as delusion, rather than ignorance, to better represent the passage in English. Although "delusion" is the conventional translation for *moha*, and not *avidyā*, we prefer to translate *avidyā* as delusion so that *ajñāna* is not rendered as nescience, which is awkward in English prose.

not heard, it would not be different. That kind of incident has now become a regular part of life. It is to the point that we cannot finish speaking of such news, and if there is a day when there are no such unpleasant incidents, we should remark on the news of such civilisation for the sake of the day when there are no longer such incidents. As such, a wrong state of affairs has come above, the blame must be placed on ignorance.

Unrest occurs constantly in each house. Income is not sufficient. If there is income, it is not enough. Whenever there is income, without noticing, it comes to be insufficient. It comes to be, as it is said, that "money is everything." People come to do any manner of work for the sake of money. Brothers quarrel. There are even nasty quarrels between husbands and wives. There are quarrels between father and son. There are quarrels between mothers and sons and daughters.

Long ago, having seen animals in the jungle, people must have become suspicious. People, even having mutually joined together, must have been afraid of animals in the jungle, with the eventuality that they would be snatched away. Now, that is not the case. Instead of that, now, *creatures* are in the situation of being suspicious when they see *humans*.

The forests and jungles have come to be destroyed. The works that we rejoice in are like undercutting our own legs and feet. Planting is not done at a seasonable time. The weather and environment have entirely changed; landslides have become too common.

Drinkable water has become scarce. There have come to be many impurities within the water. It is said to be a natural law that "drinking water is necessary for life." But having drunk water, we are struck by the rise of cholera, typhoid, meningitis, and other deadly diseases. Moreover, there is always a possibility that the ground might split in an earthquake.

There is unrest. And seeing that unrest, even more great unrest comes. The term "vicious circle of poverty" means that suffering arising amidst suffering becomes, as is seen in the great confusion of the environment, a financial affair, a social affair, a political affair, and a universal affair.

According to Buddhism, the root of all these things is delusion. We must realize that in our world, human suffering causes delusion. In the world, if there are humans, there will be more or less delusion. However far the darkness of that delusion goes, that far the light of wisdom will come to rise.

The Root of Knowledge and Prajñā | *jñāna va prajñāyā mū khaṃ*

Anyone can realize release from such a state. Here, regarding such a delusional state, we shall look at the meaning of "ru." We shall inquire into the meaning of the syllable "ru," which is the second syllable of the word "guru." In the same way, there is also a meaning for "ru." In Sanskrit[ii] the meaning of "ru" is said to be "to call," which means, it is written, "to give sound." Being given sound, i.e., knowledge, is not the normal state of affairs when one is in delusion.[3] Thus, the need to seek [knowledge] implies the need for a seeking strategy. Therefore, you could say the meaning of "ru" here is a light for us who are seeking a light for those of us [who are seeking knowledge]. Light is said to be the opposite of darkness. It is white. Darkness represents delusion. Light represents wisdom. If it is said that ignorance leads to delusion, then we shall say that knowledge leads to wisdom. The antonyms of delusion, ignorance, lack of learning, darkness, and so forth are brightness, wisdom, knowledge, learning, initiation, and so forth. For all of these words, in Buddhism, we use the word "Prajñā." The letter "ru" of "guru" indicates the knowledge of this Prajñā.

[3] Or, this is not delusion as it is.

"Ru" is thus the means to break through the obstacle of ignorance. Knowledge is needed to solve the problem of ignorance. It is said that among living things, for humans, knowledge is very, very important. Humans without knowledge cannot move out of the deep mud. But humans with knowledge are like lotuses, who can arise out of the dirt of the mud. Humans attempt to solve political, social, and financial problems with knowledge.

In Buddhism, knowledge is very important. The importance of Prajñā is even greater. It is necessary to obtain omniscience. In this way, it is said that to obtain buddhahood is to attain the Prajñāpāramitā. Thus, the Buddha was "such a skilled researcher."[4] Śrī Śākyamuni, Gautama, abandoned the royal palace and his household to end suffering, and having found a way, the dispensation he gave as his instruction to the quarters of the world is worth remembering here.[5]

The Meaning of Guru | *guruyā artha*

Having joined "gu" and "ru," we get the word "guru." So, the meaning of guru is darkness and brightness. Dark first, and later bright: the guru is he whose task it is to bring light to a dark place. Guru is the term used for he who brings knowledge to a place of ignorance. Guru is the term for he who shows the path. Guru is the term for he who brings learning. Guru is the term for he who brings initiation. In Buddhism, the guru is the person who shows one the path to the relinquishment of suffering. The guru is the one who teaches one the knowledge for attaining

4 "*kiṃ kuśala gaveśaka*"

5 We would usually translate *pranidhāna* in a Buddhist context as vow, though in the Nepali sense, it is institution or establishment; in this sense, it seems to indicate what the Buddha established in this world, rather than his vows. Therefore, we translate it as "dispensation."

liberation. The guru is the one who teaches and shows one the things one does not know.[6] Thus, the guru is a person who brings out new theories, i.e., "the propounder of a new doctrine."[iii] Before all things, the *Abhidharmakośa* performs an homage to the guru, writing thus:

yaḥ sarvathā sarvahatāndhakāraḥ
saṃsārapaṃkāj jagadujjahāra |[7]

He who dispels all darkness in every way and uplifts the world from the mire of cyclic existence…

Thus, it is written, meaning "one who saves." He thus accomplishes the destruction of the state of darkness in every way. The guru is the teacher who uplifts the world from the foundation of the suffering of cyclic existence.[iv]

When respectfully addressing the guru, one calls him "*guruju.*" In the old Newar language, the same meaning as guru is indicated by "*bharāṇḍo*;" even today, we read the word "*bharāṇḍo*" in old books. "*Bharāṇḍo*" is also read in *caryā* songs. For "*bharāṇḍo*," later it was said as "*bhāro*."[8] And, based on the sound of "*gurubhāroju*," just "*gurubhāju*" is said. And, having removed the "*bhā*" from "*gurubhāju*," we just say "*guruju.*" And having removed the "ru" from "*gurubhāju*," we say "*gubhāju.*"

By customary rule, when saying "*guruju*" or "*gubhāju*," it indicates those people who professionally perform rituals for

---

[6] There is not a clear way to distinguish the subtlety between *masaḥgu* and *masiugu*, or *sayekā* and *siikā* in English. "*masaḥgu masiugu khaṃyāta kyanā sayekā siikā biimha guru jula.*"

[7] Prahlad Pradhan, ed., (1967), *Abhidharmakoṣbhāṣyaṃ of Vasubandhu*, Patna: K.P. Jayaswal Research Institute, TSWS, 1.

[8] *Bhāro* is a common word in old Newar. It can be an honorific (*bhāro guru*, "the honorable guru"), a title for an aristocrat and even a name (e.g., the Nepalese guru of Tibetan Rā Lotsāwa).

ritual sponsors. In Hindu *śāstras*, the term "*guru*" is also used for those who perform the *karmakāṇḍa* rituals. In Apte's *Sanskrit-English Dictionary*, he gives this reading. That is: "technically a Guru performs the purificatory ceremonies over a boy..."[v] It is also customary to call the person who gives initiation in Vajrayāna the "guru."

Definition: *Vajrācārya | paribhāṣāḥ vajrācārya*

In ancient Nepal, properly speaking, "*guruju*" indicated a *vajrācārya*. *Vajrācārya* is a synonym of *guruju*. The definition of a *vajrācārya* is given as follows:

vajraścāsau ācāryaḥ vajrācāryaḥ ।
evaṃ jñānadhāraṇaṃ niyamācāraṃ astīti ācāryaḥ so vajrācārya ।
ārāt dūraṃ pāpakebhyaḥ dharmebhyaś caratīty ācāryaḥ ।
yad vā vajramārgadeśaka so vajrācāryaḥ ।[9]

This can be paraphrased as follows:

The *ācārya* who performs Vajrayāna practice in the Dharma of the Vajrayāna is a *vajrācārya*. Having borne such knowledge regarding that Dharma, an *ācārya* who performs its conduct according to rule will be called a *vajrācārya*. Having come to delight in Dharma practice, far from the deeds of evil doers, the *ācārya* who is near to such good work and, moreover, has taught the path of the Vajrayāna, is the *ācārya* who can teach the teaching of such knowledge, and is thus called a *vajrācārya*.[vi]

---

[9] *Kriyāsamuccaya*: Parallel in § "*atha vajrācārya lakṣaṇa*." Yagyaman Pati's quoted text varies from what is recorded in Chandra's edition.

Such a definition is also written in the introduction to Āśākājī Vaidya's *Bodhisattvāvadānamālā*. As follows:

yad vā vajramārgeṇa deśakayo vā ācāryaḥ so vajrācāryaḥ |[10]

This can be translated as follows:

Whosoever, having obtained *vajra*-consecration and who can teach the Vajrayāna path well: it is just such an *ācārya* who is said to be a learned *vajrācārya*.[vii]

Before saying a *vajrācārya* is a matter of caste: a *vajrācārya* is a guru. There is a customary saying on the matter of a *vajrācārya*:[viii]

One who shows the truth: that one is a guru.

Of truth, there is also conventional truth and the constant ultimate truth. That which is true for now, but which later cannot be said to be the case, is still truth. But that kind of truth is conventional truth. That is a temporary truth. Temporary truth is just like seeing the moon's reflection in water or showing it. When watching the TV, viewers might only see a picture of humans. But that is not really the truth. It is only showing something fleeting. After seeing something fleeting, when it comes to truth, that which is seen is all unreal. Gurus are those who can tell us about many matters of conventional truth like that.

The ultimate truth is that which remains unchanging, is always true regardless of time, and will continue to be true in the future. We must obtain knowledge of such ultimate truth. One who can see that kind of ultimate truth will undoubtedly become omniscient. Such people are rare gurus. Bhagavān Buddha was

---

[10] Āśākājī Vaidya, *Bodhisattvāvadānamāla*, i. Publication details unknown. Ashakaji Bajracharya's version supports that given by Yagyaman Pati just above.

omniscient. After he obtained knowledge of *samyak-saṃbodhi*, he became one with knowledge of the three times. Thus, he became omniscient. There are no such gurus as him at present. Moreover, he attained *nirvāṇa*. Now only his words remain.

One with Knowledge of the Three Times and Ten Directions: Guru | *daśadig va trikālasarśī: guru*

In the *Gurupañcāśikā,* composed by Aśvaghoṣa, it is written that the guru knows the ten directions: the four quarters, the four intermediate directions, the highest point, and the lowest point. It is also written that the guru also knows of the three times, that is, knowing the three times of past, present, and future. As it is in this *śloka*:

> *abhiṣekāgralabdho hi vajrācāryas tathāgataiḥ* |
> *daśādigbaloka dhātus yais trikālam etya vandyate* ||[11, ix]

> Having come during the three times, the *vajrācārya* who has obtained the highest consecration by the *tathāgatas*,
> Who are established in world systems of the ten directions, is honored.

Internal Guru | *adhyātmika guru*

Up to here, we have taken the matter of our remarks and discussion of a guru who has hands and feet, who can undergo birth and death, etc. But in Vajrayāna, there is also an internal guru. After Bhagavān Buddha entered *nirvāṇa*, he left the words spoken by him. "*Evam me suttaṃ*," meaning "Thus have I heard,"

---

[11] Janardan Pandey, ed., "Gurupañcāśikā," in *Bauddhalaghugranthasaṅgraha*, Sarnath: Central Institute of Higher Tibetan Studies, 1997, v.2.

is used for that which is remembered of his words. This "*Evaṃ me suttaṃ*" utterance itself has also taken on the form of a guru.

Considering the book as one's own guru, worshiping the book is also *vajra*-culture. This is also a tradition. On the Guru Full Moon day (Guru Pūrṇimā), having gathered [the requisite books], those books and we remember to worship them as they deserve. In a great ritual, methodical worship is performed, worshiping the book before one. Looking at the books, one sees that it is written within them that one should perform worship of them willingly. This is a tradition. Having looked at books as something that is set up at the heart of many ritual procedures, we must go into the matters about which they were written, which are on ritual procedures and various teachings.

Buddha, Dharma, and Saṃgha | *buddha dharma va saṃgha*

The guru is seen to take on work for the Buddha, Dharma, and Saṃgha. In the *Jñānasiddhi* of Indrabhūti, it is written in regard to the Buddha, Dharma, and Saṃgha as gurus:

> *gurur buddho bhaved dharmaḥ saṃghaś cāpi sa eva hi* ।
> *prasādāj jñāyate tasya yasya ratnatrayaṃ varam* ॥[x]
>
> The guru is the Buddha, the Dharma, and also indeed, the Saṃgha.
> By his grace, the excellent Triple Gem is recognized.

In the ritual procedure of the Guru Maṇḍala, there is no material procedure to honor the guru. The ultimate meaning of the procedure for worshiping the Buddha, Dharma, and the Saṃgha is that they are the guru. In the Guru Maṇḍala, the Ratna Maṇḍala is presented to the Buddha, to the Dharma, and to the Saṃgha. The Buddha, Dharma, and Saṃgha: these are the internal gurus. Vajradhara and Vajrasattva take on the form of the highest guru.

Explanation of the Buddha, Dharma, and Saṃgha | *buddha dharma va saṃghayā vyākhyā*

When speaking of the Buddha, Dharma, and Samgha, we are not signifying some physical human, nor are they deities. They are also not gods. They are also not physical matters related to a human. The gurus are the Buddha, Dharma, and Samgha. I will explain about them. The matter of their expansiveness will emerge from [more] context. There will then be no one in the world who will not seek refuge in the Guru Buddha, Guru Dharma, and Guru Saṃgha. Here, we shall make some remarks on the meaning of the Buddha, Dharma, and Saṃgha.

Buddha | *buddha*

The word Buddha reflects intellect [i.e. *buddhi*] and knowledge. If we say this in contemporary speech, we just say "knowledge." Everyone needs knowledge. Everyone who is doing positive work or who is also doing negative work needs intellect and knowledge. Everyone has more or less knowledge. Thieves and bandits also have it, since, to do theft or banditry, one also needs knowledge to do theft or banditry. If someone must engage in theft or banditry, the way they carry out such actions depends entirely on their own decisions and will inevitably be dishonorable. To prevent the emergence of thieves or bandits, one can adopt an alternative approach, which can be consistently applied throughout life. The key point is this: if knowledge is necessary to commit harmful acts, it is equally essential for doing good. Knowledge is unquestionably vital!

Buddha—this word is used for the one who, in this world, obtains buddhahood. Buddhahood means knowledge of perfect and complete awakening. That is omniscience. Therefore, Buddha is a title. Prajñā is hidden in the word Buddha. Wisdom (*vidyā*) is also hidden in it. The qualities of knowledge are also hidden in it.

Within the materialistic, convenience-enjoying society of the twenty-first century, there is also a lot of knowledge. Without a sliver of knowledge, there would not be so much civilization and material development. Those who have knowledge are called knowledgeable. Those who have intellect are called intelligent. Those who have wisdom are called wise. Knowledge, intellect, wisdom, and so forth are all attained in buddhahood, and one who attains buddhahood is called a buddha. Those who don't have a little bit of intellect have come to be called "fools," and here we must not forget this. One with enough intellect imagines they are in a state of fulfillment, wherein they don't need to develop more intellect, having seen how much intellect they have. One also performs acts of such imagination in a state without a little bit of intellect. These two states are not those of the wise. Nowadays, not having even a little bit of knowledge, there is only imagination. Wisdom has come to be entirely unheard of.

Humans are just between the state of the fulfillment of higher knowledge and the state of not having even a little bit of intellect. Some have a lot of intellect, and some have less intellect. We are thus speaking about them: those who do not have a lot of intellect[, i.e., who have intellect but don't think they need more], and those who, having seen them, have less intellect. This means that now, in our world, we are all between being both a buddha and a fool. Regarding intellect, of those who attain buddhahood, all have intellect. Therefore, they all become buddhas. And, indeed, it is not difficult. You, me, we are all buddhas. However many things there are in *saṃsāra*, they are all in the stream of knowledge. They are all buddha. Thus, however many grains of sand in the Ganges River there are, that many buddhas there are in *saṃsāra*. The *Bhadracarī*, which is about bodhisattva conduct, is an essential verse in the field of Vajrayāna. In this verse, it is written that

ekarajāgri rajopamabuddhā buddhasutāna niṣaṇṇaku madhye[12]

> On a single dust-mote, buddhas, equal to the number of dust motes, are seated amidst sons of the buddhas.

The meaning of what is written is that, on each and every dust mote (on each particle of dust) of a buddha field, as many buddhas are seated as there are dust motes. Whosoever there is, before them are buddhas. There are buddhas [before] whoever has even a little intellect. However much intellect humans have, that much peace they have. Whichever humans have only a little bit of intellect, they will also only have a little bit of peace. Peace is one of the signs of civilization. Therefore, it indicates great knowledge. Just this is the quintessence of Buddhism. There are no humans who do not need to rely on knowledge. Those who have faith in the Buddhist Dharma come to say "*buddhaṃ śaraṇaṃ gacchāmi*" [I go to the Buddha as my refuge]. Theravādans say "*buddhaṃ saraṇaṃ gacchāmi*" not once, but two times.[13] Not only two times but up to three times. They have the procedure that they must say "*buddhaṃ saraṇaṃ gacchāmi*" three times. Among Mahāyānists, we say "*buddhaṃ śaraṇaṃ gacchāmi*" up until the end of our lives. The method for this is to say "*yāvajjīvaṃ buddhaṃ śaraṇaṃ gacchāmi*" [I go to the Buddha as my refuge as long as I live].

---

[12] P.L. Vaidya, ed., (1960) *Gaṇḍavyūhasūtra*, "Buddhist Sanskrit Texts No. 5," Darbhanga: The Mithila Institute, 428.

[13] We edited this to fit the Pāli spelling and switched these passages to Sanskrit when speaking in the Mahāyānist contexts.

When we see how this matter is thought about, there are those outside of the Buddhist path who have learned or have not learned that this is going for refuge to the Buddha. Whether one utters "*buddhaṃ śaraṇaṃ gacchāmi*" with one's lips or does not, this is going for refuge in the Buddha. There are none here who do not need to take one step towards taking refuge in the Buddha.

Dharma | *dharma*

The Dharma is also not a god. It is just a kind of teaching. In the classifications of science, it is "Normative Science, i.e., what ought to be and what ought not to be." It has two types: what should and should not be done. Deeds that must be done and deeds that are good to do, are all Dharma. Deeds that are not good to do are all the opposite of the Dharma and are wrong deeds. Not doing good deeds and not doing deeds that must be done are also in the realm of the undharmic. In this way, if one must do deeds that are not good, and one does not do what one does not need to do, it is not necessarily correct to say those are within the realm of the Dharma.[14]

Thus, it is said that the Dharma is positive morality. It is a road. Where we are going, that is a path. The Buddha is knowledge, and the Dharma is the path. The Buddha is the light, and the Dharma is the path on which the light is used. To go on the path, you definitely need a light. In the day, it will be there; in the evening, it will be there; at night, it will be there; in the dark half of the month, it will be there: the light that you always need. Now, to draw distinctions, if the Buddha is a light, and the Buddha is knowledge, and the Buddha is Prajñā, then the Dharma is the method by which one uses the light for the use of knowledge and for the attainment of Prajñā. If you do not need a

[14] I.e., they are indefinite, not necessarily positive.

light, then there is no use for it in this world. Useless knowledge is not knowledge. If Prajñā is not fully linked with Upāya [means], then it is only like a picture hung on the wall.

Therefore, in the Buddhist religion, the proximity of Prajñā and Upāya in collections is so great in importance that without Prajñā, there is no Upāya. When there is Upāya, at that very moment, there also comes Prajñā. Prajñā impels Upāya; Upāya also impels Prajñā. In this way, the picture of the state of today's present world of the twenty-first century, joined with materialism and the enjoyment of conveniences, is fully explained by these maxims, [as it has been so] since the start of the age of humans. In later centuries, in the form of this constant process, it will also come to be and abide.

Wherever a Buddha will be, there also will be the Dharma of such a form. And wherever the Dharma will be, there also will be a Buddha. If there will not be the Dharma, there will also not be a Buddha. And if there will not be a Buddha, there will also not be the Dharma. Therefore, there was a Buddha from the beginning. There was the Dharma from the beginning. Now, also, there is a Buddha. Now, also, there is the Dharma. Even later, a Buddha will be. Even later, the Dharma will be. As long as this universe exists, there will be a Buddha and the Dharma.

No one can abide unless one goes for refuge in such a Dharma. Those who have faith in the Buddhist Dharma come to say "*dharmaṃ śaraṇaṃ gacchāmi.*" Theravādans have the custom of saying "*dhammaṃ saraṇaṃ gacchāmi*" up to three times. Mahāyānists have the method of saying "*yāvajjīvaṃ dharmaṃ śaraṇaṃ gacchāmi,*" i.e., we take refuge until the end of our lives.

When we see how this matter is thought about, there are those outside of the Buddhist path who have learned or have not learned that this is going for refuge to the Dharma.[15] Whether

---

[15] The text said "Buddha" but it must be a misprint.

one utters "*dharmaṃ śaraṇaṃ gacchāmi*" with one's lips or does not, this is going for refuge in the Dharma. There are none here who do not need to take one step towards taking refuge in the Dharma with this passage.

In the arrangement of what is called the Dharma Maṇḍala, there is no structure of images using figures which have hands and feet anywhere in the Dharma Maṇḍala. Instead, sacred texts, i.e., Dharma texts, are considered to constitute the Dharma Maṇḍala. Namely, the *Noble Prajñāpāramitā* in so many (e.g. eight, twenty-five, hundred) thousand lines, the *Gaṇḍavyūha*, the *Daśabhūmika*, the *Samādhirāja*, the *Laṅkāvatāra*, the *Saddharmapuṇḍarīkā*, the *Tathāgataguhya*, the *Lalitavistara*, the *Suvarṇaprabhāsa*, and the other eighty-four thousand Dharma texts in assemblage are all the Guru.

Saṃgha | *saṃgha*

We will also explain the Saṃgha in this manner. The Saṃgha is the third gem of the Triple Gem. The Saṃgha is also not a god. It is also not represented in an icon. We don't see an icon of the Saṃgha anywhere. Just as we speak of a Buddha Maṇḍala and a Dharma Maṇḍala, we also speak of the concept of a Saṃgha Maṇḍala. So, what the Saṃgha is cannot be settled upon [as one thing, as a maṇḍala consists of various things]. It has red, blue, white, yellow, and black figures, so how can it be assigned one color? How many heads does it have?[16] How many hands? That is also not known by anyone. It also cannot be seen written anywhere. If one actually sees it, the Saṃgha does not have a material form.

Saṃgha: this is only a resource. An icon alone is not enough to perform a particular task. "It will be done like this," just deciding in this manner is also not enough. To do that task, the

16 Literally, how-many-necks heads.

support of others is also necessary. One needs a resource. In addition to that, one needs an association: one needs a Saṃgha. The Saṃgha and an association: these are the resources.

Śākyamuni, Gautama Buddha, also did not propagate the Buddha Dharma by himself. He was assisted by many, many people who became mendicants. Gautama Buddha wandered abroad to many different countries. The kings in various places also gave him support. It goes without saying that those of lower castes who came before him also supported him. Gautama Buddha was always collaborative. Bhagavān Buddha regularly took up the alms bowl (*bhikṣāpātra*) to eat just as we eat, to drink, and to wear. Did not the Bhagavān Buddha take only material things into his alms bowl? That is goodwill and support: these are gathered in his alms bowl.

There are two kinds of support. One is in the form of individuals. The other is associational support. The Bhagavān, Gautama Buddha, placed associational support above personal support. Therefore, he gave requests for associational support. He never liked to place the good of just himself above [that of others]. He instead saw to it that all living beings are improved and benefitted.

It is also true that, compared to an individual's lifespan, the lifespan of an organization can be very great. Having done personal work, the lifespan that work achieves will be minimal. There is selfishness in that. Selfish work is momentary. But having done associational work, the lifespan that work achieves will be very significant. There is no selfishness in that. Work that is achieved selflessly will last a long time.

Therefore, as great as the Saṃgha is, that much will the Saṃgha be good. That much there will be selflessness. And whatever work is achieved will be easy. And it will also abide for a long time. I will go for refuge to such a Saṃgha, and you will also go. All will go.

No one can abide unless one goes for refuge in such a Saṃgha. Those who have faith in the Buddhist Dharma come to say "*saṃghaṃ śaraṇam gacchāmi.*" Theravādans have the custom of saying "*saṃghaṃ saraṇaṃ gacchāmi*" up to three times. Among Mahāyānists, we say "*saṃghaṃ śaraṇaṃ gacchāmi*" up until the end of our lives. The method for this is to say "*yāvajjīvaṃ saṃghaṃ śaraṇaṃ gacchāmi,*" [I go to the Saṃgha as my refuge as long as I live].

When we see how this matter is thought about, there are those outside of the Buddhist path who have learned or have not learned that this is going for refuge to the Saṃgha.[17] Whether one utters "*saṃghaṃ śaraṇaṃ gacchāmi*" with one's lips or does not, this is going for refuge in the Dharma. There are none here who do not need to take one step towards taking refuge in the Saṃgha.

There is an arrangement for the Saṃgha Maṇḍala. It is written in detail concerning the Saṃgha Maṇḍala, that together with Āryāvalokiteśvara and Maitreya Bodhisattva, there are Ānanda Bhikṣu, Upagupta Bhikṣu, Jayaśrī Bhikṣu until all of the gurus of the Saṃgha are there.

The Buddha, Dharma, and Saṃgha have a Firm Union | *buddha dharma va saṃgha lā va lusi theṃ kvātūgu sambandh*

Just the a Buddha's kindness is not enough; he also needs the Dharma. Just the Dharma's kindness is not enough; it also needs the Saṃgha. Without the knowledge of the Dharma and Saṃgha, a Buddha could not do his work. And indeed, without a Buddha and Saṃgha, the Dharma is lifeless. Once again, without a Buddha and the Dharma, what work would the Saṃgha do?

[17] Again, here the term is misprinted as Buddha, when it must be Saṃgha.

Indeed, this entire world is a Buddha. In this world, the Dharma must be explained. And the world must find it within the Saṃgha. In this way, the Buddha, Dharma, and Saṃgha are the gurus. Therefore, the Triple Gem of the Buddha, Dharma, and Saṃgha are considered the immaterial Guru and are within the Guru Maṇḍala:

> *guru buddha guru dharma guru saṃgha tathaiva ca, guru vajradharaś caiva tasmin śrī gurūbhyaḥ namaḥ, gurūbhyaḥ namaḥ, gurūbhyaḥ namaḥ*
>
> Guru Buddha, Guru Dharma, and Guru Saṃgha, and indeed the Guru Vajradhara. To those Noble Gurus, homage! Homage to the Gurus! Homage to the Gurus!

Thus, it is said.

Vajradhara | *vajradhara*

The Root Guru is called Vajradhara. Vajradhara means the one who bears the *vajra*. Bearing the Bhāva *mudrā*, he holds a *vajra* with his right hand and a bell (*ghaṇṭā*) with his left hand. His left and right hands are crossed, and he embraces himself at his chest, performing the "*mudrābhāva*." This mudra is also called the *mudrā* of the *vajra* syllable HUṂ (*vajrahūm̐kāramudrā*). Vajradhara is the Ādi Buddha [primordial Buddha].

Vajrasattva: The Highest Guru | *vajrasattva: param guru*

When considered as the Ādi Buddha, Vajradhara is called Vajrasattva. The objects held by Vajrasattva are the *vajra* and bell, just as Vajradhara. Regarding the Bhāva *Mudrā*, the bell is in the left hand upturned, whereas the right hand holding the *vajra* is kept displayed at the chest. The meaning of *vajra* is an invulnerable form, which means that after a long, long time, it will always exist. It signifies truth itself, which means it is eternal and the fundamental element.[18] Sattva is also the truth. Therefore, Vajrasattva means that until the end, it is the ultimate truth.

Vajrasattva is the Lord of the Guru Maṇḍala. While doing the cultivation of the Guru Maṇḍala, flowers are placed all around it. And, in the end, a flower is placed in the central spot of the maṇḍala, and one says, "OṂ homage for the guru who is Vajrasattva" (*oṃ vajrasattvagurubhyo namaḥ*). When looking at this cultivation all around the maṇḍala of Vajrasattva, in the ritual procedure of the Guru Maṇḍala, we do not see any material recognition of the guru. Vajrasattva is immaterial. The Five dhyāni buddhas are also recognised as Vajrasattva. In his report on Advayavajra, Doctor Haraprasad Shastri writes on the subject of Vajrasattva:

> ... the other four Dhyāni Buddhas have the stamp of a miniature Akṣobhya on their crown and Advaya explains this fact by stating that the other four Buddhas cannot be known without Akṣobhya or the stamp of Vijñāna.

In this way, Doctor Shastri analyzed the matter:

> But Akṣobhya again is stamped with the miniature figure of *Vajra*-sattva which is something like a sixth Dhyāni Buddha. But what is *Vajra*-sattva? If Vijñāna is more important than the other four Skandhas, *Vajra*-sattva must be still more important. Yes, he is. *Vajra* means Śūnyatā and Sattva means Jñāna-mātra, i.e., knowledge only. So *Vajra*-sattva means the pure knowledge of Śūnyatā.[xi]

[18] Yagyaman Pati is using *prakṛti* in a Sāṃkhya sense here.

In Advayavajra's work, *A Description of the Mudras of the Five Tathāgatas*, he writes a Sanskrit verse as follows:

> *vajreṇa sūṇyatā proktā sattvena jñānamātratā* ।
> *tādātmyamanayoḥ siddhaṃ vajrasattvasvabhāvataḥ* ॥
>
> Emptiness is proclaimed by the "*vajra*," pure knowledge by the "*sattva*."
> The identity of both is the accomplished self-existence of Vajrasattva.[xii]

In the *Hevajra Tantra*, Vajrasattva is defined in the following way:

> *abhedyaṃ vajram iti uktaṃ sattvam tribhavasyaikatā* ।
> *anayā prajñā yuktyā vajrasattva iti smṛtaḥ* ॥
>
> Indivisible, and so called, "*vajra*," a "*sattva*" awkward in English, and not in the Skt is the unity of the three states of existence. By this union, which is Prajñā, he is remembered as "Vajrasattva."[19]

This means that because it cannot be split, it is called "*vajra*." And because the truth is in the three times of the past, future, and present, it is called "*sattva*." One who has such knowledge is Prajñā, and that is Vajrasattva. In the *Kriyāsamuccaya*, the Lord of the Guru Maṇḍala is Vajrasattva. It is written that he is the highest guru.[xiii]

---

[19] Snellgrove, David L. *The Hevajra Tantra*. London, New York: Oxford University Press, 1959, Part II, p. 2. Chapter 1, v.4.

Therefore, the root of Guru Maṇḍala cultivation is Vajrasattva. This is an eternal truth. Therefore, one worships Vajrasattva and then performs various other tasks in the ritual procedures.

---

i. Vaman Shivram Apte, *The Student's Sanskrit English Dictionary*. Delhi: Motilal Banarsidass. pp. 189.

ii. *ibid.* pp. 470.

iii. *ibid.* pp. 190.

iv. Ācārya Narendra Deva, tr. Ācārya *Vasubandhukṛta Abhidharmakośa*. Allahabad: Hindustānī Ekeḍemī Uttar Prades̓, 1958. pp. 3.

v. Apte, *Op. Cit.*, pp. 190. [V.S. Apte (1890), *The practical Sanskrit-English dictionary, containing appendices on Sanskrit prosody and important literary & geographical names in the ancient history of India, for the use of schools and colleges.* Poona: Shiralkar, 463a.]

vi. Vajrarāja Śākya, Lotus Number 13. Lalitpur: Lotus Research Center, pp. 34.

vii. Áśākājī Vaidya, *Bodhisatvā Vadānamālā*, pp. *ḍ* [*xi*].

viii. Yajñamān Pati *Vajrācārya*, *Vajrācārya: Pulupālū*, Lotus Number 13. Lalitpur: Lotus Research Center, pp 19.

ix. *ibid.* pp. 32.

x. Indrabhūti Viracita's *Jnānasiddhi*, "First Section", 24 in Vajravallabha Dvivedī & Samdoṅg Rinpoche, eds., *Guhyādi-Aṣṭasiddhi Saṃgraha*. Sārnāth, Vārāṇasī: Durlabha Bauddha Grantha Śodha Yojanā, Kendrīya Ucca Tibbatī Śikṣā Saṃsthān. 1988.

xi. Shastri, Haraprasad, ed., *Advayavajrasaṁgraha*, Baroda: Oriental Institute, 1927, xxx. [the block quote just preceding this is from the same page of Shastri's *Advayavajrasaṃgraha* edition but is not cited in the original.]

xii. Shastri, *Op. Cit.*, pp. 23.

xiii. Lokesh Chandra, ed., *Kriyā-Samuccaya*, New Delhi: Sharada Rani, 1977.

2.

The Guru's Importance: Sphere and Demarcation | *guruyā mahatva kṣetra va sīmā bandī*

The Importance of the Guru in the Buddhist Dharma | *bauddha dharmay guruyā mahatva*

The place of the guru in Buddhism is essential. Without a guru, there is no practice at all. If there is to be a practice, one should wait upon the instruction of the guru, and if there is no instruction from a guru, there is not to be any practice that one can do alone. If a practice was taught or learned by oneself, one should also wait for the guru's explanation. Whenever one takes a step, the guru is required. Whatever practice there is, the guru is needed. We can never say the guru is unnecessary for this or that practice. The guru is necessary for everything. A guru is also needed for one who will seriously learn something imminently. Even a person who has already learned and been taught much needs a guru. There are these three types of people. 1. To those with a high grade of knowledge, 2. to those of a middle grade, and 3. to those with dull intellect. These three types of people need a guru: that is just how vital the guru is in Buddhism.

1. Buddhism | *bauddha darśan*

Buddhism is entirely concerned with the creation of Prajñā to help with delusion. Thus, it involves a serious attempt to extract oneself from delusion. Therein, what is really needed is a light, and here, that light becomes an illuminator. It becomes the guru.

2. The Founder of Buddhism had a Guru | *bauddha darśanayā pravartakayā naṃ guru du*

Śākyamuni, after completing his great going forth as Gautama, needed a guru: someone to tell him about the path of bliss, someone to teach him. In his own life, he took as his gurus Āḷāra Kālāma and Udraka Rāmaputra.[1] If the originator of Buddhism, Śākyamuni, had a guru, it is natural that the followers of Buddhism also need a guru.

3. The Mendicancy System | *pravrajyā vyavasthā*

It is established that the followers of the Buddhist Dharma must go into mendicancy. This system, in Theravāda countries, continues the practice of mendicancy of Gautama Buddha. In Vajrayāna, we also engage in mendicancy for four days after tonsure (*cūḍākarma*).[2] In this way, the status of guru is allocated to those who confer mendicancy.

---

[1] These are the *śramaṇa* gurus of the bodhisattva, both of whom he eventually leaves, having spiritually surpassed each in turn.

[2] In Newar Buddhism, boys undergo *cūḍākarma* wherein their hair is shorn and they are initiated into the sangha as monastics. Unlike other forms of Buddhism where such ordination involves a lifelong commitment, Newar Buddhist ordination involves a temporary period

4. The System of Initiation | *dīkṣāyā vyavasthā*

The practice of conferring knowledge is an important affair. So important is the practice of conferring knowledge and performing the officiation of knowledge that it is a practice that must be ritually authorized (*ādhikārika*). The term "initiation" (*dīkṣā*) is used for such a special ritual. It is also called "consecration" (*abhiṣekha*). The person who confers initiation is not an ordinary person. It is a person with remarkable accomplishments. In this way, the status of guru is allocated to those who impart initiation.

5. Symbolic Expression | *soṃketik bhāy*

In Buddhism, especially in Vajrayāna, symbolic or secret expressions are used. In such a case, when reading one thing, the meaning on face value is different from the meaning in practice. In such expressions, when seeing a meaning of conventional truth, while that may be on one matter, the meaning in terms of the ultimate truth will be different. In such cases, there can be no practice without the instruction of a guru.

6. The Role of the Guru in Buddhist Literature | *bauddha-sāhityay guruyā bhūmikā*

If we look at Buddhist literature, discourses on this and that matter are at the fore of the text. There is the guru. There is also the disciple. These discourses present the disciple before the guru,

---

of mendicancy followed by a return to lay life. However, in Newar Buddhism, those who underwent *cūḍākarma* are regarded as still members of the sangha, albeit embodying the ideal of a married householder bodhisattva or tantric priest.

cf. David N. Gellner, "Monastic Initiation in Newar Buddhism" in Richard Gombrich (ed.), *Indian Ritual and its Exegesis* (Delhi: Oxford University Press, Oxford University Papers on India, 1988), Vol. 2, Part I, 1988. pp. 53.

filled with curiosity. And the guru, in the form of the Bhagavān, explains matters to the disciple. Thus, Buddhist literature is a guru-disciple discourse. The influence of this is one reason that the guru has such a valued position in the Buddhist Dharma.

The methods taught in Vajrayāna are seen as being of three types. These are as follows:

1. Gestation (*garbhin*): This means that which is obtained from another, such as knowledge given to the disciple from the guru.
2. Profound (*gambhīr*): This is knowledge that, having been taught and learned, is felt for oneself.
3. Self-existent (*svabhāva*): This is non-dual, self-arisen knowledge.

"Gestation" is what one knows or is taught by others, such as education, wisdom, or methods taken in consecration. For instance, what is said by a guru and understood by a disciple. Or what is said by a friend and understood, or taught by a mother to a child and known by the child. Such matters are learned and instilled in a child as habits that become rituals. Here, a mother, friend, teacher, and so forth all take on the form of a guru. Here, it is taken that the form of a guru is a great and not a trifling matter. The matter comes that the elderly, too, must teach children. Moreover, a father who daily [teaches] his son in verses is considered a guru, which is a valuable thing. It is not the case that only friends must take on the form of a guru. Those who happen to be bitter enemies are gurus. A single activity of an enemy teaches us the path of vigilance. These are gurus in material terms.

"Profound" is also what one knows or what methods one takes. But here, this is not a directly material guru. And its method is not a matter of that which is taught or learned by someone. Its method is feeling for oneself that which one has been taught or learned. For instance, having smoked a cigarette and seen that [smokers] consume suffering, one understands that smoking cigarettes is not good. Others become rich. So, one thinks one wants to become rich oneself. Others became intelligent and came to be very honored. So, one wants to become very knowledgeable and clever. In this way, there are gurus all around this world. There is no place without a guru. In this category, we are not talking about a guru in material terms, since we are speaking about immaterial gurus. Immaterial gurus [can also be] self-existent.

The "self-existent" is the best and most excellent type. In Anuttara-yoga-tantra, there is no requirement for a guru in material form. If there is the state of a guru therein, that is the guru of oneself. Besides oneself, there is no other guru. The Bhagavān, Gautama Buddha, did not take anyone as his guru in attaining the knowledge of complete and total awakening (*samyak-saṃbodhi*). No one instructs one in the method of attaining buddhahood. Having fully learned everything that Ācārya Āḷāra Kālāma had to teach with austerities, he took on Udraka Rāmaputra as his guru. With Udraka Rāmaputra unable to fulfill his wishes, he vowed, with the valuable thought, "Now I shall work for Prajñā by my own intellect and considerations, without relying on another." Here, Śākyamuni Gautama became his own guru and became his own disciple.

The knowledge of the unexcelled complete and total awakening (*anuttara-samyak-saṃbodhi*) is not attained by oneself by working somewhere. A "somewhere" is not needed, and "to go" is also unnecessary. One also does not need to go to see anything here or there. It is within our own body. And knowledge abides within each person's body. That knowledge is of such a subtle form that it is not enough to attempt to find it instrumentally.

One only needs a guru in the "gestation" and "profound" states. And, there is only a guru of a material form in the "gestation" state. There is no material guru on the level of the "profound" state. There, the environment that surrounds all around us becomes the guru for us. On the "self-existent" stage, buddhahood can be attained by all people, and people are said to bear the ability from their birth as it is their basis. There is just the matter of opening or not opening the contents of one's treasury oneself. There is just the matter of being able or not able to go and seize whatever contents there are in the obstructed and covered treasury of buddhahood. Śākyamuni Gautama thus, having taken out all of the contents that were obscured, became able to distribute them, and so became the Buddha.

The Guru in the Theravāda | *theravāday guru*

1. The Directions

Regarding what is written about the directions, in Theravāda, gurus are placed in the highest direction[3] out of the six directions.[i] One morning, the Bhagavān Buddha was heading to the city of Rājagṛha for alms from Veluvana Monastery. On the way, there was a young man who had just bathed in the deep river, and having come out, he was paying homage to the four directions. He also looked at and paid homage to the highest direction and again paid homage to the lowest direction towards the earth. Seeing such a sight, the Bhagavān Buddha asked what he was doing, and that youth heard him. He answered, "When my father died, he instructed me that after paying homage to the four

[3] This is the zenith direction. The other five directions are respectively the four compass points and the lowest (nadir) direction.

directions, I should do so to the *devatās* in the highest direction and the demons (*piśācas*) in the lowest direction to make them all happy. I am worshiping in accordance with that." The Bhagavān Buddha explained the meaning of the six directions in order: The meaning of the eastern direction is rising for our mothers and fathers who gave birth to and raised us; the meaning of the southern direction is learning and studying what is taught by gurus, having learned aspects of knowledge from them; the meaning of the western direction is said to be providing support and nutrition to one's own children and wife; the meaning of doing homage to the northern direction is said to be treating our friends and kinsmen kindly; the meaning of the highest direction is giving hospitality, as appropriate, to monks (*bhiksu*) and gurus; finally, paying homage to the lowest direction means, having considered servants and workers, that we must place in mind the fact that our ease and convenience are provided by those who are below. Thus, it is made clear, and it is seen how gurus are placed in the southern direction and monk-gurus are placed in the highest direction.[ii]

2. The Saver from Fear

As one who gives mantras, magical spells (*vidyās*), and so forth to liberate one from the fear of serpents and other deadly, venomous animals, the guru is also called a "saver from fear." When disciples have doubts about something told to them, and the guru tells them something that helps the disciple, then the disciple respects the words given them, and for that reason also [a guru] is called a "saver from fear."[iii] It is recognised that the Bhagavān Buddha, before he obtained his own buddhahood, took as his gurus Āḷāra Kālāma and Udraka Rāmaputra. It is seen that the knowledge they taught him did not satisfy him, and for that reason, he abandoned them and went to practice asceticism.

3. Being One's Own Guru

In the Bhagavān Buddha's last journey, being his own guru, he became extremely and severely ill. He suppressed the intense feeling with his own power of meditation. He did not succumb to the illness through the power of his effort. Then, on the day that he became sick, he returned to the monastery and sat on his seat beneath a tree. And there, as the Bhagavān was sick, Bhikṣu Ānanda expressed his extensive grief and pain to the Bhagavān. The Tathāgatha (Buddha) then gave his last teaching and wished for him to listen. In that place, the Bhagavān Tathāgata addressed Ānanda Bhikṣu thus:

O Ānanda, you should not have any hopes regarding the Bhagavān. "*Natth' ānanda tathāgatassa dhammesu ācariyamuṭṭhi*," meaning, "O Ānanda, there is no closed teacher's fist regarding the Dharma for a *tathāgata*." What must be taught, I have entirely finished teaching. Live as an island unto yourself,[iv] as a refuge unto yourself. Look upon the Dharma as an island; do not look upon anything else as a refuge.[v]

What is meant here is a symbol of independence (*svatantratāyā pratīk*). Just abiding in one's own instruction and training is to say, one is independently disciplined. In being self-reliant upon the Buddhist teachings, that which is not necessary is abandoned. Therefore, there is no compulsory requirement for a guru here.

4. Non-Requirement for a Guru

Regarding the matter of there being no need for compulsion or superstition, there should be no requirement for a guru in terms of being in association with one or another person. For instance, a certain lay man (*upāsaka*) arrived one day before the Bhagavān Buddha. He was taught in a personal manner—everyone was taught individually in a personal manner. He explained that one must do something oneself. Whether we listen to these three things or we don't listen to these three things, this is the answer the Bhagavān gave to him who was before him:

1. One must act in accordance with one's own words. One does not need to do something indiscriminately just because others have said it.
2. You do not need to do whatever was said or spoken just because it was written in this *śāstra* or that *śāstra*.
3. You do not need to do whatever was said by accomplished people. If one must do such a thing, and if one understands it in one's own mind, then one should do it. Having had a reason and cause for something, and [knowing] it will have a good result, one must do it. Then, such an individual is self-reliant. Thus, one must also look to the "guru" for such matters. Indeed, the highest and best guru is oneself. Therefore, one does not need a material guru on a higher level. Someone who can look within themselves is indeed a suitable guru. Indeed, one's own Prajñā is one's own guru.

5. Gurus of the Tipiṭaka

In expounding the Tipiṭaka,[4] the books or commentaries[vi] that constitute it each had their own individual gurus on particular subjects. That is to say, the *Vinayapiṭaka* (*Basket of Discipline*), the *Sūtrapiṭaka* (*Basket of Discourses*), and the *Abhidhammapiṭaka* (*Basket of Higher Doctrines*) are each said to have an *ācārya* tradition of gurus, and it is written that they are as follows:[vii]

---

[4] This is the Pāli name for the *Tripiṭaka* (three baskets) that constitute the basic textual canon of Buddhism: Sūtra, Vinaya, Abhidharma.

Vinayapiṭaka (Basket of Monastic Regulatory Discourses):

1. Bhikṣu Upāli	2. Bhikṣu Dāsaka	3. Bhikṣu Sopāka
4. Siggava	5. Bhikṣu Moggaliputta Tissa	

Sūtrapiṭaka (Basket of Narrative Discourses):

While it is not written in the commentaries, it is customarily held that the following were responsible for the willing recitation of these:

1. Ānanda: *Dīghanikāya* (*The Collection of Long Discourses*)
2. Sārīputta's disciples: *Majjhimanikāya* (*The Collection of Middle-Length Discourses*)
3. Mahākassapa: *Saṃyuttanikāya* (*The Collection of Linked Discourses*)
4. Anuruddha: *Aṅguttaranikāya* (*The Collection of Numbered Discourses*)
5. the *Khuddakanikāya* (*The Collection of Minor Discourses*) was not the responsibility of anyone in particular

Abhidharmapiṭaka (Basket of Philosophical Discourses):

1. Sārīputra	2. Bhaddaji	3. Sobhi
4. Piyajālī	5. Piyapāla	6. Piyadassī
7. Kosiyaputta	8. Vigga	9. Saṃdeha
10. Moggaputta	11. Tissadatta	12. Dhammiya
13. Dāsaka	14. Soṇaka	15. Revata

The Guru in the Vajrayāna | *vajrayānay guru*

There are many symbolic forms in Buddhism, and we shall look to explain a variety of them. There is worldly form (*laukika rupaṃ*) and superworldly form (*alaukika rupaṃ*), which are matters of conventional truth (*saṃvṛtisatya*) and ultimate truth (*paramārthasatya*), individual/micro form (*ekākī rupaṃ*) and collective/macro form (*samaṣṭi rupaṃ*), and various other such correspondences. These are mixed in tantric yoga (*tāntrikay yogayā miśraṇa jū*), and a guru must directly supervise the disciple's progress. Therefore, in Buddhist tantra, there is the utmost respect for the guru. On the subject of the guru, there are explanations of the importance of the guru, such as the *Jñānasiddhi* (composed by Indrabhūti), the *Prajñopāyaviniścayasiddhi* (composed by Padmavajra), the *Advayasiddhi* (composed by Lakṣmīṃkārā) and so forth.[viii]

The Great Grace of the Guru | *guruprasād taḥdhaṃ*

1. In Lakṣmīṃkarā's own "*Advayasiddhi*," verse number 33, on the greatness of the subject of the guru, she writes:

   ācāryāt paratararṃ nāsti trailokye sacarācare |
   yasya prasādāt prāpyante siddhayo anekadhā budhai |[ix]

   Benoytosh Bhattacarya explains this as follows:

   "In the whole of moveable and immovable, there is nothing better than a Guru through whose kind offices the wise obtain many kinds of perfections."[x]

   In this world, with its moving and unmoving things, there is nothing greater than the guru. Through his grace, filled with compassion, one can attain liberation.

2. Padmavajra also expressed this. In his "*Guhyasiddhi*," he gave utmost import to the guru:

   ācāryāt paramaṃ nāsti ratnabhūtaṃ tridhātuke |
   asya prasādāt prāpyante siddhayo anekadhā budhai |[xi]

   There is nothing greater than the *ācārya*, a veritable jewel in the Triple Realm,
   By his grace, the learned obtain various accomplishments.

3. Indrabhūti also expressed the matter as such in his "*Jñānasiddhi*:"

   guruprasādo yasyāsti sa labhet tattvam uttamam |
   anyathā kliśyate bālaś cirakālavimohita |[xii]

   He who has the grace of the guru obtains the supreme truth,
   Otherwise, the foolish struggle, deluded, for a long time.

4. The disciple who honors and expresses respect to the guru without criticism will receive the guru's grace and knowledge of the truth. As it is written in the "*Guhyasiddhi*:"

   paryupāsya ciraṃ kālaṃ kāyavākcittato dṛḍham |
   ācāryā sarvabhāvena yāvat tuṣṭiṃ parāṃ gataḥ ||
   tataḥ prāpnoti nirvighnaṃ gurupādaprasādataḥ |
   śiṣyaḥ sunirmalaṃ tattvaṃ saṃpradāyavyavasthitam ||[xiii]

   Having served for a long time steadfastly, with body, speech, and mind,
   And having pleased the *ācārya* with all one's being,
   Then, unobstructed, by the grace of the guru's feet,
   The disciple obtains the perfectly stainless truth and is established in the tradition.

The Necessity of Performing Guru *Pūjā* | *guru pūjā yāyemāḥ*

1. In Padmavajra's "*Guhyasiddhi*," it is also emphasized that one must perform *pūjā* for the guru:

   samayānāṃ ca sarveṣāmuttamaṃ gurupūjanam |
   śrīsamājaṃ tathā cānyaṃ buddharatnakaraṇḍakam ||[xiv]

   Of all the *samaya*s, the guru *pūjā* is supreme,
   Along with the noble assembly, the other basket of the Buddha Gem.

2. It is also written in the *Jñānasiddhi* by Indrabūti that if one is to perform one's practice without distraction and if one is to generate an increase in merit, it is emphasized that it is necessary for one to perform *pūjā* to the guru:

   ārādhyo anekadhā śiṣyaiḥ satsamapadamabhīpsubhiḥ |
   akṣīṇapuṇyakāmaiś ca sarvavighnavināyakaiḥ |
   sarveṣāṃ samayānāṃ hi samayo ayaṃ niruttaraḥ |
   rakṣyo ayaṃ bhavatā nityaṃ sarvasaṃpatpradāyakaḥ ||[xv]

   [He] is to be worshiped in many ways by disciples who long for his properly even feet,
   And by those wishing for undiminishing merit and the removal of all obstacles.
   Among all *samaya*s, this is indeed the unexcelled *samaya*,
   And must be observed by you constantly, for it bestows all fortune.

3. First, when performing the *pūjā*, one must worship the guru full of devotion. And after, one must perform one's practices keeping him in one's mind, as written in the *Guhyasiddhi*. That verse is as follows:

natvā guruṃ bhaktipūrva pūjākāle prayatnataḥ |
paścād dhyāyeta taccittāgyaṃ buddhasiddhipradaṃ śubham |[xvi]

Having bowed to the guru filled with devotion at the time of *pūjā* with diligent effort,
Afterwards, one should think of him foremost in mind, as auspicious, and as granting the accomplishment of buddhahood.[5]

The Secret of Tantra is in the Guru | *guruyāke tantra rahasya du*

1. The lips of the guru indeed reveal the knowledge of the truth. There should not be any doubts about this matter, as it is also written in Lakṣmīṃkarā's *Advayasiddhi*. That is expressed thus:

yattadavyakyarūpaṃ tu sarvasattveṣu saṃsthitam |
guruvaktrāt paraṃ tattvam prāpyate nātra saṃśayaḥ ||[xvii]

That whose unmanifest form abides in all beings,
One obtains that highest truth from the guru's mouth without any doubt.

2. In Padmavajra's *Guhyasiddhi*, it is written that the secret of tantra is entirely in the mouth of the guru. It is written thus:

rahasyaṃ yatparaṃ tantre guruvaktre pratiṣṭhitam |
buddhasiddhipradaṃ dipyaṃ tatsarva kathitaṃ mayā ||[xviii]

That which is the highest secret in tantra is situated in the guru's mouth,
Illuminating and granting the accomplishment of buddhahood; I have told all that.

---

5 Literally, "of a buddha."

The Highest Deva | *param deva*

1. Lakṣmīṃkarā held her brother, King Indrabhūti, to be a guru, calling him the Lord of the World. In his verses composed by him in his "*Jñānasiddhi*," it is written:

   gurureṣa samākhyātaḥ sarvabuddhaiḥ savajribhiḥ |
   sa eva sarvasattvānāṃ śāsako lokanāyakaḥ ||[xix]

   The guru is the one declared by all buddhas and tantric Buddhist practitioners (*vajrins*),
   As he who is the instructor of all beings, the Lord of the World.

2. In Lakṣmīṃkarā's "*Advayasiddhi*," verse number 34, it is emphasized that it is suitable to do *pūjā*s to the guru as the same as the highest god (*deva*). It emphasizes that the guru is awake regarding the whole world, and no one else is like him. It is as follows:

   cāryaḥ paramo devaḥ pūjanīyaḥ prayatnataḥ |

   The *ācārya* is the highest deva and should be worshiped with *pūjā*s diligently.

3. In the *caryā* song by Līlāvajra called "*Hāḍābharaṇa*," he expresses to his guru that "without you, the eyes of this country are dark." If you do not have a guru, you would be just like a blind person in this world. Such a sentiment is evident [in his text].

The One who Shows the Ultimate Truth is the Guru | *paramārtha satyayā khaṃ kanīmha guru he khaḥ*

In chapter seven of the *Caryāmelāpakapradīpa* (*The Lamp for Integrating the Practices*), composed by Āryadeva, considering the guru from the perspective of conventional truth, he is praised as the teacher of ultimate truth. He explains that one cannot do without the words of the guru. His verse is as follows:

yathā dīpo ghaṭāntaḥstho bāhye naivāvabhāsate |
bhinne tu taddhaṭe paścād dīpajvālābhibhāsate ||
svakāya eva hi ghaṭo dīpa eva hi tattvakam |
guruvaktreṇa saṃbhinne buddhajñānaṃ sphuṭaṃ bhavet ||
gaganaṃ gaganodbhūtam ākāśākāśaṃ sa paśyati |
tathaiva hi guruvaktrāt prayogo ayaṃ pradarśitaḥ ||[xx]

Just as a lamp inside a pot does not shine outside it,
But once it is broken, the light of the lamp illuminates,
One's own body, similarly, is like a pot, and truth is like a lamp,
When broken by the words of the guru, Buddha-knowledge becomes apparent,
And that one sees the sky arisen from sky and space from space.
Thus, indeed, is this practice revealed from the guru's mouth.

That is to say, if one lights a lamp and puts it into a pot, the light will not come out. But having broken the pot, [or] if one takes the lamp out of the pot, only then does the light work. Our bodies are just like that pot. There is Prajñā within us. Only when the guru's words break our body, which is like a pot carrying us on his back, can Prajñā be brought out. Thus, one must be pleased with the guru. One can make the Gana Mandala methodically after receiving the guru's instruction. One must offer the well-practiced *mudrās* to the guru. In such a manner, one must perform the *pūjās* humbly. One must serve the guru, thinking of him as a *tathāgata*.

The Guru as a Boat | *duṃgā samān guru*

In the *Vyaktabhāvānugatatattvasiddhi* (*Attainment of the True Clarity of Phenomena*) composed by Yoginī Cintā, she likens the guru to a ship that can grant passage across the ocean of existence:

asmād aghoratarād anantaviṣayād durvāramārārṇavāt |
saṃsārād yadi no bhavanti guravaḥ potopamāstāyinaḥ ||[xxi]
From this most terrible, endless, impassible ocean;[6]
From *saṃsāra*: there would be no saviors if no gurus served as boats.

Lakṣmīṃkarā's brother, King Indrabhūti, also wrote on the topic of the guru's role in the section on the disciple's characteristics in his *Jñānasiddhi* in verse number four. He emphasized that the guru is the one who frees one from *saṃsāra*, which is the web of illusion of existence. As follows:

guruḥ karṇadharo vidvān naukā dharmaḥ prakāśitaḥ ।
saṃsārapāragantaṇāṃ vajrasattvena deśitam ॥

The guru is the learned helmsman, and the ship is the Dharma he revealed,
Taught by Vajrasattva to those crossing beyond *saṃsāra*.

1. In this way, Līlāvajra's disciple, Ḍombī Heruka (c. 777 CE), expressed that his guru gave the way across the stream, writing thus:

gaṃgā jaunā mājhe re vahaī nāī |
tāhīṃ baḍili mātī poīā līle pāra kareï ||[xxii]

Between the Ganges and Yamuna, there goes his boat.
There dwells the mother, and her sons are brought across by Līlā.

---

[6] More literally, the adverbial durvāram would be something like "insurmountable."

The Importance of the Guru | *guruyā mahatva*

The topic of the importance of the guru, on a theoretical level, has been raised in various ways. One method is that, when performing the excellent *pūjās* of the Vajrayāna, the root *ācārya* is viewed as the guru by the disciples. The beginning of *caryā* songs, the "Rāga Mālā," begins with the disciples reading a separate section of verses for the guru. In these verses, it is written that one always, and at all times, bows one's head down to the feet of the guru, as one must perform humble supplication. As follows:

> *yā sā saṃsāracakraṃ viracayati manaḥ saṃniyāgātmahetoḥ*
> *sā dhīryasya prasādād diśati nijabhuvaṃ svāmino nisprapañcam* ।
> *tattvaṃ pratyātmavedyaṃ samudayati sukhaṃ kalpanājālamuktaṃ*
> *kuryāta tasyāṅghriyugmaṃ śirasi savinayaṃ sadguroḥ sarvakālam* ।

> That which fashions the cycle of *saṃsāra* is the mind because of its attachment to the self,
> The Master shows, by the grace of his intelligence, the inherent world, free from discrimination.
> The truth, which is to be personally realized, gives rise to bliss, freed from the web of imagination;
> May you, at all times, humbly place the good guru's two feet on your head.

This is an extract from one of Sarahapāda's song as it appears written in Rāhula Sāṃkṛtyāyana's *Dohākoṣa*. There is a commentary on it in Yogīśvara's *Vajragīti*."[xxiii]

Special Characteristics | *viśeṣatā*

[Based on our discussion so far, it is clear that the guru in the Vajrayāna has the following special characteristics:][7]

1. The guru has great grace.
2. The secrets of tantra are hidden in the mouth of the guru.
3. The guru is the highest *deva.* He is the guide of the world.
4. The guru will make one's practice free from obstruction.
5. The guru is the one who gives passage beyond saṃsāric existence.

The System of the Inner Guru | *adhyātmaka kathaṃyā guru vyavasthā*

Here, it is worth knowing about the place of the cultivation of the inner guru. It should be seen that various scholars emphasized this matter in their writings.

King Indrabhūti described the necessary satisfaction with the guru in Indrabhūti's own *Jñānasiddhi*, where he writes that the gurus are the Buddha, Dharma, and the Saṃgha:

> *gurur buddho bhaved dharmaḥ saṃghaś cāpi sa eva hi |*
> *prasādāj jñāyate tasya yasya ratnatrayaṃ varam ||*[xxiv]
>
> The guru is the Buddha, the Dharma, and also indeed the Saṃgha.
> By his grace, one discerns the three supreme gems.

---

[7] These have been reordered to better match the order in which they were discussed above.

Līlāvajra | *līlāvajra*

Līlāvajra was a tantric master (*tantravid*). In the field of tantra, in the various stages of tantra, a guru is only required in Action tantras (*kriyātantra*), Conduct tantras (*caryātantra*), and Yoga/ Union tantras (*yogatantra*).[8] But for those on the stage of the Unexcelled yoga tantra (*anuttara-yoga-tantra*), there is no requirement for a guru in material form. At that stage, one is adept at: 1. the self-existent (this is non-dual, self-arisen knowledge) and 2. the profound, which, having been experienced just by oneself, one teaches and instructs to bring others to the same level of knowledge. Līlāvajra, also being one who was an adept on the stage of Unexcelled yoga tantra, after that, did not need a material guru. Having experienced that just for himself, he became one who could teach and instruct. In such a state wherein one has become wise in the state that one can teach self-arising knowledge, one becomes one's own guru, which we can say is not natural [i.e., is an exceptional case].

The Bhagavān Buddha's Gurus[9]

A guru in the material state is necessary on the stage where one proceeds towards attaining the knowledge of unexcelled complete and total awakening. The Bhagavān Buddha also, before attaining buddhahood (meaning, when he was living life in the form of a bodhisattva), experienced consecration and learned from each guru in this way. They were thus:[xxv]

---

[8] These are the first three groups of the Vajrayāna tantra corpus, moving from exoteric to esoteric.

[9] Section created so that the following headings are not subsections of the Līlāvajra section.

1. Gurus of the Initial Period | *pārambhika kālayā gurupiṃ*

When Sarvārthasiddha[10] was born, eight *brāhmaṇas* inspected the marks on his body and performed the purificatory rites of the child. Their names were Rāma, Dhaja, Lakkhaṇa, Manti, Yajña, Suyāma, Subhoja, and Sudatta. These were the gurus of the life-cycle rites of the initial period.

2. Educational Guru | *śikṣā guru*

His father Śuddhodhana, to give an education to his own son, handed over his son Sarvārthasiddha to the *brāhmaṇa* called Sabbamitta (or Viśvāmitra), who was well-versed in reasoning, vocabulary, and grammar.[11] This Brahmin Sabbamitta was the guru who gave an education to Sarvārthasiddha.

3. The Guru Who Gave Inspiration for the Great Renunciation | *mahābhiniṣkramaṇayā preraṇā dāyaka guru*

Having become particularly distracted from matters of material enjoyment and the various affairs that are the domain of illusory delusion and the bondage of existence, having thought about how he should act and what he should do, Bodhisattva Sarvārthasiddha immediately left the palace. On the way, he encountered mendicants who inspired him, who were, in fact, deities (*devatās*). Those deities were also on the same rank as a guru.

---

[10] Sarvārthasiddha (or Sarvārthasiddhi) is the standard way for rendering Śākyamuni's name in the Newar tradition. Siddhārtha is used, but it is uncommon.

[11] It seems that the *Lalitavistara* has Viśvāmitra. As for "Siddhārtha," we opted to record Sarvārthasiddha for consistency, as with the following sentence.

4. Āḷāra Kālāma | *ālārakālāma*

After Sarvārthasiddha became a mendicant, he thoroughly learned everything that Ācārya Āḷāra Kālama had to teach with austerities.

5. Uddaka Rāmaputra | *uddakarāmaputra*

Sarvārthasiddha, also not being able to fulfill his wishes with Uddaka Rāmaputra, vowed, with the valuable thought, "Now I shall work for Prajñā by my own intellect and considerations, without relying on another."

6. The Bhagavān Buddha as his Own Guru | *bhagavān buddha svayam guru*

The Bhagavān Gautama Buddha's attainment of buddhahood was accomplished without relying on the instruction of any guru. The gurus written about above were for matters before the attainment of buddhahood. They only gave education on matters of worldly knowledge. They had no involvement in the Buddha's supramundane knowledge.

The attainment of insights within the unexcelled complete and total awakening come solely from within oneself; neither a specific location nor the act of going somewhere is required. There is no necessity to venture out to observe anything in any place. This knowledge resides within our own body, present in every individual. Its nature is so delicate that seeking it through external means is insufficient.

On this matter, something Bhagavān Buddha said himself is worth remembering. It is this:

After finishing the attainment of complete and total awakening, the Bhagavān first went to the Deer Park in Ṛsipaṭana, in Sāranātha, when a naked ascetic called Upaka saw him. He walked to the Bhagavān, and having seen his characteristics and constantly peaceful form, the ascetic was amazed. As he became curious, he asked the Bhagavān:

> "*Ko vā te satthā*," meaning [in Pali] "Who is your teacher?"
> "*Kassa vā tvaṃ dhammaṃ rocesi*," meaning, "Whose Dharma do you prefer?"

The Bhagavān answered thus:

> "*Vimutto sayaṃ abhiññāya*," meaning, "Having attained higher-knowledge myself, I have become liberated."
> "*Na me ācāriyo atthi*," meaning, "I do not have any *ācārya* (guru)."
> "*Ekomhi sammāsambuddho*," meaning, "I, just by myself, have become a complete and fully awakened one (*samyak-saṃbuddha*)."[xxvi]

This, being the state of the attainment of the knowledge of unexcelled complete and total awakening is also called "knowledge of Prajñā" (*prajñājñāna*).[12] For Prajñā Devī, there are no impurities in the saṃsāric world (*sāṃsārik jagatay*). This is because there are no real things (*vastu*) in this saṃsāric world. There is also no one who can show this. This is because the material eye is not able to see this. This is self-existent purity. This is a single state without the boundaries of artificiality. Thus,

---

[12] *Prajñājñāna* is a concept in Vajrayāna with several interpretations. One interpretation, not advocated in the Newar tradition, is that this refers to the stage in tantric initiation (*prajñājñānābhiṣeka*) wherein the initiand has knowledge of the wisdom consort (i.e., he engages in coitus with a female partner). Yagyaman Pati's interpretation of *prajñājñāna* is related entirely to the understanding of liberating wisdom as non-metaphorical, and his discussion of covering nakedness makes clear the rejection in the Newar tradition of the literal interpretation of transgressive language.

it is an entirely naked state. This is because external coverings only apply to that which is lower.

Līlāvajra's Caryā Song: "Hāḍābharaṇa" | *līlāvajrayā hāḍābharaṇa nāṃgu cacā*

In the *caryā* song "Hāḍābharaṇa," Līlāvajra expresses the sentiment of devotion in the form of devotion to Prajñā Devī, who wears clothes on her lower body. In this regard, one's own skeleton is covered. This is also a covering with clothes of that which is lower. This is what the author of the "Hāḍābharaṇa" is indicating. One or two examples here will be valuable.

A. "Without you, the eyes of this country are dark." |
ka. tumha vinu deṣ mi andhārāa

This is one verse in the *caryā* song "Hāḍābharaṇa." "Without you, the eyes of this country are dark," means, "Without you, it is as if we are people without eyes." This is preceded by, "Without the guru, how sour is knowledge" (Middle Indic *vina guru jñāna kaise pāü*). Such words indeed look like those of someone speaking to a woman he likes. But here, having looked at the letters being used, it must be found that this is indeed directed towards Prajñā Devī. One who is an accomplished person, if they have not been able to be devoted to Prajñā Devī or to understand her [teachings], it is indeed sufficient for them to do that to become one who obtains knowledge of *Anuttara-samyak-saṃbodhi*. When one sees Prajñā Devī dwelling within oneself, one will obtain the state of bliss and experience "*sahaja*" (spontaneously born or co-born) bliss. Thus, in short, the essence of this *caryā* song is that Prajñā Devī is concealed and covered, and if one is without her or does not have her, then one's life is in vain. "*Adya me saphalaṃ janma jīvitañ ca me!*" ("Today, my birth and my life are worthwhile!") It comes to be that one can say such a thing.

B. "The Bed of the Three Forms." | *kha. triyaṃ dhāu khaṭa hūṃ*[13]

This is another verse in the "Hāḍābharaṇa." Here, there are three forms that are indicated as being a [single unit he describes as a] bed. These three limbs indicate material forms. When considering the meaning of "form," someone would not automatically think of a bed. The three limbs of the form are body, speech, and mind. Body, speech, and mind, in the state in which they are unified into one mass, bring about a triangular cultivation. Thus, in that triangular state, having received a vision of Prajñā Devī, one

[13] Our translation of *khaṭa* is derived from the meaning in a *vajra* song in Munidatta's c. 1300 CE collection, normally titled *Caryāgītipāda*. In song 28, attributed to Śabara, a similar image to Līlāvajra's is given. In an erotic scene, Śabara's lovemaking with Śabari is described. Śabari represents Nairātymā, indicating that Śabara's embrace with Śabari is a metaphor for his embrace with the concept of no-self. In the description, the bed (*khāṭa*) that the couple embraces is on is said to be made from the three *dhātus* (body, speech and mind). The relevant line reads: *tia dhāu khāṭa paḍilā sabaro mahāsuhe seji chāilī*, translated by Yagyaman Pati as "A cot made of the three materials was laid, Śabara spread the bed with great pleasure." The English word "cot" is actually etymologically derived from the Bangla "*khāṭa*," which appears in these parallel *vajra* song verses. Incidentally, a Newar word for bed is *khāṭā*. Given that the Hāḍābharaṇa involves Prajñā Devī, the song may involve a metaphorical lovemaking similar to that detailed in the song attributed to Śabara. We cannot be conclusive in this regard, however, as we are only aware of the lines from the song given by Yagyamapati. We thank Pronoy Chakraborty for drawing our attention to the verse in Munidatta's *Caryāgītipāda*. The appearance of the verse in the original version is "*triyaṃdha u khaṭa hūṃ*," and "*triyaṃ dhāu khaṭa hūṃ*" is our minor emendation. Our emendation is based not only on the corpus, which has the parallel in the *Caryāgītipāda*, but also on Yagyaman Pati's own explanation of the verse, in which he clearly understands "*tridhātu*" (three materials/forms) and not "*tryandha*" (three blindnesses).

experiences *sahaja* bliss suited to one's state in that bed.[14] This is what is meant by the poetic phrase "The Bed of Three Forms."

In the "Hāḍābharaṇa" *caryā* song, there are many verses expressed with poetic language. When considering this, one must acknowledge Līlāvajra as an accomplished literary figure. Furthermore, in this *caryā* song, many words in the Apabhraṃśa language[xxvii] are used. For instance, after the previously mentioned "Without you, the eyes of this country are dark," there are words like "*chādiṃgela*," "*śālinja*" and so forth. Therefore, Līlāvajra certainly knew the Apabhraṃśa language. In a passage on the commentary on omniscience, called "*Amṛtakarṇikā*," composed by the monk Raviśrījñāna, he cites Līlāvajra's verse in the Apabhraṃśa language: "*Sahājananda ca catukkhaṇa ṇia sambeaṇa jāṇa*,' thus says Līlāvajra."[xxvii] Here, it becomes apparent, as with other places in his *caryā* songs, that he was also accomplished at the Apabhraṃśa language. In summarizing the topics of the *Guhyasamāja* (which concerns the three secrets of body, speech, and mind, and that in uniting these three into one part, called a *samāja* or assembly, by methods involving much "*sahaja*," or innate bliss, one obtains liberation), which are included in the "Hāḍābharaṇa" *caryā* song, and having shown that they are as important as one's own body, it must be said here that one of his specialities is making compact the necessary maxims of his own guru Lakṣmīṃkarā. In this *caryā* song, it is not expressed that a deity is here or there using colors (i.e., describing his forms). Such only describes saṃsāric truth. These *caryā* songs are thus an important style of śāstric literature.

If there is any large or smaller secret *pūjā*, it is not enough to just sing this "Hāḍābharaṇa" in words. When performing a *caryā* song, there is also the tradition of performing *caryā* dance.

---

[14] The bed is a metaphor for the awakened state that occurs when body, speech and mind are in perfect conjunction and the practitioner has a direct experience of *prajñā*, personified as a goddess.

Usually, within the *caryā rāga*, the Ahemdī tune[15] is sung. This is primarily about the guru and liberation obtained by the guru's grace.

In various forms, the guru has various positions in the Buddhist Dharma. They have it in Theravāda, and they also have it in the Mahāyāna Vajrayāna. As for the idea of the internal guru, it is thus present in both the Theravāda and Vajrayāna.

---

i. Amṛtānanda Bhikṣu. *Gṛhī Vinaya Teśro Saṃskaraṇa.* Kathmandu: Ānandakuṭī Vihāra Guṭhī, VS 1995 [1938 CE]. pp. 72.

ii. Buddhadāsa Bhikkhu. *Bālopayogī Sacitta Buddhajīvanī,* tr. Bhikṣu Vinpassī Dhammārāmo. Thailand: Bonajñānja Samūha, 1999. pp. 17-19.

iii. Amṛtānanda Bhikṣu, *Op. Cit.*, 73.

iv. "*Dvīpa*" [here translated as "island"], can mean a cremation ground, an island, and also a refuge. Thus, when saying "Jambudvīpa," [the Sanskrit term for the southern continent of our world, see Chapters 7, 8 and Appendix B] it must [figuratively] mean Jambu-refuge. Thus, it is a jewel-island, a refuge of good qualities.

v. Amṛtānanda Bhikṣu. *Saṃkṣipta Buddha-Jīvanī.* Kathmandu: Ānandakuṭī Vihāra Guṭhī, V.S. 1994 [1937 CE]. pp. 124.

vi. There are two terms for *Tipiṭaka* commentaries, one is "Aṭṭhakathā," and the other is "Aṭṭhavaṇṇā." Sujī Puññānubhāva. *Sampūrṇa Buddhavacana Tipiṭakayā Sāra,*

---

[15] This refers to a particular tune that *caryā* songs may be sung in accord with.

tr. Bhikkhu Sumedha Dhīrasugaṃdho. Saddharma-pracāraka Pucaḥ, n.d. pp. 28.

vii. This tradition was passed on up to the year 234. Sujī Puññānubhāva, *Op. Cit.* pp. 21.

viii. Bhārataratana, Mahāmahopādhyāya, Pāṇḍura Vāmaṇa Kāṇe. *Dharmaśāstrakā Itihāsa,* Part Five. tr. Arjun Chauve Kāshyap M.A. Lucknow: Uttar Pradesh Hindi Institute (Hindi Committee Division), 1984. pp. 31, pp. 8.

ix. Yoginī Lakṣmīkarā Viracitā's Advayasiddhi, pp. 164, v. 33 in Vajravallabha Dvivedi & Samdhong Rinpoche, eds., *Guhyādi-Aṣṭasiddhi Saṃgraha*. Sārnāth, Vārāṇasī: Durlabha Bauddha Grantha Śodha Yojanā, Kendrīya Ucca Tibbatī Śikṣā Saṃsthān. 1988.

x. Benoytosh Bhattacarya, ed., *Sādhanamālā*, vol. II. Baroda: Oriental Institute, 1968. pp. lvi.

xi. Vajravallabha Dvivedi & Samdhong Rinpoche, eds., *Op. Cit.*, "Part Nine," v. 11.

xii. *ibid.*, Indrabhūti Viracita's *Jñānasiddhi*, pp. 95, "Part One," v. 23.

xiii. *ibid.*, Padmavajra Viracita's *Guhyasiddhi*, pp. 52, "Part One," v. 51.

xiv. *ibid.*, "Part Nine," v. 8.

xv. *ibid.*, Indrabhūti Viracita's *Jñānasiddhi*, "Part One," vv. 30-31.

xvi. *ibid.*, Padmavajra Viracita's *Gṛhyasiddhi*, "Part Nine," v. 25.

xvii. *ibid.*, Yoginī Lakṣmīkarā Viracitā's *Advayasiddhi*, v. 30.

xviii. *ibid.*, Padmavajra Viracita's *Guhyasiddhi*, v. 88.

xix. *ibid.*, Indrabhūti Viracita's *Jñānasiddhi*, "Part Thirteen," v. 12.

xx. Janārdan Śāstrī Pāṇḍey, ed., Āryadevaviracitam Cayamilāpakapradīpam. Sārnāth, Vārāṇasī: Durlabha Bauddha Grantha Śodha Yojanā, 2000. pp. 61.

xi. Vajravallabha Dvivedi & Samdhong Rinpoche, eds., *Op. Cit.*, Yoginī Cintā Viracitā's *Vyaktabhāvānugatatattvasiddhi*, Chapter on being stuck in *saṃsāra* (*saṃsāravyavasthā paṭala*), pp. 172.

xxii. Yajñamān Pati *Vajrācārya*, *Līlavajra*, working paper (Saturday, 18 Māgha 2051 VS = 1 February 1995 CE), presented at the Lotus Research Center. This is a working paper on guru devotion and disciples.

xxiii. "Lupta Bauddha-vacana Saṅgraha," *Dhīḥ*: A Review of Rare Buddhist Texts 1, 1986. pp. 78.

xxiv. Vajravallabha Dvivedi & Samdhong Rinpoche, eds., *Op. Cit.*, Indrabhūti Viracita's *Jñānasiddhi* "Part One," v. 24.

xxv. Motikājī Śākya, tr. *Milinda Praśna*, Part Two. Kathmandu (Śrīghaḥ): Dharmakīrti Bauddha Adhyayan Goṣṭhī, VS 2051 [1994/1995 CE]. pp. 228.

xxvi. S.N. Goenka. *Chimekī Deśaharūsaṃga Sneha Sambandha.*, VS 2545 [1988 CE]. pp. 69. This was a Buddha Jayanti commemorative publication.

xxvii. The Apabhraṃśa language was active in India from the sixth century until the twelfth century. Apabhraṃśa was spoken in north and east India. The official story is that it first came out of a *caryā* song called "Kollāyire," which was written in Apabhraṃśa. This is discussed at length in the above cited working paper on *caryā* songs.

xxviii. Dr. Banārasīlāla, ed., Āryamañjuśrī-nāmasaṅgīti of Raviśrījñāna, Āmṛtakarṇikākhyaṭippaṇi of Vibhūticandra, *Amṛtakarṇikodyotavibandhena* ca Sahitā. Sārnāth, Vārāṇasī: Central Institute of Higher Tibetan Studies, VS 2538 [1994 CE], pp. 63.

3.

Selecting a Guru | *guru varaṇa*

Establishing a Guru | *guru sthāpanā*

Here, the topic is that of the material (*bhautik*) guru. The non-material (*abhautik*) and the transcendent guru are not here considered. Regarding the material guru, his responsibilities include teaching general knowledge for living (*śikṣā*), teaching esoteric knowledge (*vidyā*) and performing initiations. He is neither profound nor self-existent, those being traits of the non-material transcendent guru. In Buddhism, the material guru is absolutely necessary. A guru should be established. Since there are various types of gurus, one therefore chooses the kind that is the best fit. This is the most important thing. "Praise of the guru is for the acceptance by the guru"; every detail should be in such a way. This is also said about the obtainment of the guru.

Obtaining a guru in such a way means one should have already chosen a prospective guru. In the selection of a guru, one chooses a guru who is beloved; it is said that a guru who is disliked is rejected. The qualities possessed by the prospective guru must be examined. The acceptable guru is one who has developed the requisite qualities of a guru, and the guru who lacks the requisite qualities should not be accepted. So, therefore, here in this chapter the qualities possessed by the prospective guru are examined.

Good qualities of a benevolent guru | *bhiṃmha guruyā bhiṃ-lakṣaṇa*

The qualities cultivated by a benevolent guru are not base but noble. Now, those qualities are listed for the reader's benefit.

1. Inspiration to find a guru | *prekaraṇā dāyaka guru*

There must be a desire to locate one's own guru and a desire for oneself to be a disciple. The disciples themselves tend to be among the Buddhist lay population. There cannot be any doubt concerning the guru in the minds of any potential disciple, as it is said that the disciple is instructed by a guru on many issues. Therefore, the prospective disciple must have confidence in the discourses of the prospective guru. And the guru should speak well to give strong confidence to the disciple.[i]

2. Fully Protecting | *saṃrakṣak juiphugu*

Everyone makes mistakes. So when it comes to mistakes, a guru should not abandon an immature disciple [who errs]. The thought should be made by the guru, "kindness is useless for the immature disciple; it only results in failure for yourself." Therefore, they should censure an immature disciple for committing a mistake, but they should not censure that disciple in their heart. Anger arises for most, but for someone filled with pity, anger does not arise in the same way. As it is said:

> *"kṛpākrodhaṃ mahāraudra"*
>
> "Pitiable anger and great wrath"

Anger arises after pity.[1] Since "anger burns intensely" by slowly losing the characteristic of kindness towards the immature disciple and letting anger steadily burn, the guru is potentially led by that anger. The anger of the guru Tilopa for the disciple Naropa grew over 12 years. Despite the scolding and abuse suffered by Naropa, he committed no serious mistake, continuing to serve the guru and always keeping him in mind. All this occurred in the midst of a guru test. Naropa undertook a guru test for Tilopa. After all the hard work (Nep. *mehanat*), Tilopa opened up. Finally, Naropā was an accomplished disciple.[ii]

3. The Honorable *Vajrācārya* | *vajrācārya juiphumha*

In the *Kriyāsamuccaya*, the *ācārya* Jagaddarpaṇa stated the traits which make a guru. The *vajrācārya* is explained to be the guru. It is explained that in the *sādhana* of the Prajñā maṇḍala of the honorable *Mañjuśrī*, the *bhāvanā* (meditative visualization) of a guru is, in effect, the *bhāvanā* of a *vajrācārya*. This is explained in the following way:

> *gurupāda sadā natvā vajrācārya tathaiva ca praṇamyādau*
> *likhiṣyāmi mañjuśrīryena sidhyati* |[iii]

> Having perpetually bowed to the feet of the guru, the *vajrācārya*, I write regarding the various obeisances one accomplishes with the aid of Mañjusrī.

The guru, as construed by Aśvaghoṣa in his *Pañcāśikā*, described the concept of a guru as referring to a *vajrācārya*. This is the verse:

> *tasmāt sarvaprayatnena vajrācārya mahāgurum* |[iv]

> So with every effort, the *vajrācārya* is a great guru.

---

[1] This seems to be Yagyaman Pati's gloss of "kṛpākrodhaṃ mahāraudra."

In the *Kriyāsamuccaya* of the *ācārya* Jagaddarpaṇa, the characteristics of a guru are explained:

1. The guru is one who knows the three times. He is one who knows the past, present and future. He must be very clever as regards gain and loss in any activity.
2. The *vajrācārya* is the teacher who shows the tantric Buddhist path. He must understand the benefit of being shown the gnosis that comes from adherence to the Vajrayāna.
3. He is one who works on the sinner. "The activity is set in motion due to the results from great transgressions of the past" means in order to work on the sinner, he must be one who remains engaged in auspicious activity based on events that occurred in the past.[2]
4. He is always skilled regarding both the material and non-material. "The *ācārya*, having clarified both mundane and supramundane activity". He must always skillfully act towards the physical and the transcendent, performing each activity according to how it is to be performed, and he should beneficently explain the philosophy surrounding both physical and transcendent activity.
5. Someone who serves the highest goal—He is established as one who sets in motion the vessel that is his own living form so that service to the highest goal should always come to mind.

According to the *Tattvaratnāvalī* of the *Advayavajrasaṃgraha* (*Compendium of Advayavajra*), this characteristic [of service to the

---

[2] Yagyaman Pati interpreted "*dharmebhyaś caratītyā cārya*" to refer to dharmic activity (*dharmācāray*), rather than dharmas as results of transgressive actions.

highest goal always coming to mind] is obtained along with the aid of the guru:

pratipaṅgannapulaśūnyācintyatālakṣaṇama
ācāryasvayambhūjñānavipaśyānā samarthaḥ,[v]

meaning:[3]

1. He is one who abides with a mind directed towards emptiness.
2. He is one for whom liberating knowledge is self-produced.
3. He is capable in having insight (*vipaśyanā*) [into ultimate reality].

In the Inquiry of Milinda (New.: *Milinda Praśna*; Pali: *Milindapāñha*)

The Inquiry of Milinda is a Buddhist literary text in which several questions arise. In the inquiry of the senior monk (New. *thakii meṇḍaka*) facts were put forth to do with established customs (*vyavahāra*) regarding how the guru *ācārya* should act towards the disciple. The guru *ācārya* Nīnyāgū (Nāgasena) demonstrates such qualities [of how a guru acts].[vi] Here they are now:[4]

---

[3] *pratipannapudgalaśūnyācintyatālakṣaṇān ācāryasvayambhūjñānavipaśyanāśamathaḥ*. Quoted in Gerloff, Torsten. "Advayavajra's 'Tattvaratnāvalī': A Newly Revised Critical Edition." *Journal of Indian Philosophy* 46, no. 5 (2018): 805–43. pp. 822.

[4] In Khuddaka Nikāya, milindapañhapāḷi, meṇḍakapañhārambhakathā, ācariyaguṇaṃ: idha, bhante nāgasena, [1] ācariyena antevāsimhi satataṃ samitaṃ ārakkhā upaṭṭhapetabbā, [2] asevanasevanā jānitabbā, [3] pamattāppamattā jānitabbā, [4] seyyavakāso jānitabbo, [5] gelaññaṃ jānitabbaṃ, [6] bhojanassa {bhojanīyaṃ (syā.)} laddhāladdhaṃ jānitabbaṃ, viseso jānitabbo, pattagataṃ saṃvibhajitabbaṃ, [8] assāsitabbo 'mā bhāyi, attho te abhikkamatī'ti, [9] 'iminā puggalena paṭicaratī'ti {paṭicarāhīti (ka.)} paṭicāro jānitabbo, [10] gāme paṭicāro jānitabbo, [11] vihāre paṭicāro jānitabbo, [12] na tena hāso davo kātabbo {na tena saha sallāpo kātabbo

1. He benevolently takes care of the disciple.
2. "The disciple cultivates certain things and avoids certain things"; he will give the disciple that beneficial instruction.

(sī. pī.)}, tena saha ālāpo kātabbo, [14] chiddaṃ disvā adhivāsetabbaṃ, [15] sakkaccakārinā bhavitabbaṃ, [16] akhaṇḍakārinā bhavitabbaṃ, [17] arahassakārinā bhavitabbaṃ, [18] niravasesakārinā bhavitabbaṃ, [19] 'janemimaṃ {jānemimaṃ (syā.)} sippesū'ti janakacittaṃ upaṭṭhapetabbaṃ, [20] 'kathaṃ ayaṃ na parihāyeyyā'ti vaḍḍhicittaṃ upaṭṭhapetabbaṃ, [21] 'balavaṃ imaṃ karomi sikkhābalenā'ti cittaṃ upaṭṭhapetabbaṃ, [22] mettacittaṃ upaṭṭhapetabbaṃ, [23] āpadāsu na vijahitabbaṃ, [24] karaṇīye nappamajjitabbaṃ, [25] khalite dhammena paggahetabboti. Yagyaman Pati's number 13 is not in the Pali version. Horner's translation of the Pali is as follows (bracketed numerals added): "When a pupil is practising rightly the teacher should rightly practise twenty-five special qualities of a teacher. What twenty-five special qualities? As to this, revered sir, [1] the teacher should constantly and continuously keep a guard over his pupils; [2] he should let each know what is not to be followed and what is to be followed [3] he should let him know about slothfulness and diligence; [4] he should let him know the occasions for lying down; [5] he should let him know about illness; [6] he should let him know what food he may accept or reject; [7] he should let him know a particular quality (in food ?); he should share with him what has gone into his bowl; [8] he should console him, saying: 'Do not be afraid, the goal is approaching for you'; [9] thinking: 'He is visiting this man/ he should let him know about the visit; [10] he should let him know about a visit to a village; [11] he should let him know about a visit to a monastery; [12] he should not hold (foolish) conversation with him; [14] having seen a defect he should have patience with it; [15] he should be zealous; [16] he should do nothing partially; [17] he should keep nothing secret; [18] he should hold nothing back; [19] he should arouse the attitude of a begetter, thinking: 'I have begotten him in the crafts; [20] thinking: 'How should he not deteriorate ?' he should arouse an attitude for growth; [21] thinking: 'I will make him strong with the strength of the rules of training,' he should arouse the attitude (for strength); [22] he should arouse an attitude of friendliness; [23] he should not forsake him in distress; [24] he should not be slothful in anything to be done; [25] by means of the rule he should befriend him if he stumbles" (Horner 1969, 130-131).

3. He convincingly relays information regarding what the disciple should give special attention (*viśeṣa dhyān*) to and what he should not.
4. He ensures that the disciple has an appropriate resting place.
5. He gives the disciple exercise and administers medicine so the disciple is not unhealthy.
6. He makes sure that the disciple is vigilant concerning what is and is not to be eaten or drunk.
7. He is appropriately attentive concerning the matter of the particular diet (*viśeṣa ruci*) of the disciple.
8. He always acts to encourage the mind of the disciple.
9. He clarifies the company the disciple should meet with and the company to avoid.
10. He informs the disciple regarding which villages to go to and which villages to not go to.
11. He informs the disciple regarding what kind of monasteries he should go to and what kind of monasteries he should not go to.
12. He should not joke around with the disciple.
13. He works to alleviate the situation of the disciple's suffering before his own.
14. He is patient regarding any fault of the disciple.
15. He is ever diligent for the sake of the disciple.
16. He upholds religious practice appropriately for the sake of the disciple.
17. He does not keep any secret information from the disciple.
18. He teaches the entirety of the teachings for the sake of the disciple; nothing is held in the closed hand of the guru (*gurumuṣṭhii*).

19. He considers the disciple as the same as a son thinking, "The competence of the disciple reflects his maturity."
20. He skillfully directs the path of the disciple.
21. "Gracious in giving knowledge," he is joyfully charitable towards the disciple.
22. He will act while filled with affection for the disciple.
23. He does leave the disciple alone in a time of need.
24. He always performs his teaching duties for the disciple when he has the chance (*maukā*) to instruct.
25. He immediately guides what the disciple should do in the case that the disciple does not do the correct action.[5]

Testing the Guru | *guru parīkṣaṇa*

The topic of testing the guru may be particularly surprising to some. It may be surprising to say that whenever a guru tests the student, the disciple examines the guru. But in Buddhism, the

---

[5] १. शिष्ययात बाँलाक्क हेर विचार याइ। २. शिष्यं छु याये मजिउ छु याये जिउ धकाः, शिष्ययात बाँलाक्क कना बिइ। ३. शिष्यं विशेष ध्यान बिइमाःगु म्वाःगु खँ ध्वाथुइका बिइ। ४. शिष्यया निंतिं पाछि जुई कथंया च्वनेगु थाय्या व्यवस्था याइ। ५. शिष्य उसाँय् मदुसा माः कथंया वासः यायेगु ज्या याना बिइ। ६. शिष्यं इलय् ब्यलय् नये त्वने खं मखंया चिन्ता यानाच्वनी। ७. शिष्यया विशेष रूचि पाखे पाछि कथंया ध्यान बिइ। ८. शिष्यया मन त्याकेगु कथं न्ह्याबलय् नं ज्या यानाच्वनी। ९. शिष्यं सुनाप संगत याये जिउ, सुनाप याये मजिउ ध्वाथुइका बिइ। १०. शिष्य गन गामय् वने जिउ, गन गामय् वने मजिउ कनाबिइ। ११. शिष्ययात गजाःगु बिहारय् वने जिउ, गजाःगु विहारय् वने मजिउ कनाबिइ। १२. शिष्यनाप ख्याः यायेगु ज्या याइमखु। १३. शिष्यया न्ह्योने थःगु दुःखया खँ कनाः विस्मात याइमखु। १४. शिष्यया दोष दुसा क्षमा याना बिइ। १५. शिष्ययात न्ह्याबलेसं उत्साह विया हे च्वनी। १६. शिष्ययात छसिकथं शिक्षा व्युब्युं यंकी | १७. शिष्ययात छं कथंया खँ मकंसे सुचुका तयेगु ज्या याइमखु। १८. शिष्ययात फुक्कं शिक्षा स्यनाबिइ कनाबिइ, गुरुमुष्ठिइ तया तइमखु। १९. शिष्यया क्षमता ब्वलंकाःगु दु धकाः भाःपिनाः शिष्ययात थः काय् समान भाःपी। २०. शिष्यया लँपु बाया मवनीगु उपाय याना हे च्वनी। २१. शिष्ययात विद्यादान याना च्वनागु धकाः हर्ष एवं आनन्दित जुयाच्वनी। २२. शिष्ययात स्नेहपूर्वक व्यवहार यानाच्वनी। २३. शिष्ययात आपद विपद अवस्थाय् याकःचा त्वःती मखु। २४. शिष्ययात छुं स्यनेगु मौका दयेवं उध्रिमे स्यने कनेगु ज्या याइ। २५. शिष्यं यायेमाःगु ज्या कर्तव्य मयाइगु अवस्थाय् उध्रिमय् न्वानाः लॅ क्यना बिइ

guru-disciple system is based on reciprocity. Therefore, this topic should not cause surprise.

It is not enough to only benefit the student. The guru should also benefit. In a guru-disciple lineage, are the guru and the disciple equal? Gurus provide the connection that is the access point for students. Their time is sacred. This is because they do not engage in any activity that is inauspicious. Therefore, the guru is given pride of place. When it comes to the guru, he is considered equal to the highest god. According to the *Advayasiddhi* of Lakṣmīṃkarā, the guru should be fully praised. Furthermore, the female guru Yoginī Cintā wrote that the guru may be likened to the vessel that is guided across the ocean to the opposite shore.

Having made an investigation of the guru, the disciple determines the fit of the guru; the choice should be made. If a guru is greedy (*lobhī*), selfish (*svārthī*) and base (*ḍhoṃgī*) by nature (*prakṛtyāmha*), the chosen disciple will be developed according to the learning taught by that stupid guru, so he will be accordingly misinformed and confused. In the *Jñānasiddhi* of Indrabhūti, a good and complete (*savistāraṃ*) explanation is given on the topic of faults (New. *kharāva*) to be considered in the assessment of a guru. It occurs in the *Jñānasiddhi* following the test for the good or bad (*sadasad*) guru.[vii] In the section on proper order in the *Kriyāsamuccaya* of Maṇḍalācārya Darpaṇa, it says, "the master is one who observes the rite correctly" (*ācārya lakṣaṇavidhiḥ*).[viii]

Introducing the religious teaching of the living guru and looking at the face of the guru | *guruyā khvāḥ svaye guruyā arti upadeśaṃ he guru mhasīkegu*

Guru selection cannot happen without looking at the face of the guru. The matter of the guru is to be taught with sufficient measure. There was a discourse given by the Lord Buddha in

Rājagṛha concerning appropriate activity. At that time, a renunciant named Sañjaya was also staying there. He had many disciples. Among them were the disciples named Upatissa (Śāriputra) and Kolita (Maudgalyāyana). After they first obtained the true dharma (*amṛta-dharma*),[6] they discussed gaining liberating knowledge (*jñānāmṛta*),[7] it is written that they both wandered together searching for a guru to teach methods for the creation of liberating knowledge (*jnānāmṛta*).

One day in Rājagṛha, Upatissa saw a monk named Assajita going for alms. He observed the monk's conduct. He observed everything about the monk's disposition as he went for alms: the monk's walking, standing, and sitting. Everything he contentedly observed brought on a feeling of joy.

Upon seeing such kindness, in the mind of Upatissa arose the thought that he must come to know this man's guru. "So that such knowledge will be given, there will become a desire that there will be such a venerable guru." This was said in the vicinity of the monk Assajita.

His compassion aroused, the monk Assajita told this short teaching (*saṃkṣipta*) for the sake of instruction—Whatever comes into being, all that has a cause (*gugu naṃ vastu dakvasiyā naṃ hetu (kāraṇa) du*). So too is the destruction of everything (*athe tuṃ ipiṃ dakvayāgu nirodha (nāśa) juyāvanīgu naṃ khaḥ*). This was established by the teacher, the great renunciant, the guru (*thajāḥgu khaṁ (siddhānta) kanīmha he mahāśramaṇa (guru) khaḥ*). According to the tradition, it was said in this way:

---

[6] *Amṛta-dharma* appears to be a synonym for *saddharma*.

[7] *Jñānāmṛta* comes from the Newar translation of the Pāli consulted by Yagyaman Pati. We contend that it refers to the liberating gnosis (Skt. *jñāna*/Pāli *ñāna*) that brings awakening and *nirvāṇa*. Understanding it in this way incorporates *-amṛta*, to capture its meaning of "deathless" in relation to *nirvāṇa*.

1. *ye dhammā hetuppabhā teṣām hetu tathāgato āha* |
   teṣāṃ ca yo nirodha evamvādi mahāsamano ||[ix]
2. *ye dharmā hetuprabhavā hetuṃ teṣāṃ tathāgato hyavadat* |
   teṣāṃ ca yo nirodha evaṃvādī mahāśramaṇaḥ ||[x]

This *śloka* is in the *āryā* meter. Furthermore, it is listed in such a way in the completion of a handwritten book, that is, a handwritten manuscript:[8]

3. *ye dharmā hetuprabhavā hetusteṣāṃ tathāgataḥ* |
   hyavadatteṣāṃ ca yo nirodha evaṃvādī mahāśramaṇaḥ ||[xi]

In *Blue Annals*, it is translated into English.

> "Of those things which spring from a cause, the cause has been told by the Tathagata;
> And their suppression likewise, the great Sramana has revealed."

Upon hearing this (i.e., "*ye dharmā hetu...*"), Upatissa immediately became contended and moved since he had never heard such a profound teaching before and learned how to worship a guru through the act of *darśan*. Having thought, "In this way an appropriate guru is to be worshiped," the wish was fulfilled. Then he went to his best friend Kolita. Kolita was also

---

[8] The difference here appears to be that it is written as a single sentence, with *hyavadat* and *teṣāṃ* combined due to the orthography required in handwritten Nepalese and Nāgarī scripts. However, there is still a *daṇḍa* breaking the *śloka*, so the difference is not immediately clear. All spacing has been left to preserve it as it appeared in the Devanāgarī of the Newar book. In a footnote Yagyaman Pati note that, when a *caesura* is made this way, the first section of the verse is in the *anuṣṭubh*, while the second section has the 30 *mātra*s of the *āryā* meter.

moved by the same teaching. They went together for *darśan* in the presence of the Lord Buddha. The two of them became the primary disciples (*agraśrāvaka*) of the Lord Buddha, named Śārīputra and Maudgalyāyana, since the teaching of the equal, *amṛta* dharma is never destroyed. Though this dharma has arisen, it will not be destroyed. Śārīputra and Maudgalyāyana, now having established a guru, listened to the religious instruction of the guru in his presence.

In the thirteenth chapter of his *Jñānasiddhi*, the esteemed Indrabhūti brings up a characteristic that is not possessed by a true guru (*sadyaguru*). What was said by him is, "Some gurus are greedy. One should never engage such a guru." What is written in the *Jñānasiddhi* is:

> *anye ye guravaḥ khyātā mithyājñānābhimāninaḥ* |
> *lobhādyarthaṃ prakurvanti dharmasya deśanāṃ parām* ||
> *pāpamitrāś ca te bālā: sattvanāśe pratiṣṭhitāḥ* |
> *mārapākṣikagotrās te aparātmāno vināśakāḥ* ||[xii]

> Others are famed teachers who are arrogant due to their erroneous knowledge.
> They preach the supreme teachings of the dharma for the sake of worldly gain.
> And they are childish friends of sin who bring about the destruction of what is good.
> Members of factions of *māras*, they bring about the ruin of others.

---

i. Bhikṣu Amṛtānanda. *Gṛhī-Vinaya*. Lalitpur: Kumārī Pāṭī Yala, VS 2055 [1998/1999 CE]. pp. 58.

ii. Ṭhākura Sena Negī. *Vajrayānī Anuttara Yoga*. Vārāṇasī: Kendrīya Ucca Śikṣā Saṃsthān Sārnāth, 1999. pp. 491-492.

iii. Yajñamān Pati *Vajrācārya. Vajrācārya Pulupālu* [Light on the *Vajrācārya*]. Number 13. Lotus Research Center. pp. 32.

iv. *ibid.*

v. Shastri, H.P., ed. *Advayavajrasaṁgraha.* Gaekwad's Oriental Series 40. Baroda: Oriental Institute, 1927. pp. 16.

vi. Motikājī Śākya, tr. *Milinda Praśna.* Kathmandu (Śrīghaḥ): Dharmakīrti Bauddha Adhyayan Goṣṭhī, VS 2059 [2002/2003 CE]. 1.5-6.

vii. Indrabhūti's *Jñānasiddhi*, pp. 130, "Part Three: Gurulakṣaṇa Chapter." in Vajravallabha Dvivedi & Samdhong Rinpoche, eds., *Guhyādi-Aṣṭasiddhi Saṃgraha.* Sārnāth, Vārāṇasī: Durlabha Bauddha Grantha Śodha Yojanā, Kendrīya Ucca Tibbatī Śikṣā Saṃsthān. 1988.

viii. The Ācāryalakṣaṇavidhi in the *Kriyāsamuccaya* of Maṇḍalācārya Darpaṇa.

ix. *Dhīḥ* 23, pp. 127; Vinaya Piṭaka: Mahāvagga 1.17.39.

x. *Dhīḥ* 20, pp. 90; Vinaya Piṭaka, Mahāvagga 1.23.40; Vrajavallabh Dvivedi and Samdhong Rinpoche, eds. *Op. Cit.* "Introduction," pp. 54.

xi. If it is divided this way [with the caesura following *tathāgataḥ*] then the first verse is in the *anuṣṭubh* meter and the second verse [beginning with *hyavadat*] is in the āryā meter.

xii. *ibid.* Indrabhūti's *Jñānasiddhi*, "Chapter Thirteen," v. 13-14.

4.

Examination of the Disciple | *śiṣya parīkṣaṇa*

A Disciple's Praiseworthy or Blamable Conduct must be told to the Good Disciple | *śiṣyapiṃke dayemāḥgu guṇa va nindanīya śiṣya-vyavahāra*

In the guru-disciple tradition, the role of the guru is to see, up to now, how far the disciple's conduct has reached and whether it has gone to excess. If the disciple's conduct has been good, the guru will also be a successful guru. If the disciple's behavior is not proceeding well, that is as far as he can go relying on the guru's knowledge [at that time]. If the disciple's conduct is good, he will obtain accomplishments. He will be one who can be taught the knowledge of the truth. One who can undergo such teaching according to the guru's wishes can become a disciple. Those who cannot engage in good conduct for the guru would not be fit for the guru's compassion. As a disciple, such a person would not be able to receive the knowledge of Prajñā from a guru. No matter how much one reads books, that alone will not give rise to practice. It is necessary that the teachings concerning practice come directly from the mouth of a guru. All the secrets of tantra are concealed in the words of the guru. Since such things come from a guru, one must become a dear disciple of a guru.

There are also various types of disciples. These type are evident from what previous scholars have said about there being such and such disciples.

Disciples Must Comply with a Code of Conduct | *śiṣyapisaṃ pālana yāyemāḥgu ācāra saṃhitā*

After choosing a guru, an apprentice must also look upon their guru with a sense of humility. According to the book of Anaṅgayogī (Anaṅgavajra), called the *Ḍākinī Guhyasamaya Sādhana*, one should not leap beyond the reasoning and plans of the guru, which are as a *vajra* cage, and one also should not disobey the instructions of the guru. If one does so, one will undoubtedly have a troubled life, and in the next world, one will certainly end up in hell, and so forth. So it is written. One must then recant, prostrating at the feet of the guru's wife, uttering one's recantation. On this subject, a verse is written as follows:

guroś chāyāṃ na laṃghayed gurupatnī ca pādukām ।
satataṃ ye laṃghayanti ne narāḥ kṣuradhāriṇaḥ ॥
susiddho api mahāśiṣyo gurorājñāṃ na laṃghayet ।
iha loke bhavet kaṣṭa paraloke narakaṃ vaset ॥

One should not overstep the shadow of the guru nor the sandals of the guru's wife.
Those constantly overstepping are not men but are bearers of razors.
Even the well-accomplished great disciple should not overstep the guru's command;
He would face hardship in this world, and in the next world, he would dwell in hell.

As said in such books, the disciple must always be absorbed in guru devotion. One must receive the guru's commands to accomplish such an accomplishment [i.e., *sādhana*]; this point is well emphasized. On this topic, there is a verse as follows:

evaṃ matvā sadā śiṣyo gurubhaktiparāyaṇaḥ ।
sādhayed vipulāṃ siddhiṃ guror ājñāprayatnataḥ ॥[i]

Considering this at all times, the disciple who is absorbed in guru devotion
Would accomplish extensive accomplishment by diligently following the guru's commands.

Before taking on a disciple, the guru engages in various examinations of the disciple. Only if they are entirely suitable in the guru's eyes will they be taken on as a disciple, and if not, they will not. Thus, after the guru examines and sees one as his own son, if he says something is not to be done to one whom he has accepted as his disciple, whatever he says should not be done: that should not be done. King Indrabhūti himself made his own son Padmasaṃbhava his own disciple and told him he should not go where he wanted or do what he wanted (Padmasaṃbhava is also called Indrabhūti's Dharma-son). Thus, Padmasaṃbhava, having gone against his own father in his mind, having been exiled from his own country, [had to] leave the country and went to Lhāsā. The people of Lhāsā regarded him as the highest guru. Even today, the lama gurus (i.e., Tibetan gurus) of Lhāsā are performing *pūjā*s to Padmasaṃbhava as a guru.

It appears that the development of treatises on the method of the guru-disciple examination has a particular form. It features substantial cultivation of the guru-disciple relationship such that it is seen as the relationship between the father and son in one's own household. It goes so far as the guru abandoning his own son [by blood] as there is the son of another who must take refuge in him as a disciple. There are sons by blood made worldwide, but the disciple-son is one to whom a lamp is transmitted; thus, one cannot feel astonished at such a thing.

Many disciples willingly come to accept the theory of a guru. In this regard, Līlāvajra was one such person. Līlāvajra's guru was Lady Lakṣmīṃkarā, the author of the *Advayasiddhi*. Lakṣmīmkarā, having seen an image of a deity, declared that humans are great and introduced something new. It was reported that she created an image of wood, clay, stone, metal, and so forth, unlike any human before. Līlāvajra was the one who verified this report. Having researched that report for 500 months, upon finally verifying it, he understood.

Līlāvajra, having declared how great the body of a human was, was taught and made to know about it.[1] After he imported this learning to Nepal, he established the custom whereby it is said that one must worship one's own body.[2] A saying goes, "Blessed is it to obtain a body."[3] It is extremely blessed just to bear a body. Also, "Today, my birth has been fruitful; I have easily obtained a human existence,"[ii] the essence of which is that "I have attained a human birth." Having heard and told this, a tradition with a practice was created relating to this, which one must undertake. Therein, one must take, if available, vermillion, flower, yogurt,

---

[1] It is unclear if this means he saw the image and then understood, but this seems to be the idea: Lakṣmīṅkarā taught Līlāvajra about the greatness of the human body.

[2] This refers to the Newar Buddhist practice *mha pūjā*. *Mha pūjā* (body worship) is performed on the first day of the Newar year, which occurs in the Autumn. One creates a maṇḍala and then offers this maṇḍala to their own body, and treat their body as the object of veneration. It is meant to build good fortune in the New Years for the participant. The various foods detailed in this passage are also eaten at the celebration of the New Year.

[3] This saying may come from the *Rāmcarit Mānasaḥ*.

egg, fish, cloth (and if not available, a sacred thread, *jajaṅkā*). Thus, to settle whatever new work or challenge one has, or if one must go out somewhere, having done this "Body Worship" (*kāy*[4] *pūjā*, New. *mha pūjā*), no obstacle or annoyance will come. This gave us the custom of the Sagaṃ festival.[5] If you are fearful, [doing this ritual,] you will come to have substantial fortune; having thought [one's fear] to be nothing more than the deception of an eyebrow hair in the eye; having given these things during Sagaṃ, one's body will be fortunate likewise. Thus, this practice of making fortunate and pacifying whatever destruction may come is also a cultural tradition of Nepal.

Therefore, before the start of the Nepāl Saṃvat era (879/880 CE), it is said that the country was one large city which burned, whereupon people ran away this way and that way. It appears that the fire did not reach Bū Bahāḥ in Lalitpur, and without any reliable vessels [for water to put out the fire] and the fire having reached various places in the town, it appears that they came from the great city and gathered together there.[iii] Everyone spoke dearly to one another and were pleased. Although the country was in an emergency and a disaster, they performed propitiation for fortune and peace (*svasti śānti*) on the bright half of the month of Kārtika. The countryfolk all mutually had the same meal and methodically performed worship of their bodies, which is also taken to be part of Sagaṃ. This continues today in the form of a nationwide celebration ("*Denakhaḥ*") called "*Mha Pūjā*" (Body Worship). When one says "fortune and peace" (i.e., *svasti śānti*) quickly with

---

[4] Typically in Newar, *kāy* means a son. But in this instance, *kāy pūjā* plainly refers to well-established practice of worshiping one's own body (*mha pūjā*).

[5] The *sagaṃ* meal is mentioned throughout Löwdin, Per. *Food, Ritual, and Society: A Study of Social Structure and Food Symbolism Among the Newars*. Kathmandu: Mandala Book Point, 1998. A dedicated description is found on pp. 95..

the mouth, the "*sva*" from "*svasti*" (fortune) and the "*nti*" from "*śānti*" (peace) are joined, and one just says "*svanti*," which indeed is also still a way in which the idea of a nation-wide celebration ("*Denakhaḥ*") is expressed in Newar.[iv] In this manner, the [establishment of the] practice of *Mha Pūjā* in the country of Nepal was the doing of Līlāvajra.

Guru devotion is also seen in his composition of *caryā* songs, wherein we can observe his particular manner of guru devotion. Līlāvajra composed these *caryā* songs for his gurus:

"satgurucaraṇena ārādhye"

"The Worshipful Feet of the True Guru" — *Hāḍābharaṇa*

"satgurucaraṇakamalaprasādā"

"The Grace of the Lotus-like Feet of the True Guru" — *Jvalitavajrānala*

"satguru ājñā śiregata dhariyā"

"Bearing the Command of the True Guru on the Head" — *Vajramayabhūmi*[6]

In Padmavajra's *Guhyasiddhi*, it is written in a special preface that those who blame the guru will not obtain the truth. It is written that disciples who will obtain knowledge of the truth must perform good conduct. Another *siddha*, Anaṅgavajra, writes in his *Prajñopāyaviniścayasiddhi* that those who show respect to the guru will obtain the truth, that the conduct of evil disciples cannot warrant the compassion of the guru and that only good disciples can receive the favor of the guru. Thus, King Indrabhūti

[6] These three lines by Līlāvajra appear to be invocations to the guru sung at the start of each respective song.

also emphasized in his *Jñānasiddhi* that one only receives knowledge of the truth in the guru's grace. He made a separate section on the topic of the necessary characteristics of disciples, which are manifold.

There is a kind of conduct for disciples who are not dear to the guru. There are also different types of disciples:

1. There are even disciples who are too shy to accept a guru. In the story of the disciple called Dharmaśrīmitra, he gradually and slowly came to be examined for discipleship under Mañjuśrī; not having known the behavior of those who listen to Mañjuśrī's teachings, he was too shy to accept Mañjuśrī as a guru. After Mañjuśrī finished giving a Dharma teaching, when all of the laymen and laywomen (*upāsaka*s and *upāsikās*) who were listening to his teaching had departed, he bowed down to that guru's feet. If such a disciple goes alone to a guru, he may perform homage, but if he is in a group, he may not be able to honor the guru. This story is written in the *Svayambhū Purāṇa*.[7]

2. There are also disciples who criticize the guru. Obstinate disciples cannot obtain the truth. Padmavajra wrote verses about such people who criticize in his *Guhyasiddhi*,[v] [writing that] those who criticize cannot obtain the knowledge of the truth. One must think of the guru and Vajradhara as being the same person. [Doing so], if one was formerly an obstinate disciple, they will obtain accomplishment by such consideration. If one does not know the qualities of knowledge, one should continue honoring the guru. After learning and being taught the qualities of knowledge, there is nothing that one does not know, owing to the guru. When such people are going out alone, they will still bow down to the guru. This means that they don't bow down before

---

[7] This is in Chapter 6 of the *Svayambhū Purāṇa*.

anyone else in society [except the guru]. This is explained, part by part:

paśyanti ye hy anānātvaṃ guror vajradharasya ca ǀ
prāpnuvanty atra te tvaṃ siddhisaṃdohalakṣaṇam ǁ
ye punar māninaḥ krūrāḥ śaṭhā dhūrtāḥ prapañcakāḥ ǀ
rāgādyābattaḥ ciktaś ca kuto labdhaṃ kuto na tu ǁ
śāṭhacena tu guruṃ tanvā chidrānveśaṇatatparam ǀ
mithyābhimānino duṣṭā vāgvādeṣu sadā ratāḥ ǁ
vajrabhrātṛgurūṇāṃ ca vañcanābaddhacetasaḥ ǀ
prāpnuvanti na te sattvāstatpadaṃ siddhidaṃ param ǁ
anya api cātra dṛśyante paryupāsya gurūn dṛḍham ǀ
praṇāmapūjāsatkāraiyavit prāptaṃ samīhitam ǁ
prāpte tu tatpade divye purane api vyavasthitam ǀ
na jānanti durātmānaḥ ko ayaṃ kasmād ihāgakataḥ ǁ
dṛṣṭvā apy ekākinaṃ dūre praṇāmaṃ kurvate dṛḍham ǀ
bahūnāṃ tu punar madhye svāgate api daridratā ǁ
evaṃ vidhāstu ye sattvāḥ prāpnuvanti na te padam ǀ
paraṃ paramanirvāṇaṃ yad uktaṃ bhūtavādinā ǁ
anya api cāpare sattvā dṛśyante gurunindakāḥ ǀ
tyaktajjā durācārāḥ saṃbhūtaguṇadūṣakāḥ ǁ

For those who see the unity of the guru and Vajradhara,
Here, they obtain the abundance of the characteristics of accomplished beings.
But those who are arrogant, cruel, deceitful, cunning, false,
Whirled by passion and so forth, how can they obtain understanding?
And those who are deceitful to the guru, having bowed down to fault-seeking as the highest good,
Defiled by false pride and consistently delighting in verbal disputes

With their gurus and *vajra* brothers, and with minds bound by deceit,
They do not obtain the state of truth or the highest accomplishment.
Here also, others are seen who firmly worship gurus,
With prostrations, rituals, and respect, they obtain what they desired.
But, upon [the respectful disciples] obtaining that divine state, even though [this system was] established in the past,
The wicked do not know who they are or how they came to attain [that state].
It is seen [that the respectful disciples] perform prostrations [to the guru] firmly from a distance, even though alone;
Even though welcomed among many, [the wicked remain] in poverty.
Such beings as these do not obtain that state,
The highest and supreme Nirvāṇa, which is spoken of by the speakers of the real.
Here, also, other beings are seen criticizing the gurus,
And having died and been born, those wicked ones are born with bad qualities.

This is also described in the *Prajñopāyaviniścayasiddhi* composed by Anaṅgapāda: Evil disciples cannot obtain accomplishment. The guru has compassion on good disciples. An expression of this compassion can be seen written in the following *śloka*:

niravagrahacittena guruṇā api kṛpālunā ।
śiṣyasya grahaṇārthāya saṃgrāhyaṃ taddhitāya ca ॥[vi]

Also, by the compassionate guru with an ungrasping mind,

For the sake of accepting the disciple, who is to be accepted for his benefit...[8]

3. There is also the matter of the selfish disciple. To become an *ācārya* or a *yogī*, the evil disciple goes into the guru's presence. But it cannot be thought that they will obtain buddhahood. After obtaining knowledge from the guru, they will leave [and consider themselves] to be equal to the guru. If they do not get knowledge from the guru, they will also leave the guru. On this topic, Anaṅgapāda wrote in his *Prajñopāyaviniścayasiddhi*:[vii]

yogitā ācārya saṃjñā ca katham asmākam astv iti ।
etat mātrapravṛttās te buddhatvaṃ pratinārthinaḥ ॥
kathaṃcit prāpya te jñānaṃ mānayante na guruṃ purā ।
jñātāro vayam ity āhurmattaḥ kecin na cāpare ॥
anye ca kupitāḥ prāhuḥ gṛhāṇaitat samarpitam ।
ahaṃ na tava śisyo asmi na bhavān sāmprataṃ guruḥ ॥
kutas teṣāṃ bhavet siddhiḥ saukhyaṃ caiveha janmani ।
guruvañcanacittā ye te bhramanti viḍambitāḥ ॥

"How can there be the yogic ability and title of an *ācārya* for us?"

Devoted only to this thought, they have no intention of attaining buddhahood.

If somehow they obtain knowledge, they do not respect the guru as before,

Some arrogantly declare, "We are knowledgeable," whereas others do not.

And others, being upset, say, "Take this, which is offered;"

[8] Translation following the Sanskrit in Bhattacharyya, Benoytosh ed., *Two Vajrayāna Works*, Baroda: Oriental Institute, 1929, p. 14 v.34cd:

"*śiṣyasyāgrahanāśāya grāhyaṃ tasya hitāya ca.*"

"I am not your disciple;" "You are not the guru now."
Where would there be accomplishment or happiness for them in this life?
Whoever has their minds deceitful towards the guru, they wonder vexed.

This truly means that to obtain root knowledge, one must be stalwart towards the guru. One must not criticize the guru. Thus, in the first section of the *Guhyasiddhi*, verses 51 and 52, it is written as follows:

paryupāsya ciraṃ kālaṃ kāyavākcittato dṛḍham ।
ācārya sarvabhāvena yāvat tuṣṭiṃ parāṃ gataḥ ॥
tataḥ prāpnoti nirvighanaṃ gurupādaprasādataḥ ।
śisyaḥ sunirmalaṃ tattvaṃ saṃpradāyavyavasthitam ॥

Steadfastly having served, for a long time, with body, speech, and mind,
The *ācārya*, in every way, until utmost satisfaction is reached,
One then obtains, by the grace of the guru's feet, non-obstruction,
And the disciple, truly and stainlessly, is established in the tradition.

It is also written thus in the *Prajñopāyaviniścayasiddhi* composed by Anaṅgapāda that the guru is the lord of the world. Thus, one must abandon arrogance and honor the guru to do what is wholesome. Only then will one obtain the jewel of truth:[viii]

ataeva sadā sadbhiranta phaladāyakaḥ ।
ācāryaḥ sarvabhāvena ātma śreyo arthavāñchibhiḥ ॥
īrsyāmātsaryamutsṛjya mānāhaṃkāram eva ca ।

māyāśāṭhyaṃ tathāpāsya saṃbodhai kṛtaniścaryaḥ ॥
sadā parahitasyaiva caryayā akampyacetasā ।
paryupāsyo jagannātho guru sarvārthasiddhidaḥ ॥
mānaṃ śāṭhyaṃ kapaṭapaṭalaṃ sarvam utsṛjya dhīraiḥ ।
yeḥ sāmnāyaiḥ gurusamayaḥ śraddhayā sevya te atra ॥
agrāḥ prāptāḥ sakalasugatā yat samāsādya bodhim ।
nūnaṃ tat tair jinaguṇapadaṃ prāpyate tattvaratnam ॥[ix]

Thus it is always [considered] by the virtuous seeking their own welfare:
The *ācārya*, in every way, is the bestower of endless fruits.
Having indeed cast aside envy and jealousy and even pride and arrogance,
And having thus discarded illusory deceit, he is resolved on perfect awakening.[9]
Always with an unshakable mind and conduct for the sake of others,
The worshipful lord of the world, the guru, gives accomplishment for the sake of all.
The wise, having abandoned all pride, deceit, and the mass of hypocrisies,
According to tradition, undertake the guru *samaya* (commitment) here with faith.
Having attained the highest and having approached awakening like every buddha,
Indeed, the state of the qualities of the jinas is obtained by them, which is the jewel of truth.

The *Jñānasiddhi* was composed by the esteemed Indrabhūti. Therein, he also describes the good and bad gurus.

It will be seen that each guru, before accepting a disciple, must perform their examination. They will perform the observation of

[9] Reading "*saṃbodhau kṛtaniścayaḥ.*"

one or two interesting things. After examining the lineages of the five buddhas, they will perform the name-giving ceremony (*nāmābhiṣeka*), and they will be named in accord with their buddha lineage.

These days, there is also the disciple's examination. It developed in the past establishment of the guru-disciple tradition. In the development of the training institution (e.g., a *vihāra*), there were also examinations of disciples. Long ago, there was a direct examination between the guru and disciple. That is not the case these days. Thus, we should look at the circumstances between former times and today. Each *vihāra* and *mahāvihāra* has a principal deity. We see in the later development of the institution of the *vihāra* in the medieval period, where this ancient establishment was brought to be a new educational institution's "entrance examination," that the examination of the disciple became the task of the principal deity of a *vihāra*.

---

i. "*Guhyasamayasādhanasaṅgraha*," *Dhīḥ: A Review of Rare Buddhist Texts* 1 (1986), pp. 40.

ii. Yagyaman Pati Bajracharya, "Mhapūjā: Bhiṃtunā," in *Bhiṃtunā*, edited by Jagdish Manandhar. Kathmandu: Bhiṃtunā Prakāśana, NS 1116 = 1995 CE, pp. 14.

iii. Buddha Jayanti Celebration Committee Yasodhar Mahavihar, eds., *Vidyādhara Saṃskārita Yaśodhara Mahāvihāra Saṅgha*, Study, no. 2537. Lalitpur: Bu Bahāḥ, NS 1113 = 1992 CE. pp. 20-21.

iv. Satyamohan Joshi, *Nevāḥtay Dakalay Taḥjigu Nakhaḥ Mhapujā* (A study on the thoughts of people dwelling in various places), (Lalitpur: Lok Sahitya Parishad 11 & 48 Bakhauṃ Bāhāḥ, n.d.), 21-23.

v. Vajravallabha Dvivedi & Samdhong Rinpoche, eds., *Guhyādi-Aṣṭasiddhi Saṃgraha* (n.d.), "Padmavajra Viracita *Guhyasiddhi*," pp. 8-9.

vi. *Ibid.*, "Śrī Anaṅgapāda Viracita *Prajñopāyavinaścayasiddhi*," "Part Three," 2, v. 34.

vii. *Ibid.*, "Śrī Anaṅgapāda Viracita *Prajñopāyavinaścayasiddhi*," "Part Two," vv. 18–21.

viii. *Ibid.*, "Śrī Anaṅgapāda Viracita *Prajñopāyavinaścayasiddhi*," "Part Two," vv. 24-26.

ix. *Ibid.*, "Śrī Anaṅgapāda Viracita *Prajñopāyavinaścayasiddhi*," "Part Two," v. 34.

5.

The Guru-Disciple Tradition | *guru-śiṣya paramparā*

The Clan of the Guru | *gurukula*

Gurukula (the clan of the guru) is in the old language.[1] A long, long time ago, the custom was to live in the guru's *āśrama* and learn there. Not until he was at the *āśrama* of the guru did the disciple develop sufficient learning. It would not be the case that the disciple goes to his own home. Not only was his residence in the home of the guru, but the disciple would be staying inside the

[1] *Gurukula* refers to an educational system wherein all disciples were in residence at the home of their teacher, with *kula* the Sanskrit term for a clan or extended family. This *gurukula* educational system is a normative model for Brahminical education in South Asia. The word *kula* gains further purchase in a Mahāyāna setting, wherein all buddhas are identified with a particular buddha clan or family (*buddhakula*). The meaning contained by *kula* is deepened even further in a Vajrayāna setting, wherein all initiates become a member of a particular *buddhakula*. Finally, the meaning of the term is deeper still in Newar Buddhism, wherein most tantric initiations double as life cycle rites which are determined according to the family of one's birth (*janmakula*). Yagyaman Pati invokes all of these meanings of *kula* in this brief discussion.

physical space of the guru's home at all times. Essentially, his life was spent in the *āśrama* of the guru. In this situation, he would consider the *gurukula* to supersede the clan of his birth (*janmakula*). The affiliation of the disciple becomes whatever the affiliation of the guru is. A saying regarding the lineage that respectable people say is "the disciple of which guru?". This expression is said to refer to the *gurukula* since it is well-known terminology (i.e., "the disciple of such-and-such guru" is a part of the related *gurukula*). When in Kapilavastu, the Lord Buddha was not a son of the Śākya clan (*śākyakula*) of his father, King Śuddhoddhana. Rather, we are told that he was of the buddha clan (*buddhakula*). Here it is pertinent to bear the distinction in mind between one's *janmakula* and one's *gurukula*. The relationship between the guru and disciple is comparable to and as important as the relationship between a father and son. It is said that the disciple performs the death rites of the guru. He is as a son.

The Guru-Disciple Tradition in the Tripiṭaka | *tripiṭakay guru-śisya paramparā*

The guru tradition laid out in the Tripiṭaka became the established tradition. This tradition is very ancient and is still around. In Vajrayāna, the tradition is passed on from the guru directly to the disciple. Nowadays, the word for tradition (*paramparā*, also meaning a lineage) refers to tantric initiation (*dīkṣā*). In this situation (i.e., *dīkṣā* by *paramparā*), the older sense of the word *paramparā* is absent.

The Guru-Disciple Lineage in Vajrayāna | *vajrayānay guru-śiṣya paramparā*

There is also a guru-disciple tradition in Vajrayāna. The training (*śikṣā*) and initiation (*dīkṣā*) in Vajrayāna are extremely serious. This is because through initiation into and proper training in Vajrayāna, it is possible to obtain buddhahood in a single lifetime, rather than practicing across many lives in the hopes of attaining buddhahood. Initiation into the Vajrayāna is such a serious thing because the causes and conditions necessary to provide a person such an opportunity are exceedingly rare. It is exceedingly rare because it is naturally (*svābhāvika*) hidden (*gupta*). The guru-disciple lineage itself also developed in an extremely secret manner. Therefore, although the saying is "the disciple of which *guru*[*kula*]?", the person asking the question and the person providing an answer do not actually know to which group a person belongs since the secrecy is maintained up to the present day.

The secret content is passed on from one individual to another individual. The passage of a mantra in *dīkṣā* will be passed from the lips of the guru directly into the ear of the disciple. A verse was written regarding this very thing, the compact (*mela*) between a disciple and a guru. This topic is recorded in texts such as the *Amanasikāra*:

> *...śiṣyānugrahe jivhāyāṃ mantrābhilikhya svahrdaśminādaṃ praveśya āveśayata*[i]

> Having inscribed the mantra upon the tongue of the disciple, having entered into the disciple's heart, the disciple is as one possessed.

The guru-disciple lineage according to texts | *grantha kathaṃyā guru-śisya paramparā*

Within Vajrayāna, there are many śāstric texts. The discourse on tantric methods and ritual arrangements (*vidhi vidhāna*) varies depending on the individual śāstric text consulted. In the same way, the guru-disciple lineage of the Vajrayāna given by individual *śāstras* and books varies. For example, the *Guhyasamājatantra*, *Cakrasamvaratantra*, *Vajravārāhītantra*, *Kālacakratantra*, *Caṇḍamahāroṣaṇatantra*, *Kriyāsamuccaya*, and so on. Nowadays in Nepal, the custom to pass on the lineage is called "giving *dīkṣā*." But not all *dīkṣā*s are like this one. There are various methods and arrangements for giving *dīkṣā*. Most take *dīkṣā* in their own area and do not shift to receive *dīkṣā* in another area (i.e., Kathmandu tradition, Lalitpur tradition, etc.). For example, the tradition of Om Bahāḥ is said to be the one used in the Kathmandu (Yeṁ) area. Members of a clan (*kulaputrata*) based on their area of habitation (*thāy*) are forbidden to take *dīkṣā* in just any area; they are compelled to take *dīkṣā* only in the clan associated with their area of habitation.[2]

---

[2] This refers to the Newar Buddhist institution of the *digu pūjā guthi* (one's lineage worship organization). One receives initiation related to their lineage deity (*digu dyaḥ*), and this lineage deity is connected to the individual's family's ancestral home. Even if a Newar moves away from the area of their ancestral home and settles down in an area associated with a different deity, they are compelled to receive an initiation related to their familial lineage deity associated with the geographic location of the individual's ancestral home. "Traditionally all Newars have a lineage deity (New. *digu dyaḥ*) inherited patrilineally. Followers of the same lineage deity are exogamous and considered to be blood relatives, even if they are not obviously related by blood. Like membership in a death *guthi*, it is compulsory to have a lineage deity, which have *digu pūjā guthi*s associated with them. Although compulsory, the practice of lineage deity *pūjā* has waned significantly since the latter half of the 20th century. In the past, these deities were worshipped annually, with this worship financed by the *digu pūjā guthi* associated

The Guru-Disciple Lineage of the *Guhyasamājatantra* | *guhyasamājatantrayā guru-śiṣya paramparā*

The *Guhyasamājatantra* is the oldest tantric text (New. *nhāpāṃgu tantra saphū*) of the Vajrayāna. This best of books was revealed to Asaṅga (280-360 CE). Lama Tārānātha also reported that the guru-disciple lineage of the *Guhyasamājatantra* was transmitted secretly for around 300 years. Following this totally secret transmission, it is said that the *Guhyasamājatantra* was disseminated outwardly, thereby becoming accessible to everyone.[ii] It is said that the guru-disciple lineage starting with Asaṅga went up to the venerable Dharmakīrti. Who were the gurus in the period between Asaṅga and Dharmakīrti, and furthermore, who were the students? Those belonging to this initial lineage are unknown.

The Guru-Disciple Lineage of the *Cakrasamvaratantra* | *cakrasambaratantrayā guru-śiṣya paramparā*

A serious effort should be made to learn the list of the guru-disciple lineage of the *Cakrasamvaratantra*. But how many lists appear up to today? They are all mixed up and scattered about,

---

with that particular lineage. Sometimes the *guthi* had landholding as a source of income, but more typically they were funded by members. Like death *guthis*, lineage deities are connected to particular geographic locations. However, unlike death *guthi*s, where a member can ostensibly pay into another *guthi* after moving to a new location, when a follower of a particular lineage deity and member of its *digu pūjā guthi* moves, that follower/member retains that same lineage deity. For example, many Kathmandu *vajrācārya* families have their lineage deity as the *caitya* at the Sankhu Vajrayoginī temple, suggesting that in the distant past their ancestors moved from that area, a culturally-strong Newar town in the north of the Valley, to Kathmandu" From Grimes, Samuel M. *Resilience and Reinvigoration: Histories of the Buddhism of the Nepal Valley*. PhD Dissertation. University of Virginia, 2022. pp. 189-190.

and there is not a single, authoritative list. Below the various lists are given in an attempt to approach what the authoritative list may be.

The List of Benoytosh Bhattacharya | *vinaytoṣ bhaṭṭācāryajuyā dhalaḥ*

Benoytosh Bhattacharya gives two guru-disciple lists in the introduction of the second volume of his *Sādhanamālā* edition. His second list corroborates the one postulated by the *Cakrasamvaratantra* textual tradition.[3]

A. First List | *ka. nhāpāṃgu dhalaḥ*[iii]

1. Padmavajra (693 CE)
2. Anaṅgavajra (705 CE)
3. Indrabhūti (717 CE)
4. Lakṣmīṃkarā (729 CE)
5. Līlāvajra (741 CE)
6. Dārikāpā (753 CE)
7. Sahayoginī Cintā (765 CE)
8. Ḍombī Heruka (777 CE)

[3] These two, different, lists given by Bhattacharya, highlight two *paramparās* that are intended, in their respective traditions, to show *paramparās* for the whole of Vajrayāna. The "First List" beginning with Padmavajra is related to the dissemination of the *Hevajratantra*, revealed by Padmavajra. The "Second List" beginning with Saraha is related to the dissemination of the *Cakrasamvaratantra*. Yagyaman Pati gives both of these lists to highlight the confusion that arises when attempting to systematize the various guru-disciple lineages into a single, cohesive list.

B. Second List | *kha. lipāgu dhalaḥ*[iv]

1. Saraha (633 CE)
2. Nāgārjuna (645 CE)
3. Śabatīpā (657 CE)
4. Luipā (669 CE)
5. Vajraghaṇṭā (681 CE)
6. Kachāpā (693 CE)
7. Jālandharīpā (705 CE)
8. Kṛṣṇācārya (717 CE)
9. Guhya (729 CE)
10. Vijayapā (741 CE)
11. Tilopā (978 CE)
12. Naropā (990 CE)

It is recorded that there are 237 years between Vijayapā and Tilopā. This gap is between the guru and the disciple. But it is not recorded who fills this gap. When examining the list, other than this gap between Vijayapā and Tilopā, there are 12 years between each guru and disciple listed. Each person named on the list was the disciple of whomever preceded them, and the guru of whomever followed them. No such name is given for a disciple of Vijayapā, or for a guru of Tilopa. Whoever the guru of Tilopā was, it was not a human. It is explained in this way, written in the song that he made himself in the Newar language:

I, Tilopā (tilīyā), do not have a human guru.
My guru is Mahāvajradhara.[v]

The Guhyādi-aṣṭasiddhi (8 siddhi texts beginning with "Guhya") | *guhyādi aṣṭasiddhii*

The time of Vijayapā and Tilopā is identical; this is not controversial. One might be wondering, between Vijayapā and Tilopā, who is the guru and who is the disciple? Therefore, a list is given in the introduction to the *Guhyādi-astasiddhi* book. This list with the corresponding dates of the guru-disciple lineage is given as a table below. And this is it:

1. Saraha (858 CE)
2. Nāgārjuna (870 CE)
3. Śabatīpā (882 CE)
4. Luipā (894 CE)
5. Vajraghaṇṭā (906 CE)
6. Kachāpā (918 CE)
7. Jālandharīpā (930 CE)
8. Kṛṣṇācārya (942 CE)
9. Guhya (954 CE)
10. Vijayapā (966 CE)
11. Tilopā (978 CE)
12. Naropā (990 CE)

However, regarding this list, it is to be borne in mind that there could have been many divergences that could be anywhere along the line from the ancient, revealed texts up to the later, human-authored books.

Snellgrove's List | *snelgrobhyā dhalaḥvi*

The record given by Tārānātha is supported by the list given in Snellgrove's introduction to the *Hevajratantra.*

Indrabhūti (the first)	Aśvapāda
Mahāpadmavajra	Vilāsavajra
Anaṅgavajra	Vajraghaṇṭā
Saroruha	Kampala
Indrabhūti (the second)	Indrabhūti (the second)

In his study, Snellgrove notes that Indrabhūti (the second) received *dīkṣā* and teaching from both Saroruha and Kampala. Although the table above does not make clear whether or not Saroruha and Kampala shared a similar time, it should be noted that they were contemporaries and thus known to have appeared at the same time. Indrabhūti (the second) received training and *dīkṣā* from both Saroruha and Kampala. Both of them are recorded in a single text: the *Hevajratantra*. Neither of these two personages is anywhere else, and it is said that they are not a single person [in the *Hevajratantra*].

This issue is potentially resolved in an argument made by Bhattacharya. According to Bhattacharya, Padmavajrapāda and Kambalapāda are the same person. Here, there are many possibilities regarding both the Kampala of Snellgrove and the Kampalapāda of Bhattacharya. Furthermore, "Saroruha" and "Padmavajra" refer to a single person.[vii]

Līlāvajra and his disciples[viii] | *līlāvajra va līlāvajrayā śiṣyapiṃ*

Līlāvajra is the main *siddha* to be associated with Nepal. He also started the guru-disciple lineage in Nepal. It is remembered here that he and his disciples launched the Buddhist tradition. The disciples of Līlāvajra are given as:

Dārikāpāda aka Karuṇācala (753 CE)
Ḍombīheruka (777 CE)
Buddhaguhya
Vimalamitra[ix]
Buddhaśrījñāna
Mañjuśrī Mitra

The *Kriyāsamuccaya* Guru-Disciple Tradition | *kriyāsammucaya: guru-śiṣya paramparā*

The Guru Maṇḍala is in the *Kriyāsamuccaya*. The *Blue Annals* record information in support of the guru-disciple lineage detailed in the *Kriyāsamuccaya*. Vajradhara is shown by this *śāstra* to have been the premier and primordial guru. This suggests that Vajradhara became a guru for himself/all on his own (*svayam*, i.e., he had no teacher). He is the first one on the line of gurus and disciples that eventually ends with Dharmasvāmin. Furthermore, it is written that the Tibetan disciples were given *dīkṣā* by Mahābodhi. This is the lineage it provides:[x]

1. Vajradhara
2. Jñānaḍāka
3. Darpaṇācārya
4. Samantabhadra
5. Jñānajyoti
6. Śrīhanumata
7. Śrīmañjubhadra
8. Śrīlakṣmībhadra
9. Dharmajyotibhadra

10. Manojīvabhadra
11. Srotrama Śrībhadra
12. Śrīvijayabhadra
13. Śrīmadanabhadra
14. Śrīlakṣmībhadra
15. Gaganabhadra
16. Udayajīvabhadra
17. Śrīharṣabhadra
18. Abhāgabhadra
19. Jagadānandajīvabhadra (Nepalese *paṇḍita*)
20. Mahābodhi (Jagadānandajīvabhadra's son)
21. Mātipā Phags-pa gZon-nu-blo-gros (also known by the name of Ma-li-pan-dhen)
22. Dharmasvāmin

Countless subsequent individuals make up the lineage of training given in the *Kriyāsamuccaya*.[4]

---

[4] The original text includes the following passage, quoted from the Blue Annals, after giving the list in the Blue Annals. For simplicity's sake, we have moved this passage to the notes. "This is the lineage (*aṃśa*) from the *Blue Annals* of Buston Rinpoche-The Lineage of the great rite of the maṇḍala called *Kṛyāsamuccaya* [sic.] (*Vajrācāryakṛyāsamuccaya*, [sic.] Tg. rGyud, No. 3305), composed by the *siddha* named Dar-paṇ (Darpaṇa-ācārya), whose teeth had changed twenty times and who had lived for a thousand two hundred years, through which the initiation was transmitted: Vajradhara (rDo-rǰe-'čhaṅ), Jñānaḍāka (Ye-śes mkha'-'gro), Darpaṇa-ācārya, Samantabhadra, Jñānajyoti, Śrī Hanumat, Śrī Mañjubhadra, Śrī Lakṣmībhadra, Dharmajyotirbhadra, Manojīvabhadra, Śo-traṃ Śrībhadra, Śrī Vijayabhadra, Śrī Madanabhadra, Śrī Lakṣmībhadra, Gaganabhadra, Udayajīvabhadra, Śrī Harṣabhadra, Abhāgabhadra, the Nepālese paṇsita of Ye-raṅ—Jagadānandajīvabhadra, his son the paṇḍita Mahābodhi, Sabzaṅ 'Phags-pa gŽon-nu blo-gros (also known by the name of Ma-ti paṇ-čhen), the Dharmasvāmin Kun-

Here, in this chapter, an attempt was made to systematize the various lists into a version that adequately captures them all. But, as should be made clear, the various lineages are not always in accordance with one another. Indeed, each tantra possesses its own lineage. Essentially, a separate guru-disciple lineage is found in each tantra. For example, there is a particular guru-disciple lineage belonging to the *Kriyāsamuccaya*. So too does the *Cakrasamvaratantra* have its own tradition regarding the foundational lineage historically passed from guru to disciple.

---

dga' bzaṅ-po, and (thus) to the Dharmasvāmin of dMar-ston rGyal-mtshan 'od-zer.

The origin of the Doctrine: Since in former times there did not exist translation of it into Tibetan, 'J̌am-dbyaṅs Don-yod rgyal-mtshan of dPal-ldan Sa-skya obtained the Sanskrit text of the *Samuccaya* from a Nepālese merchant (this very copy is preserved at the Ṅor monastery in gTsaṅ. Verbal communication by Rev. dGe-'dun Chos-'phel). This book was then found in the possession of Kun-spaṅs Chos-grags-dpal-bzaṅ-po. It was translated at the latter's request and with his assistance by Mañjuśrī, a great paṇḍita of Vikramaśīla, and the Tibetan translator (lo-tsā-ba) Sa-bzaṅ-pa bLo-gros rgyal-mtshan. While they were unable to find any one from whom they could obtain its initiation and "permission" (luṅ) to read it, they heard a report that mṄa'-ris-pa rDo-rǰe-dpal had obtained the initiation of the *Samuccaya* at Ye-raṅ (Kāṭhmāndu). 'Phags-pa gZon-nu blo-gros with his disciples, seven persons in all, proceeded to Ye-raṅ in Nepāl, and there obtained the complete initiation and "permission" (luṅ) to read the text from the paṇḍita Mahābodhi. It spread widely. Again, the Blessed gŚin-rǰe mthar-byed (Yamāntakṛt), Virūpa, Ḍombhī-pa, the brāhmaṇa Śrīdhara (dPal-'dzin), Matigarbha, Darpaṇa-ācārya who bestowed on gLo-bo lo-tsā-ba the *gŚin rǰe gśed-dmar-po'i gzuṅ* with its exposition and precepts. The lo-tsā-ba bestowed it on bLo-čhen Saṅs-rgyas. The latter on the lo-tsā-ba mChog-ldan. The latter on bKa'-bču-pa gZon-nu-seṅ-ge. Also following another Lineage [sic.], it was practised by Bu-ston Rin-po-čhe and others, and numerous living beings were nourished by it." Roerich, George N., trans. The Blue Annals, (Delhi: Motilal Banarsidass, 1945 [1976]). pp. 1045.

---

i. Vajrayoginī guru paramparā.

ii. Bhattacharya, *Guhyasamājatantra*, xxxv.

iii. Bhattacharya, *Sādhanamālā*, vol. 2, xlii.

iv. Bhattacharya, *Sādhanamālā*, vol. 2, xliii.

v. Dr. Ṭhākurasen Negī: Vajrayānī Anuttar Yog, Kendrīya Ucca Tibbati Śikṣā Sasthān, Sārnāth, Vārāṇasī, 1999, pp. 489.

vi. Snellgrove, *Hevajratantra: A Critical Study*, 13.

vii. *Guhyādi-aṣṭsiddhisaṃgraha*, Durlabha Bauddha Grantha Śodha Yojanā Vārāṇasī, 1987, 16.

viii. Yagyaman Pati *Vajrācārya*, Līlāvajra Kāryapatra: Ādaranīya Guru Līlāvajra Patricchaṁda.

ix. Dr. Banārsī Lāl "Bauddhatantra-Vāḍmay kā paricay" (Dhīḥ 15, pp. 334).

x. Roerich, *The Blue Annals*, 1045-1046.

i. Vaivoglin guru paramparā
ii. Bharadvāja Gotranām aśayaxxv
iii. Bharadvāja Sūtrakṛuṇām vol. 3. III.
iv. Bharadvāja Sūtrakṛuṇām vol. 2. xip

v. Dr. Thākūrasen Nech Kumar, an Anuṛta, V. et Look-ind, Deva
   Tibbat Sibat Sansthan, Sārnāth, Varanasi, 1994, pp. 189

vi. Spellman, Propgimasveral Crdict, Strok, 19.

vii. Govind aṃrdl Sāstri-... Buddhiśa Bauddha, Granth
     Sodha āvīrm Varanasi, 1987-70

viii. Vyomnaṁ Pari. Viśi lyo, Tibbrata Kanyapīṭh Adaršita
      Guru Dākṣiṇa Parikarṇa.

ix. Dr. Bansal, Lal "Bauddhamitra-Vādaṣit ka pariaya" (Dhih
    15. pp. 35).

x. Regedā, 4th śloka śūnat. 1053.1000.

Part Two

Maṇḍala

6. The Meaning, Importance, and Boundaries of the Maṇḍala | *maṇḍalayā artha mahatva va sīmitatā*

Now, we have discussed the matter of the guru, and it is a suitable time to study the matter of the maṇḍala, since, after finishing a discussion of the matter of the guru of the Guru Maṇḍala, [we can proceed to] the matter of the maṇḍala [proper]. One meaning of maṇḍala is that of a "circle." That is a boundary, which goes all around, and its contents. The boundary and the interior of that boundary, together, are called a "maṇḍala." In Vajrayāna, seeing a deity placed in the center of a maṇḍala is commonplace. That is the root deity of the maṇḍala. All around that root deity is its assembly. This is the case, for instance, in the Vajravārāhī Maṇḍala, Cakrasaṃvara Maṇḍala, Buddha Maṇḍala, Dharma Maṇḍala, Saṃgha Maṇḍala, and so forth. In the *Nispannayogāvalī* of Abhayākaragupta, 21 maṇḍalas are detailed, such as the Mañjuvajra Maṇḍala, and so forth. In the *Kriyāsamuccaya* of Jagaddarpaṇa as well, we see the structures of 33 or 34 maṇḍalas. There is also an explanation of the Guru Maṇḍala in the *Kriyāsamuccaya*: when the guru is seated in the maṇḍala, it is the

"Guru Maṇḍala." Thus, when we see an assembly and the root deity placed together, we use the term "maṇḍala."

The Meaning of "Maṇḍala" | *maṇḍalayā artha*

A "maṇḍala" is also said to be a treasury of the truth. In this sense, the "la" of "maṇḍala" means a container, and "maṇḍa" means true essence. So, in saying "maṇḍala," we indicate a container wherein that true essence is hoarded. Thus, Min Bahadur Shakya wrote:

> Many (but not all) etymologies in Buddhist tantra say that maṇḍala consist of "maṇḍa," the essence of content, and "la," the container. Maṇḍala, therefore, means something like "contained essence" in Buddhism.[i]

The meaning is thus given in the very letters of "maṇḍala." "Maṇḍa" and "la," joined together, become "maṇḍala." The meaning of "maṇḍa" is knowledge. Whatever knowledge there is inside and outside [the circle], it will all gradually be obtained from the maṇḍa [i.e., the essence] of knowledge at the central spot. It is like something that is covered. For example, a coconut is covered by layers. When you remove a coconut's outer layer, another layer is inside. After taking off that layer, finally, one gets to the edible part that is good to eat. The matter is one of going within to find the substance [i.e., maṇḍa].[1] This substance is the best essence of root knowledge. Now we see the sense of "la," which had been implied: this is the other matter of the "boundary." The boundary and what is within the boundary are all the form of the maṇḍala. On this matter, Alex Wayman's words are fitting, who writes in his *Yoga of the Guhyasamājatantra*:

---

[1] The Sanskrit term *maṇḍa* has a sense of essence. It refers to the scum that forms on the top of rice during boiling.

The word *maṇḍala* is uniformly defined as an inner content (*maṇḍa*) bounded by an enclosing element (*-la*). For example, the extract from the *Saṃdhivyākaraṇa* in this sub-section illustrates the word's meaning by the inner content as 'knowledge' with an enclosing element as the non-tantric statement of the path.

There is also a ritual sequence of two kinds of *maṇḍala*, the *maṇḍala* of residence (ādhāra-maṇḍala) and the *maṇḍala* of the residents (ādheya-maṇḍala); the former is the palace and the seats for gods; and the latter is the group of gods who take their places in that palace. The palace is the inner sanctum of the maṇḍala.[ii]

In the method of giving *dīkṣā* to child disciples, they are made to enter into a maṇḍala. Here, it is explained that a lotus is a "maṇḍala." In this case, the maṇḍala is the connection of leaves that make up a lotus.

Maṇḍala: The Sign of a Great Caitya | *maṇḍala: taḥdhaṃgu caityayā pratīk*

According to the words of Benoytosh Bhattacharya, the meaning of "maṇḍala" is a "magic circle." He suggests that this circle was a representation of the big *caitya*s.[iii]

Maṇḍala: According to the *Śāstra*s | *maṇḍala: śāstra*

Other things can be said about maṇḍalas if we even consider later *śāstra*s, where their essence is also expressed. Later, they had various commentaries and sub-commentaries established. This is so that by giving more details, one can even make a fool understand. We shall learn what was said on this matter in these *śāstra*s. When looking into this, the *Guhyasamājatantra* is one such *śāstra*, and it features the Guhyasamāja Maṇḍala. The

Hevajratantra also has a maṇḍala. The rites for performing all these are included in the *Kriyāsamuccaya*. Thus, the *Kriyāsamuccaya* is one presentation of maṇḍalas. On the subject of the *Kriyāsamuccaya*, one must also receive consecration and be established in the guru-disciple tradition. The *Blue Annals* introduces its author thus:

> The lineage of the great rite of the maṇḍala called *Kriyāsamuccaya* (*Vajrācaryakṛyasamuccaya* Tg.r Gyud, No. 3305) composed by the *siddha* named Dar-pan (Darpaṇa *ācārya*), whose teeth had changed twenty times and who had lived for a thousand two hundred years, through which the initiation was transmitted: [after which his lineage is given].[2]

It is also worth remembering that the teachings on the maṇḍala of Dharmadhātu Vāgīśvara in pure Kambala and the meaning of the twelve-syllable mantra of Ārya Nāmasaṅgīti were given to Mañjuśrī's very own disciple, the great paṇḍit Dharmaśrīmitra.

This was given so that he could speak on any philosophical matter related to the maṇḍala in the *Guhyasamājatantra*. Such as saying:

> *bhagaṃ maṇḍalam ākhyātaṃ bodhicittam ca mandalam |*
> *dehaṃ maṇḍalam ity uktaṃ triṣu maṇḍalakalpanā ||*

> The Fortunate One is termed a maṇḍala, and *bodhicitta* is a maṇḍala,
> The body is also said to be a maṇḍala: these are three designations of maṇḍala.[iv]

---

[2] Roerich 1945 [1976]: 1045.

The Source of the Maṇḍala | *nhāpāṃgu maṇḍalayā śrota*

The earliest structure of the maṇḍala appears to have emerged from the *Guhyasamājatantra*. All *tathāgatas*, having been in their own kind of *samādhi*, exited that *samādhi* and were established as deities in the various directions. The very first section of the *Guhyasamājatantra* is the section on the establishment of the maṇḍala of all *tathāgatas*, wherein one visualizes the maṇḍala being established from the assembly of that section into all directions. The five Dhyānī Buddhas, their five consorts, and Yamāntaka, Prajñāntaka, Padmāntaka, and Vighnāntaka are placed in this maṇḍala.[v]

It will be seen that a synonym of maṇḍala, in Newar, is "*caka*." This means "circle," from the Sanskrit "*cakra*." A suitable term for this is also the Newar, "*chacāḥ*," meaning "all around." There are also particular compound words using the term "*cakra*." For instance, "*kāyacakra*" (circle of the body), "*vākcakra*" (circle of speech), "*cittacakra*" (circle of the mind), and so forth. In this way, there are also the "*nirmāṇacakra*" (circle of manifestation), "*dharmacakra*" (circle of the Dharma), "*saṃbhogacakra*" (circle of enjoyment), and "*mahāsukhacakra*" (circle of great bliss), and so forth. When we thus look at the meaning of "*cakra*," it is "collection," which is like a "group" and an "accumulation." Thus, looking at maṇḍala as a bounded accumulation, we see that it is more than an indication of location. When we say "maṇḍala," it has an expansive signification. But when we say "*cakra*" (circle), it is more narrow in scope. This is because each part of a maṇḍala is a deity or another [important] thing. It is a *cakra* within which there are such things as deities. Taking as an example the Kālacakra Maṇḍala in the *Niṣpannayogāvalī*, the Kālacakra is one kind of *cakra*[, i.e., in principle, it is a kind of circle]. But because of the contents of the Kālacakra, [i.e., by the addition of the assembly of Kālacakra,] its meaning is strengthened, and it is called a "maṇḍala."

Types of Maṇḍala | *maṇḍalayā prakāra*

When discussing other kinds of *cakras,* they are circular shapes. But when talking about a maṇḍala, it is not necessarily circular. Maṇḍalas can be circular, semi-circular, triangular, square, and so forth. In the *Guhyasamājatantra,* there are various structures to maṇḍalas. In the cultivation of the Guru Maṇḍala, there are also the structures of the Vāyu (wind) Maṇḍala, Agni (fire) Maṇḍala, Varuṇa (water) Maṇḍala, as well as the Pṛthvī (earth) Maṇḍala. We will take a closer look at these four types of maṇḍala. The Vāyu Maṇḍala is the shape of a bow, called a "Dhanvābhaṃ," or a semi-circle. The Agni Maṇḍala has a triangular shape. The Varuṇa Maṇḍala has a circular shape. The Pṛthvī Maṇḍala has a rectangular shape. It is also the case that the Vajrayāna *vihāras* take on the form of a square maṇḍala. In fact, Vajrayāna *vihāra*s are square. A square *vihāra* implies that the length of the east and west sides will equal the length of the north and south sides. In the *Guhyasamājatantra*, measurements are given for *vihāra*s, or maṇḍalas, measuring 16 square cubits, measuring 24 square cubits, and measuring 36 square cubits.[3]

The Importance of the Maṇḍala | *maṇḍalayā mahatva*

In the minds of Vajrayāna Dharma practitioners, deities must be threaded throughout a *cakra*. In such a *cakra*, they will be placed such that they take up the entirety of one *cakra*. In a *cakra*, there is one root deity, and only one who is the lord of the *cakra*. And

---

[3] 16 cubits squared is 7.3 meters squared. 24 cubits squared is 10.9 meters squared. 36 cubits squared is 16.5 meters squared.

among the *caryā* songs that there are, most of them are about a lord of the *cakra*. But just as how there are many relatives of the solar maṇḍala [i.e. the sun] in space and the Ganges [as reflections], there are very many flocks of lesser circles [minor maṇḍalas]. These are [also] true aspects in the form of the *cakra* of the lord of the *cakra*, which is infinitely true and both immovable and moveable, and which also come to be conceived of by the Vajrayāna practitioner.[vi]

Good people are social beings. They have good families. Within their families, there are also various members. This is also the case with one maṇḍala. When we see one [root deity] having gathered their family, what was just one figure quickly becomes a great family. Viewing such a maṇḍala is exoteric (i.e., it is okay to see without initiation). They thus expand to become a district, a nation, an international nation, and thus become a maṇḍala of maṇḍalas. This world is also such a maṇḍala. It is called the "Great Maṇḍala" (*mahimaṇḍala*). All who dwell on it will come to perish. Living beings die, and their deaths will come about. Therefore, it is also called the "Maṇḍala of Death" (*martyamaṇḍala*).

Those who are born will also be those who die, and as they are born again, this is also the "Maṇḍala of Old Age and Birth" (*jarājanmamaṇḍala*). The amount of that which will be born and will die, thus, cannot be reckoned. Even whatever has been born just now, all of which will become that which dies, is unreckonable. If one collected all of the corpses of one person's [past] deaths up to now, they would pile up even taller than the height of a mountain. In this way, if one were to collect the tears cried from one's eyes from the times that one became sad after considering that those one loves will die, I am afraid that the tears would come to equal the seas and oceans. This is the Maṇḍala of Old Age and Birth. To support just this Maṇḍala of Old Age and Birth, the philosophical aspects of maṇḍalas emerged in

Vajrayāna. Between birth and death and birth and death, there is an increase in many sufferings and pleasures, and there is the accumulation of good and bad incidents. Those are also considered part of the Maṇḍala of Old Age and Birth.

We cannot say that humans arise and are isolated things. They must also eat, drink, get dressed, live, etc. They go around doing all sorts of things like this. Those are also within this Maṇḍala. If they were in isolation, they wouldn't give rise to discrimination. On this basis, in Vajrayāna, it is held that any deity in isolation is devoid of discrimination.

The different directions also have one basis. The four directions each have intermediate directions, and thus, there comes to be a total of eight directions. These directions and intermediate directions are, in fact, imagined surroundings, and thus, the form of a maṇḍala comes to take shape [through imagination]. Moreover, as it is said, wherever roads cross on the earth, there are not only those ahead and behind, right and left, but there are also the up and down directions, and these can also be seen to be good directions. Thus, regarding different directions, a direction going anywhere whatsoever is always one of the "directions."

On this basis, in not seeing a solitary deity, one sees them together with their environment and that which is situated around them, which accords to the particular tradition [of that deity]. For instance, abiding in the different directions around Vajravārāhī are Yāminī, Sañcariṇī, Santrāsinī, Mohinī, Caṇḍikā, and so forth; having placed them, it becomes the Vajravārāhī Maṇḍala, and thus they can be seen when one looks within the maṇḍala of Vajravārāhī.

Similarly, one can see the resplendent throng of Aṣṭamātṛkā surrounding Bhairava. Traditionally, one sees eight figures, such as Kākāsyā and so forth, in the different directions around Cakrasaṃvara.

The guru is worthy of worship. And there is also the cultural practice that, when performing a *pūjā*, one visualizes figures placed in different directions around the guru. This tradition continues from before.

At various opportunities, various kinds of maṇḍala rites have become prevalent. Wherever such and such an opportunity is, there will be such and such a maṇḍala ritual, as discussed by Hemraj Shakya in his introduction to maṇḍalas.[viii] Therein, various suitable opportunities [for maṇḍalas] are raised. They are as follows:

1. Viewing the maṇḍala of Dharmadhātu Vāgīśvara in pure Kaṃbala, whose meaning (that of Ārya Nāmasaṅgīti of the Twelve Syllable Mantra) Guru Mañjuśrī made clear to his own disciple, the Mahāpaṇḍita, Dharmaśrīmitra.
2. Viewing the maṇḍala of Kālacakra before the noble *caitya* at Dhānyakaṭaka, when its consecration is given to a disciple of the Vajrayāna tantras by Śākyamuni Buddha.
3. It is customary to draw the maṇḍala of Durgatipariśodhana when performing the *pūjā* for the pacification of those who have died.
4. Drawing the maṇḍala of the Five Buddhas when completing the Lakṣacaitya *vrata* fast.
5. The Graha Maṇḍala is created before performing the [first] *jyājaṃku* ceremony.
6. The Vasundharā Maṇḍala is created when performing the second *jyājaṃku* ceremony and the *tilā vrata* fast.
7. The Uṣṇiṣavijaya Maṇḍala is drawn when performing the third *jyājaṃku* ceremony.
8. The Amoghapāśa Maṇḍala is drawn during an *aṣṭamī vrata* fast and anywhere a consecration occurs on Aṣṭamī.

9. The Tārā Maṇḍala is created when performing the Dharma rite of Sahasrāvartā Pūrā Tārā.
10. The Mahākāla Maṇḍala is drawn when performing the *caturdaśī vrat* fast.
11. The Pañcarakṣā Maṇḍala is drawn for fortune and the pacification of hindrances and the obstructions of evil *māras*.
12. The Guru Maṇḍala is drawn at the beginning of any *pūjā* in Vajrayāna.
13. The Piṇḍikā Maṇḍala must be drawn during the *padasādhana* [*caryā*] *pūjā* for one day and night.
14. After making the Ratna Maṇḍala, one dedicates it as an offering to the guru and bodhisattvas.
15. A viewing of the [Vajradhātu] Mahāmaṇḍala is given when giving consecration in the Newar Vajrayāna.

When giving consecration, this last kind of consecration maṇḍala is given. In the ritual procedure of *utkrānti*[, i.e., transference of transference of the consciousness of the deceased to a good rebirth], one must perform the rite of the Vajravārāhī Maṇḍala. That is also called the Transference (*dusvaḥ*) Maṇḍala. In the rite of transference, one must perform the rite of the Transference Maṇḍala.

---

i. As quoted in Rajit Bahadur Shrestha, *Mandaḥ va Mandaḥ Kāsā*. Lalitpur: Kaulā Lakṣmīpujā, NS 1120 (1999 CE). pp. 22.

ii. Alex Wayman, *Yoga of the Guhyasamājatantra*, New Delhi: Motilal Banarasidass, 1977, 122.

iii. Ed. Benoytosh Bhattacharya, *Guhyasamāja Tantra*, 1931, pp. xxxv.

iv. Divyavajra Bajracharya, trans., Ārya Guhyasamājatantram: Guhyasamājatantrapradīpodyatanaṭīkā Padakoṭī Vyākhyā Sahita, Lalitpur: Lotus Research Center, VS 2058 (2001 CE), 623, v. 99.

v. Ed. Benoytosh Bhattacharya, *Guhyasamāja Tantra*, 1931.

vi. Yagyaman Pati Bajracharya, *Caryāgīta: Kāryapatra*, Lalitpur: Lotus Research Centre, VS 2053 (1996 CE). pp. 1.

vii. As quoted in Rajit Bahadur Shrestha, *Mandaḥ va Mandaḥ Kāsā*, Lalitpur: Kaulā Lakṣmīpujā, NS 1120 (1999 CE), 64.

7.

Maṇḍala Generation | *maṇḍala sṛjanā*

Introduction | *prasṭhabhūmi*

The Buddhist Dharma is a doctrine without a creator god (*nitānta anīśvaravāda*). There is no role for either a creator god (*īśvara*) or minor deities (New. *dyaḥ*). However, in the Tripiṭaka, gods ("*devapiṃ*") do have various roles. The Lord Buddha explained the various gods as referring to body parts, such as the hand. For the completeness of Vajrayāna, there is no need for any gods to have a role. If the gods have a role, it is only their role to appear as an image (*mūrti*). The image is a sign of emptiness, for the god depicted does not actually exist anywhere. In the *Advayavajrasaṃgraha*, it is written that the material appearance (*ākāra prakāra*) of a god is only to illustrate that the god is representative of emptiness. The creator (*nirmātā*) of the deity image is also just a person. Whether the god is to be or not to be is determined by the hands of a person. This is the only way it exists or does not exist. It does not come about on its own. The *mūrti* of the deity is made by a person. In the same way, the agent of the visualization of the maṇḍala is a person. The one who generates the maṇḍala is a person. On the topic of generating a maṇḍala, there are three modes in which it can be made. They are:

1. The making of the maṇḍala with a visualized form (*bhāvanātmaka*).
2. The making of the physical maṇḍala.
3. The performance of other ritual elements, such as the recitation of mantras.

1. The Maṇḍala Which is Made with a Visualized Form | *bhāvanātmaka kathaṃ dayekīgu maṇḍal*

This visualized form is the very best kind of maṇḍala there can be in a ritual. However many maṇḍalas there are, they are all completed in human ritual and have the nature of their fashioner (*karātmaka*). They are a product of yogic effort (*tapasyā*). According to the *Guhyasamājatantra*, the *sādhakas* abide in meditation. Having reached the level of emptiness in prior entrance into purified (*viśuddha*) meditation, they have had many visions in their minds. How could this be the case since, presumably, their minds are absent of all content? It is because the vision will arise (*utpanna*) from a seed syllable (*bījākṣara*). Thus, the generated form emanated from the seed syllable is the physical form of the *mūrti* that is brought into being in the *siddha*'s meditation on emptiness. Once the physical form of the *mūrti* comes about, it forms a kind of imprint (New. *chāpa*) and always exists in the *siddha*'s meditation. The embodied sense (New. *mhaṃgu khaṃ*) or the vision in a dream is forgotten. But the generated physical form of the *mūrti* in the mind of the *siddha* during the course of meditation is never forgotten. It is now perpetually (*sadāyā*) established. In that case, the *siddha* and the *mūrti* of the deity now share an identity.

And having established the deity in such a way, placed to the right and left and above and below the deity are added a number of other deities. Dangerous, pacifying deities are created, wrathful and inflamed, visualized in gross form with all their limbs. The generation of each deity, according to their respective colors—blue, white, green, yellow and red—will be done during the course of meditation. So there the group of deities is generated. The root deity is in the middle. Then the others are in the East, South, West and North, and they each have their own color. Then, in the central region of the maṇḍala, deities are situated at the northwestern, southwestern, northeastern and southeastern corners. This is the maṇḍala. There are gods situated in the primary region but also in the outside regions. Thus, there should be a second and a third outer region. Each region is itself totally surrounded by another region in the shape of a wheel. These are the mind wheel (*cittacakra*), the speech wheel (*vākcakra*), the body wheel (*kāyacakra*), the wheels containing implements such as crows and so on (*kākāśyādi*),[1] etc., etc. The edge of each wheel has a space (*puṭa*) between it and the wheel surrounding it. In this way, each wheel in the maṇḍala's form will be fully surrounded.

The gate will be at the center of the fortress of the king (*rājyayā killāy*), and a gatekeeper will be stationed at each gate. The arrangement of the gatekeepers is at each of the four doors in the four directions on the maṇḍala. This is the case for the Cakrasamvara maṇḍala, the Vajravārāhī maṇḍala and so on.

The visualized maṇḍala of the *Guhyasamājatantra* serves as an ideal example for other visualized maṇḍalas. This maṇḍala is the oldest one in the Vajrayāna. Because it is the oldest maṇḍala of the Vajrayāna, it is the one I have elected to use as an example in this book. If one mentions a king of maṇḍalas, it refers to this

---

[1] In a Newar context this refers to the outermost ring of the maṇḍala which often contains wild animals.

maṇḍala. Because there are so many deities in Vajrayāna, all those inhabitants of the maṇḍala will only be in the form of an individual part that symbolizes a particular deity. It is taught that in each direction (*digdarśana*) of the Guhyasamāja maṇḍala, the color of the deity who inhabits a respective direction's region be applied to that region along with the embodied form of the deity itself with a corresponding us color. This constitutes the simplest arrangement (New. *byūgu*) of the embodied deities in each of the directions. Therefore, it is appropriate to refer to the maṇḍala of the *Guhyasamājatantra* as king of the maṇḍalas. Any maṇḍala has the five buddhas in their respective direction, or they are indicated by a particular symbol for each. This is because it is compulsory to include all the directions when generating the maṇḍala.[i] In just this way, the Guhyasamāja maṇḍala is generated.

The generation of the visualized mantra appears in the first chapter of the *Guhyasamājatantra*. It is recorded that the generation of each respective deity during the course of each respective meditative *samādhi* is established in each respective direction.

The First Procedure | *dakale nhāpāṃgu caraṇay*

1. Vajradṛk is the buddha Akṣobhya. The region of the center of maṇḍala belongs to that exalted one.
2. Jinajik is the buddha Vairocana. The eastern region of the maṇḍala belongs to that exalted one.
3. Ratnadhṛk is the buddha Ratnasambhava. The southern region belongs to that exalted one.
4. Ārolik is the buddha Amitābha. The western region of the maṇḍala belongs to that exalted one.
5. Prajñādhṛk is the buddha Amoghasiddhi. The northern region belongs to that exalted one.

So, the form of the maṇḍala is to have a *tathāgata* at each of the four directions and the *tathāgata* Akṣobhya as the lord of the maṇḍala between the four other buddhas.

The Second Procedure | *lipāgu caraṇay*

1. Dveṣarati is a *tārā*. She should be placed together with the buddha Akṣobhya.
2. Moharati is a *tārā*. She should be placed together with the buddha Vairocana.
3. Īrṣyārati is a *tārā*. She should be placed together with the buddha Ratnasambhava.
4. Rāgarati is a *tārā*. She should be placed together with the buddha Amitābha.
5. Vajrarati is a *tārā*. She should be placed together with the buddha Amoghasiddhi.

The Third Procedure, That of the Gatekeepers | *dvārapāla kathaṃ svaṃgūgu caraṇay*

1. Yamāntakṛta refers to the protector Yamāntaka. He is at the eastern gate.
2. Prajñāntakṛta refers to the protector Prajñāntaka. He is at the southern gate.
3. Padmāntakṛta refers to the protector Padmāntaka. He is at the western gate.
4. Vighnāntakṛta refers to the protector Vighnāntaka. He is at the northern gate.

These male deities, female deities and gatekeeper deities are the components of the Saṃgha. This is the collection. The arrangement of the Vajrayāna maṇḍala (i.e., *vajradhātu* maṇḍala)[2] is the five-buddha arrangement of the maṇḍala with Akṣobhya at the center. This visualization only occurs during the generation of the maṇḍala. This is a mentally-generated maṇḍala (*bhāvanāmayīmaṇḍala*).

2. The Making of the Physical Maṇḍala | *bhautik sāmagrī chyalāḥ dayekīgu*

The reason for making the physical form is to serve as a template for the mentally-generated maṇḍala. This physical form of the mentally-generated maṇḍala is also depicted in paintings (*paubhāḥ*). At the time, it is necessary to make the *paubhāḥ* according to the custom and to place the maṇḍala accordingly. And in order to give a living form to the *paubhāḥ*, the custom is that the deity is ritually established (New. *palisthātaka*) in the physical painting. In this way, the painted maṇḍala is made in absolute secrecy. For example, the Cakrasamvara maṇḍala, Vajravārāhī maṇḍala and so on.

In this way, the maṇḍala is established as a drawing. This is still the method today to complete a *paubhāḥ*. This is a secret maṇḍala, not one that can be seen by anyone and everyone anywhere, like the *vajradhātu* and *dharmadhātu* maṇḍalas that are installed in public *caityas*. Or, for example, the Svayambhū *mahācaitya*, which is made of durable materials. If necessary, when one is drawing the maṇḍala, one is also allowed to draw it on a wooden medium.

A maṇḍala may also be made of powder ("*dhū-raṅga* (Dust Colour)"). A maṇḍala made with various colored powders serves

---

[2] The Vajradhātu maṇḍala has Akṣobhya at the center and Vairocana in the East. The Dharmadhātu maṇḍala has Vairocana at the center and Akṣobhya in the East. The former is the more esoteric, the latter the more exoteric.

as a template for a visualized maṇḍala. Such a powder-made maṇḍala will not be nearly as stable as a maṇḍala on a *paubhāḥ*. Accordingly, it is made unstable due to one's [lack of] effort. The custom is to make the maṇḍala-to-be-offered out of powder. It is said that a day after you draw the maṇḍala it dies. Because of this, the dismissal is performed at the completion of the maṇḍala rite.[3]

The construction of the maṇḍala also involves materials such as uncooked rice, wheat barley as *caitya*s and food offerings, popped rice and so on. But in this way, the maṇḍala is extremely unstable. This is because this maṇḍala only exists in a single location, namely, where it is physically constructed. On the subject of the Guru Maṇḍala, it is written in the *Kriyāsamuccaya*:

> *anena maṇḍalamadhye aṣṭhadalakamalaṃ likhet* |[ii]
>
> By this, an eight-petaled lotus should be drawn in the middle of the maṇḍala.

3. The Performance of Other Ritual Elements, Such as the Recitation of Mantras | *mantra ādi prayoga yānāḥ dayekīgu*[4]

The generation is done during the course of *pūjā*, when one will make a maṇḍala. In this instance mantras are used. Furthermore, during the rite of generating the maṇḍala, *mudrā*s are made by

---

[3] After it has been constructed, and a deity summoned into it, the maṇḍala is said to be "alive." Following the dismissal it is "dead."

[4] This was originally section 4, and there was a section 3 entitled "3. The Application of Hand *Mudrās* | *hasta mudrā jyānāḥ dayekīgu*." Other than the first sentence, that section includes a description of the types of persons according to the Candrakīrti who authored the *Pradīpodyotana*. An identical section includes in the chapter on the Ratna Maṇḍala. The section in the Ratna Maṇḍala chapter (now an appendix) has been kept in our translation, but the section here has been removed, with the relevant sentence on *mudrās* appearing in this current section 3.

arranging the hands in various ways. A single mantra is uttered when the corresponding deity is imagined, at which point the *yogin* also places a flower in the appropriate location. In the correct order a flower is placed in each respective direction along with the recitation of the corresponding mantra. In such a way, a flower is last placed in the Northwest corner during the generation of the maṇḍala [following a *pradakṣiṇa* laying out of flowers].[5] This is referred to as the flower installation (*puṣpanyāsa*). In just this way is the procedure of constructing the Guru Maṇḍala done:

1. Inside the maṇḍala
2. East (New. "*vaṃtā*")
3. South (New. "*yetā*")
4. West (New. "*itā*")
5. North (New. "*yaṃtā*")
6. Northeast corner, the *iśāna* (New. "*yaukulī*")
7. Southeast corner, the *āgneya* (New. "*vaṃkulī*")
8. Southwest corner, the *nairṛtya* (New. "*vayakulī*")
9. Northwest corner, the *vāyavya* (New. "*yaṃkulī*")

In each of these places, flower petals will be distributed and fixed with a mantra. This concludes the generation of a maṇḍala, which should be visualized.

---

i. Benoytosh Bhattacharya, ed. *Guhyasamājatantra*, pp. xxxv.

ii. Lokesh Chandra, ed. *Kriyāsamuccaya*, New Delhi: Sharada Rani 1977, pp. 316

---

[5] The flowers laid out to form the maṇḍala are placed in a clockwise (*pradakṣiṇa*) direction.

8.

The Guru Maṇḍala | *gurumaṇḍala*

It is the guru who gives knowledge because of the ignorance of his disciples. The honorable guru is very worthy of respect (*pūjanīya*). The performance of *pūjā* for the sake of the guru has been practiced since an ancient period. Worshiping the guru does not only involve giving food offerings, but also incorporates song, dance and recitation. The ritual functions as a kind of cleansing. The ritual *pūjā* performance causes a splendid mental visualization (*virājamāna*) of the maṇḍala for the sake of the guru; this is the complete development of the mental ascertainment of the maṇḍala in Vajrayāna. The tradition treats the Guru Maṇḍala ritual as something which must be preserved (*aparihārya*) since it is considered to be of the utmost importance for the guru. The main reason for doing the Guru Maṇḍala is that it is pleasing to the guru. If it is not pleasing to the guru, there will be no favor from the guru. Without the favor of the guru, there cannot be any success. The guru of the Guru Maṇḍala is not that human master. He takes on a visualized form for the sake of the Buddha, Dharma and Saṃgha. The guru to be considered in this case is the Ādibuddha, the guru Vajradhara.

Vajrasattva is the supreme guru. Each of these two gurus is engaged in the rite of the Guru Maṇḍala.[1]

This is the order in which the actions of the rite occur:[2]

1. First all the gurus are praised.
2. Subsequently the *bhāvanā* will be purified.
3. The *bhāvanā* is stabilized.
4. The *bhāvanā* of the maṇḍala.
5. The flower installation is the splendid Vajrasattva.
6. The *pūjā* which is the offering of the Ratna Maṇḍala.
7. The confession of sins, the vow to give away all merit for the benefit of the world.
8. The spirit offering *bhāvanā*.
9. Closing rites. Any summoned deities and/or spirits are sent away with a recitation.

The Full Gurumaṇḍala | *sampūrṇa gurumaṇḍala*

(According to the form of the contemporary (*ādhyāvadhika*) Guru Maṇḍala)[i]

1. Praising all the gurus | *guruvandana*

oṃ namo vajrasattvāya namo ratnatrayāya gurubuddhaḥ gurudharma gurusaṃgha tathaiva ca guruvajradharaś caiva tasmai śrīgurubhyo namaḥ oṃ namaḥ śrī gurubhyo namaḥ[3]

---

[1] All translations and explanations of Sanskrit in this chapter are by Yagyaman Pati.

[2] None of these numerated subheadings appear in the body of the chapter in the Newar original. They appear only as a list here at the beginning. To aid the reader, we added subheadings in this section to aid in reader navigation. Most do not appear in the original Newar version.

[3] For longer mantras, we have included the entire mantra before the translation and explanation. The translation and explanation of these

oṃ namo vajrasattvāya
namo ratnatrayāya
gurubuddhaḥ

Homage to Vajrasattva
Homage to the three jewels
Guru Buddha

The Buddha is the first of the three jewels. It refers to the five buddhas Vipaśvin, Krakuchanda, Kan̄akamun, Kāśyapa and Śākyasiṃha. It refers to the seven buddhas beginning with Dīpaṅkara. All the buddhas that are measurable in number to the grains of sand in the Ganges River; they are all meant by this guru.

gurudharma

Guru Dharma

The five *tārās*—Māmakī, Locanī, Padmīnī, Tārā, Prajñāpāramitā, as well as the texts on the Dharma maṇḍala—*Sahasrikāprajñāpāramitā*, the *Gaṇḍavyūha*, the *Daśabhūmika*, the *Samādhirāja*, the *Laṅkāvatāra*, the *Saddharmapuṇḍarīkā*, the *Tathāgataguhya*, the *Lalitavistara* and the *Suvarṇaprabhāsa*—and all the 84,000 Dharma books are meant by this guru.

---

mantras are justified to the right. The original does not include the long mantras as a unit at any point; these long mantras are added by translator to help guide the reader. In the original thes mantras are only presented as chopped up sections, with the reader expected to know the mantra as a whole. In the case of short mantras, we have left these justified to the left so that the reader can distinguish them from longer ones.

gurusaṃgha tathaiva ca

And so too the Guru Saṃgha

All the various figures who in the Saṃgha but not buddhas, such as Āryāvalokiteśvara, Maitreya Bodhisattva, the monks Ānanda, Upagupta and Jayaśrī, they are all meant by this guru.

guruvajradharaś caiva

And indeed the Guru Vajraholder

This refers to all vajraholders going all the way back to the guru Vajrasattva.

tasmai śrīgurubhyo namaḥ
oṃ namaḥ śrī gurubhyo namaḥ[4]

Homage to them, the honored gurus

OṂ homage to the venerable gurus.[5]

This is an homage to all the gurus just mentioned as a collective.

2. Purifying the water, the practitioner, the offerings, and the space

oṃ āḥ hūṃ 3 vaṃ vajrodake hūṃ svāhā

The seed mantra of VAṂ is said (and placed) in order to purify the conch.

---

[4] The full Sanskit, without being chopped up, is "*oṃ namo vajrasattvāya namo ratnatrayāya gurubuddhaḥ gurudharma gurusaṃgha tathaiva ca guruvajradharaś caiva tasmai śrīgurubhyo namaḥ oṃ namaḥ śrī gurubhyo namaḥ.*"

[5] The English translation, without being chopped up, is "Homage to Vajrasattva. Homage to the three jewels. [Homage to] Guru Buddha, Guru Dharma, and so too the Guru Saṃgha, and indeed the Guru Vajraholder. Homage to them, the honored gurus. OṂ homage to the venerable gurus."

yathā hi jātamātreṇa snāpitāḥ sarvatathāgatāḥ tathāhaṃ snāpayiṣyāmi śuddhantu dibyavāriṇā oṃ āḥ hūṃ sarvatathāgatābhiṣeka samaśriye hūṃ

yathā hi jātamātreṇa snāpitāḥ sarvatathāgatāḥ[ii]

Just as all the buddhas are bathed as soon as they arise,
All the buddhas come into the vessel (New. *dhālasā*).

tathāhaṃ snāpayiṣyāmi śuddhantu dibyavāriṇā

In that same way, with divine water, I will bathe them, and they are necessarily purified.
At this point, the practitioner visualizes the buddhas being bathed by using the water poured from the conch.

oṃ āḥ hūṃ sarvatathāgatābhiṣeka samaśriye hūṃ

All the *tathāgata*s are bathed along with the practitioner's own body in an *abhiṣeka*. The practitioner conceives that he is now purified.

oṃ hriṃ svāhā x3, kāya viśodhane svāhā

OṂ HṚIM SVĀHĀ x3, the body is purified SVĀHĀ
He pours a small amount of water from the conch into his hand and puts it into his mouth in order to purify his interior (*garbha*).

oṃ sarvavighnānutsāraye hūṃ

He sprinkles the water from the conch over himself to purify himself.

oṃ namo bhagavate puṣpaketurājāya tathāgatayārhante samyakasambuddhāya tadyathā
oṃ puṣpe puṣpe mahā puṣpe supuṣpe puṣpodbhave puṣpa saṃbhave puṣpāva kiraṇe svāhā

oṃ namo bhagavate puṣpaketurājāya tathāgatayārhante samyakasambuddhāya

The fully-awakened *tathāgata*, the *arahant*, named Śrīpuṣpaketu Rājā, is the object/receiver (New. *jyāva bijyākamha*) of this mantra.

tadyathā

So then

oṃ puṣpe puṣpe mahā puṣpe supuṣpe puṣpodbhave puṣpa saṃbhave puṣpāva kiraṇe svāhā

This is performed to purify the many different kinds of flowers that are offered in the course of the *pūjā*.

oṃ āḥ hūṃ 3 trikāyādhiṣṭhānaṃ
oṃ āḥ hūṃ tiṣṭha vajrāsane hūṃ

He makes a resting place (*āśrama*) that he imagines is the *vajrāsana*.[6]

oṃ sarvapāpānapanaye hūṃ |

He throws uncooked rice (New. *jāki*, hereafter "rice") over the left shoulder as he imagines that all sins are cast away.

oṃ maṇidharivajrīṇī mahāpratisare rakṣa rakṣa māṃ hūṃ hūṃ phaṭ phaṭ svāhā |

OṂ to the great Pratisarā, the female vajra-holder, the bearer of a jewel, protect, protect me! HŪṂ HŪṂ PHAṬ SVĀHĀ

---

6 The referent of *vajrāsana* varies according to context. In this instance, the *vajrāsana* is the ritually-empowered seat upon which the practitioner is seated. In a more general sense, *vajrāsana* refers to the place where a buddha is sitting when he/she becomes awakened. The *Vajrāsana* in Bodh Gaya is where Siddhartha Gautama is believed to have sat when he attained awakening.

This is the mantra of Pratisarā, and the practitioner places a flower atop his head as he says it. This protects oneself.

oṃ vajratilakabhūṣane svāhā |

OṂ you who are adorned with the *vajra tilaka* SVĀHĀ
This refers to a *tīka* ("*cittanaṃ* (*sinha*)"), which is considered/imagined as the splendid ornament of the *pūjā*.

oṃ vajrodake svāhā | *oṃ vajragomaya svāhā* | *oṃ vajrarekhasurekhe hūṁ* |

OṂ *vajra* water SVĀHĀ. OṂ *vajra* cow dung SVĀHĀ. OṂ to the beautiful *vajra* lines HŪṂ.
The cow-dung lines of the maṇḍala made on the *vajra* earth are embellished by all the buddhas.

sarvatathāgata adhiṣṭhānādhiṣṭhite svāhā |

All the *tathāgata*s are installed and fixed SVĀHĀ
He visualizes all the reverend *tathāgata*s. He installs (*adhiṣṭhāna yānā*) them.

dānaṃ gomayamambunā ca sahitaṃ śīlaṃ ca samārjanaṃ kṣānti kṣudraṃ pipīlikā nāpanayaṃ vīryakriyā sthāpanaṃ dhyānaṃ tatkṣaṇam ekacittakaraṇaṃ. prajñāsurekho jvalāya. etāḥ pāramitāḥ ṣaḍ eva labhante kṛtvā munimaṇḍalaṃ | *bhavatu kanakavarṇaḥ sarvarogair vimuktaḥ suramanujaviśiṣṭaś candravad dīptakāntiḥ dhanakanakasamṛddho jāyate rājavaṃśe sugatavaragṛhe 'smin kāyakarmāṇaṃ kṛtvā*[7]

[7] The *munimaṇḍala* is made while acknowledging the six perfections (*ṣaḍ pāramitā*).

dānaṃ gomayamambunā ca sahitaṃ

generosity together with water and cow dung
The *dāna pāramitā* refers to the product of a cow (i.e., dung), and a VAṂ syllable is given with cow dung.

śīlaṃ ca samārjanaṃ

and discipline is gained
Having purified the VAṂ syllable by spreading cow dung over it, the *śīla pāramitā* is considered.

kṣānti kṣudraṃ pipīlikā nāpanayaṃ

patience is not destroying even the smallest ant
He does not cause fear to even tiny creatures such as ants and other insects. Killing is improper; he should be merciful. This is the *kṣānti pāramitā*.

vīryakriyā sthāpanaṃ

heroic action is established
His auspicious actions are well-known. This is the *vīrya pāramitā*.

dhyānaṃ tatkṣaṇam ekacittakaraṇaṃ

meditation refers to cultivating a single-pointed mind at each moment
To do *dhyāna* is to act always with a one-pointed mind, especially in performing worship.

prajñāsurekho jvalāya

The beautiful lines of the maṇḍala are shining with *Prajñā*
A splendor that possesses a shimmering beauty is in the writing of illuminating knowledge; the perfection of wisdom is fulfilled.

etāḥ pāramitāḥ ṣaḍ eva labhante kṛtvā munimaṇḍalaṃ

after these six *pāramitās* are obtained, the *muni* maṇḍala is generated
The *muni* maṇḍala is made at this stage as the entire result of the six *pāramitās*.

bhavatu kanakavarṇaḥ sarvarogair vimuktaḥ suramanujaviśiṣṭaś candravad dīptakāntiḥ
dhanakanakasamṛddho jāyate rājavaṃśe sugatavaragṛhe 'smin kāyakarmāṇaṃ kṛtvā

Performing bodily actions, may he be golden, freed from all diseases, distinguished among gods and humans, splendidly bright like the moon, endowed with gold and riches, born into a royal dynasty in the best house of buddhas
The practitioner is the *muni* maṇḍala itself. [Both the practitioners and the practitioner-as-maṇḍala] are born into a royal dynasty, entirely gold and like a king distinguished among gods and humans. [The *munimaṇḍala* and practitioner-as-*muni* maṇḍala] shines brilliantly like the full moon.

oṃ maṇḍalalekhasurekhe sarvatathāgatān adhiṣṭhānādhiṣṭite svāhā
One mentally establishes all the buddhas on the lines of the *muni* maṇḍala.

oṃ candrārka vimale svāhā
The moon and sun shine unblemished.

oṃ vajrasattva sarvavighnānutsāraye hūṁ
OṂ vajrasattva, cease every hindrance HŪṂ
This recitation for Vajrasattva stops every hindrance.

5. Installing the maṇḍala with flowers

oṃ vajrabhūme hūṁ sarvatathāgata adhiṣṭhānādhiṣṭite svāhā
oṃ vajrasuvarṇajaladhāre svāhā
OṂ upon the earth HŪṂ all the buddhas are compelled to sit SVĀHĀ
OṂ to the ground that bears this golden *vajra* water SVĀHĀ
All the *tathāgata*s are established on the consecrated *vajra* ground. This water that is sprinkled upon the consecrated ground is equivalent to gold.

5.1 The Center Merus

oṃ ha mahāmadhye merave namaḥ
OṂ HA homage to the Meru at the great center
The HA syllable is produced in the center is a Buddha Maṇḍala.

oṃ hrīṁ madhye merave namaḥ
OṂ HRĪṂ homage to the Meru at the center
The HRĪṂ syllable produced on the right side is a Dharma Maṇḍala.

oṃ suṁ sukṣmamadhye merave namaḥ
OṂ SUṂ homage to the Meru at the subtle center
The SUṂ syllable produced on the left side is a Saṃgha Maṇḍala.

5.2 The Four Continents

oṃ yaṁ pūrvavidehāya namaḥ
OṂ YAṂ homage to Pūrvavideha
This is the eastern continent. The continent has a size that is 8,000 yojanas across (*vistāra*). It is in the shape of a half moon. On this continent stands a mango tree (*ava simā*) that stretches upwards to 100 yojanas. The trunk (*gājana*) is 5 yojanas thick. The inhabitants of this continent are born from eggs (*aṇḍajā*).

The length of people's lives here is 250 years. The lives of the beings living on this continent are extremely blissful. The king of this continent is Dhṛtarāṣṭraka.

oṃ raṁ jambudvīpāya namaḥ

OṂ RAṂ homage to Jambudvīpa

Jambudvīpa is to the south of Meru and in the southern quadrant of the maṇḍala. The length of the continent is 7,000 yojanas across. It is triangular in shape. In the center of the continent stands a 100-yojana-tall Guphama tree. Its branches are 40 yojanas long, and its trunk is 5 yojanas thick. The inhabitants of this continent are born from womb-borne embryos (*jarāyujā*). The people here live up to 100 years. Being born on this continent is the result of very auspicious past lives. The king of this continent is Viruḍhaka.

oṃ laṁ aparagodāvarīyāya namaḥ

OṂ LAṂ homage to Aparagodāvarīya

Godāvari is the western continent. The diameter (*vistāra*) of the continent is 9,000 yojanas. It is circular shaped. In the center of the continent stands a white fig (*pilāsa*, *Ficus virens*) tree. Its branches are 40 yojanas long, and its trunk is 5 yojanas thick. The inhabitants of this island are born from sweat (*saṃśvedajā*). The people here live up to 500 years. Those born on this continent are the happiest in all the world. The king of this continent is Virupākṣa.

oṃ vaṁ uttarakuruve namaḥ

OṂ VAṂ homage to Uttarakuru

Uttarakuru is to the north of Meru and in the northern quadrant of the maṇḍala. The length of the continent is 10,000 yojanas across. It has a square shape. On the island stands a 100-yojana-tall burflower (*kadamba*, *Neolamarckia cadamba*) tree. Its branches are 40 yojanas long, and its trunk is 5 yojanas thick. The inhabitants of this continent are born from a seed (*upapādajā*). The people here live twice as long [as those in Godāvarīyā, that is, 1,000 years]. All the people on this continent are blissful and have fabulous wealth. The king of this continent is Kubera.

5.3 The Four Islands

oṃ yā upadvīpāya namaḥ
OṂ YĀ homage to the island between continents
The southeastern (*agneya*) island.

oṃ rā upadvīpāya namaḥ
OṂ RĀ homage to the island between continents
The southwestern (*nairṛtya*) island.

oṃ lā upadvīpāya namaḥ
OṂ LĀ homage to the island between continents
The northwestern (*vāyavya*) island.

oṃ vā upadvīpāya namaḥ
OṂ VĀ homage to the island between continents
The northeastern (*īśāna*) island.

5.4 The Four Being Treasure-Continents[8]

oṃ yaṁ gajaratnāya namaḥ
OṂ YAṂ homage to the elephant treasure
The elephant treasure (*gajaratna*) is in the east. The *gajaratna* is an elephant (New. *kisi*), and it is placed on the continent Pūrvavideha. It is able to cross the ocean of *saṃsāra* within a

[8] These are not in the right place or order. They are correct in the chapter on Ratna Maṇḍala (Appendix Two).

single day and night (New. *cachinhichiyā bhitre*), and it is white in color. It is the union of an elephant and a gem.

oṃ raṁ puruṣaratnāya namaḥ
OṂ RAṂ homage to the man treasure
The human treasure is in the south. The human gem is placed on the southern continent and is given as a man. He is gold-colored and handsome. He possesses the 32 marks. This man becomes the man treasure.

oṃ laṁ aśvaratnāya namaḥ
OṂ VAṂ homage to the horse treasure
The horse treasure is in the west. The horse treasure is placed on an island to the west of Godāvari. It has a green body and both ears are white (*saphed tuyūvarṇa nhayapaṃ nipā*). The horse is able to cross the ocean of *saṃsāra* within a single day and night (*cachinhichiyā bhitre*). This extraordinary horse becomes the horse treasure.

oṃ vaṁ strīratnāya namaḥ
OṂ VAṂ homage to the woman treasure
The lady treasure is placed on the continent of Uttarakuru in the North. She has a *tikā* the color of a lotus flower. This *tikā* is also smeared across her collarbone. She is beautiful. This woman becomes the lady treasure.[9]

[9] Līlāvajra, the *mahāsiddha* credited with first constructing Kashtamandap and Śika͂mū Bāhā, is said to have been able to transform himself into these four-horse, elephant, male and female (Tārānātha, 272). Along with all other members of the Śika͂mū Bāhā *saṃgha*, Yagyaman Pati claims descent directly from Līlāvajra.

5.5 The Four Item Treasure-Continents

oṃ yā khaḍgaratnāya namaḥ

The sword treasure is on the southwest island. The sword treasure continent is established in the southwest. The sword treasure is associated with collections of *māras*, obstacles and weapons (*māragaṇa vighnagaṇa śatrugaṇa*) that kill beings. This deadly sword becomes the sword treasure.

oṃ rā maṇiratnāya namaḥ

The jewel treasure is on the northwest island. The jewel treasure can be red, black, yellow, green or white. If it is the red form and put into the ocean, it turns the entire ocean red. So, too, if a black, yellow, green or white *maṇi* is dropped into the ocean, it turns the ocean to the respective color. This splendid jewel becomes the jewel treasure.

oṃ lā cakraratnāya namaḥ

The disc treasure is on the northeast island. The disc treasure is so called due to having four spokes.[10] He visualizes that this disc assails (New. *phukācoṃgu*) collections of enemies, obstacles and *māras*. This disc weapon becomes the disc treasure.

oṃ vā sarvanidhānebhyo namaḥ

The all-riches vase is the treasure continent on the southeast island. The vase in the southeast is called "all riches," and it is to be made entirely filled with *amṛta*. He visualizes the vase as he utters the mantra. The vase is associated with all riches.

---

[10] Yagyaman Pati here uses two meanings of the word *cakra*. One is that of the discus weapon, such as the one wielded by Viṣṇu. The other meaning he invokes is that of cart wheel, which has four spokes. Both are circular (another meaning of *cakra*) in shape.

oṃ candrāya namaḥ
The moon maṇḍala is on the left side.

oṃ suṃ sūryāya namaḥ
The sun maṇḍala is on the right side.

oṃ āḥ śrīvajrasattvagurubhyo namaḥ
The Guru Maṇḍala is at the center.

6. The Ratna Maṇḍala offering *pūjā*

vajrapuṣpa, vajradhūpa, vajragandha, vajradīpa, vajranaivedya[11]
[Accept this] *vajra* flower, *vajra* incense, *vajra* unguent, *vajra* light and *vajra* food.

caturatnamayaṃ merum aṣṭadvīpopaśobhitaṃ nānāratnasamākīrṇa tadanuttaradāyine gurubhyo buddhadharmebhyaḥ saṃghebhyaś ca tathaiva ca niyātayāmi bhāvena saṃpūrṇaratnamaṇḍalaṃ

> *caturatnamayaṃ merum aṣṭadvīpopaśobhitaṃ*
> Mount Meru, made up of four jewels, adorned with eight continents
> Eight islands surround Mount Sumeru, arranged as the eight petals of a flower.

---

[11] Each of these five *vajra* offerings (*pañcopacāra pūjā*) is made with a series of *caryā* dance *mudrās*. They are not part of the creation of the Ratna Maṇḍala. They are also not part of the Ratna Maṇḍala offering itself. They constitute their own offering. We include them within "6. The Ratna Maṇḍala offering *pūjā*" subheading as this seems a more appropriate place than the "5. Installing the maṇḍala with flowers" subheading.

nānāratnasamākīrṇa tadanuttaradāyine

Surrounded by various jewels; to the giver of the highest of objects/to the giver at the highest place
A horse, elephant, man, woman, disc, sword, jewel and vase filled with treasure constitute the kinds that make up the "various jewels" surrounding Mount Sumeru. This constitutes the triple world (*jhiṃsvaṃgūgu bhūvana*). There are 25 realms of existence contained within the triple world. The world as the Ratna Maṇḍala is presented to Vajrasattva, who gives the highest knowledge that fully awakens and who dwells in the realm of the gods at the peak of Mount Sumeru.

gurubhyo buddhadharmebhyaḥ saṃghebhyaś ca tathaiva ca

For the gurus Buddha, Dharma, and Saṃgha each respectively
Homage is made to the four, respectively, the guru [Vajradhara], the Buddha, the Dharma, and Saṃgha.[12]

niyātayāmi bhāvena saṃpūrṇaratnamaṇḍalaṃ

Having brought it into being, I present the entire Ratna Maṇḍala.[13]
The Ratna Maṇḍala, visualized in its entirety, is offered.

---

[12] Yagyaman Pati cites four gurus here, rather than taking "guru" as an adjective modifying each of the three jewels. This is so he is sure to include the human guru of the tantric Buddhist tradition, the *vajra* holder (*vajradhara*).

[13] The full translation, without being chopped up, is "Having brought it into being (lit. by creation), I present to the giver of the highest of objects/to the giver at the highest place, and for the gurus Buddha, Dharma, and Saṃgha each respectively, the entire Ratna Maṇḍala containing Mount Meru, which is made up of four jewels and adorned with eight continents."

oṃ āḥ hūṁ śrīmad vajrasattva guruvara caraṇakamalāya samyajjñānāvabhāsakarāya namo hūṁ namos tu te hūṃ namo namaḥ bhaktyāhaṃ tvāṃ namasyāmi śrīgurunāthaprasiddhaye

oṃ āḥ hūṁ śrīmad vajrasattva guruvara caraṇakamalāya

OṂ ĀḤ HŪṂ honorable Vajrasattva, the best of gurus, to your lotus feet
The lotus feet of the guru Vajrasattva are purified/cleaned.

samyajjñānāvabhāsakarāya namo hūṁ

And to the splendid luminescence of awakening knowledge, I bow.
Every day he bows down, covering [the feet of the guru].

namos tu te hūṃ namo namaḥ[14]

To those honored ones: homage, homage, homage.

bhaktyāhaṃ tvāṃ namasyāmi śrīgurunāthaprasiddhaye

I bow for the success of my guru, to whom I am devoted.
He will, therefore, be necessarily pleased with me.

7. The confession of sins, the vow to give away all merit for the benefit of the world

yasya prasāda kiraṇai spharitātmatatva ratnaprabhāpratikara-prahatāndhakārā paśyantunāviradṛśaiḥ savilāsam uccai tasmai namaḥ kṛtir iyaṃ gurubhāṣkarāya oṃ namo buddhāya guruve namo dharmāya tāraṇe namaḥ saṃghāya mahas te tribhyo 'pi satataṃ namaḥ sarvabuddhaṃ namasyāmi dharmaṃ ca jinabhāṣitaṃ

---

[14] We changed this from what appears in the original—*namostena tuṃ namo namaḥ*—to what appears in the ritual manuals distributed by Yagyaman Pati presently. That printed in the original had problems, whch were evidently addressed in the manuals published after the 2004 book.

saṃghaṃ ca śīlasampanna ratnatrayaṃ namastu te ratnatrayaṃ me śaraṇaṃ sarvaṃ pratidiśāmy ahaṃ anumode jagatpuṇyaṃ buddhabodhau dadhe manaḥ ābodhau śaraṇaṃ yāmi buddha-dharmagaṇottamaṃ bodhicittaṃ karomy eṣa svaparārtha prasiddhaye utpādayāmi paramaṃ varabodhicittaṃ nimantrayāmi ahaṃ sarvasatvān iṣṭāṃ carisyaṃ varabodhicārikā buddho bhaveyaṃ jagato hitāya deśanāṃ sarvapāpānāṃ puṇyānāṃ cānumodanāṃ kṛto pravāsa carisyāmi āryāṣṭāṅgī ca poṣadhaṃ mayā bālena modena kiñcit pāpam ārjjita prakṛtyā vadya śāvadya prajña pratyāvadyam eva ca tad atyayaṃ deśayām eṣa nānām agratasthita kṛtāñjalī duḥkhabhīta praṇipatya punaḥ punaḥ atyayaṃ matyayaṃ tena pratigṛnhantu nāyakāḥ na bhadrakam idaṃ nātha na kartavyaṃ punar mayā yathā te tathāgatā āryā arhante samyaksaṃ buddho buddhajñānena buddhacakṣuṣā jānanti paśyanti yatkuśalamūlaṃ yaj jātikaṃ jaḥ nikāya yaḥ svabhāvaṃ jalakṣaṇaṃ yayā dharma tathā saṃvidyate tathāhaṃ anumode yathātebhyo anujānanti tatkuśala mūlaṃ anuttarāyā samyavasambodho tathā ahaṃ parināmayāmi tathā mamānena samādhikālaṃ lokasya duḥkhaṃ ca sukhodayaṃ ca hartuṃ ca kartuṃ ca sadātuttiḥ tama prakāsaṃ yathā bhāno dṛṣṭa śruto 'nusmṛtim āgato vā puṣṭaḥ kathāyogam upāśako vā sarvaprakārajagato hitāya kuryyāmya jadhaṃ sukhasaṃhitāya

yasya prasāda kiraṇai spharitātmatatva

The light of the guru's grace develops the liberating knowledge of reality.

ratnaprabhāpratikaraprahatāndhakārā

This light of his bejeweled splendor drives away all darkness.

paśyantunāviradṛśaiḥ savilāsam uccai

In *saṃsāra* [the guru] is the one who reveals liberating knowledge.

tasmai namaḥ kṛtir iyaṃ gurubhāṣkarāya

Homage to the honorable perfect guru (*śrī sadguru*) is performed endlessly.

oṃ namo buddhāya guruve

Homage is made to the guru Buddha.

namo dharmāya tāraṇe

Homage is made to the Dharma, which helps one cross the ocean of *saṃsāra*.

namaḥ saṃghāya mahas te tribhyo 'pi satataṃ namaḥ

Homage is made to the Saṃgha, which is characterized by its discipline (*śīla*).

sarvabuddhaṃ namasyāmi dharmaṃ ca jinabhāṣitaṃ

The worshiper makes homage to all the buddhas. He or she also bows to the Dharma, spoken by buddhas.

saṃghaṃ ca śīlasampannaṃ ratnatrayaṃ namastu te

Homage is made the Saṃgha, those learned in the *śāstras*. Homage is made to the Three Jewels.

ratnatrayam me śaranaṃ sarvaṃ pratidiśāmy ahaṃ

The worshiper confesses their sins.

anumode jagatpunyam

The worshiper rejoices over all the merit in the world.

buddhabodhau dadhe manaḥ

The practitioner worships the awakening knowledge of a buddha.

ābodhau śaraṇaṃ yāmi

The *bodhicitta* now arisen, the worshiper goes to the refuge of the Buddha.

buddhadharmagaṇottamaṃ

The worshiper has gone to the refuge of the Three Jewels, the great arising of the Buddha, Dharma, and Saṃgha.

bodhicittaṃ karomy eṣa svaparārtha prasiddhaye

The worshiper does the *Saptavidhānuttara pūjā*, which is done for the sake of all beings, and develops the awakened mind. He or she accomplishes all actions in *saṃsāra*.

utpādayāmi paramaṃ varabodhicittaṃ

He or she makes the *bodhicitta* arise.

nimantrayāmi ahaṃ sarvasatvān

The worshiper extends an invitation to all beings.

iṣṭāṃ carisyaṃ varabodhicārikā

The path is one of awakened activity (*buddhacaryā caraṇapā*).

buddho bhaveyaṃ jagato hitāya

He or she becomes a buddha for the sake of the world.

deśanāṃ sarvapāpānāṃ puṇyānāṃ cānumodanāṃ

The worshiper confesses their sins and delights in their merits.

kṛto pravāsa carisyāmi āryāṣṭāṅgī ca poṣadhaṃ

A fasting vow is undertaken, as one fasts during the eight-limbed *upoṣadha vrat*.

mayā bālena modena kiñcit pāpam ārjita

If I should gleefully and immaturely commit some impure sin, *prakṛtyā vadya śāvadya prajña pratyāvadyam eva ca*

detailing this sin in its entirety, it need not be detailed in the future.

tad atyayaṃ deśayām eṣa nānām agratasthita.

Oh lord, all my various sins are elucidated.

kṛtāñjalī duḥkhabhīta praṇipatya punaḥ punaḥ

Repeated homage must be made by saying "Oh forgive me!"[15] to purify the repeatedly committed sin.

atyayam atyayaṃ tena pratigṛnhantu nāyakāḥ

Oh Lord, oh Guru, guide me away from all my missteps!

na bhadrakam idaṃ nātha na kartavyaṃ punar mayā

Oh Lord, oh Guru, from now sins will not be committed by me!

yathā te tathāgatā āryā arhante samyaksaṃ buddho buddhajñānena buddhacakṣuṣā jānanti paśyanti yatkuśalamūlaṃ

Relinquishing sin, I will obtain the liberating knowledge of a buddhas, I will obtain the eye of a buddha, and may whatever acts I perform be meritorious.

yaj jātikaṃ jaḥ nikāya̧ yaḥ svabhāvaṃ jalakṣaṇaṃ yayā dharma tathā saṃvidyate tathāhaṃ anumode yathātebhyo anujānanti tatkuśalamūlaṃ anuttarāyā samyavasambodho tathā ahaṃ parināmayāmi .

Whatever my birth will be, whatever my caste, I will have a mind on Dharma and I will obtain knowledge leading to awakening (*bodhijñāna*), and I will ever enjoy happiness. As

---

[15] Yagyaman Pati actually writes "*hā jvajalapā*," which means something akin to "Oh! Greetings!" The sense is that the person cries out to Vajrasattva for forgiveness every time they commit a sinful act.

one maintaining the highest of commitment, I will obtain this awakening knowledge. Having acquired the shelter of the *tathāgatas* (i.e., *nirvāṇa*), worshiping daily, I am transformed.

tathā mamānena samādhikālaṃ lokasya duḥkhaṃ ca sukhodayaṃ ca hartuṃ ca kartuṃ ca sadā tu saktiḥ tama prakāśaṃ yathā bhāno .

Just as the sun has the capacity to bring either light or darkness in *saṃsāra*, and make pleasure or pain for those beings languishing in *saṃsāra*, so too

dṛṣṭa śruto 'nusmṛtim āgato vā

developing this capacity by seeing, hearing and recalling,

puṣṭaḥ kathāyogam upāśako vā .

I myself may be a guide [to end the suffering of others and bring them to happiness].

sarvaprakārajagato hitāya

Having completed the necessary acts, the practitioner is always engaged for every being in *saṃsāra*.

kuryyām yajadhaṃ sukhasaṃhitāya.

For the sake of happiness, I will make offerings daily.

athaiva pāpadeśanādikaṃ vidhāya

Thus, the recitation of the confession of sins is finished.

8. The Spirit *Bhāvanā* | *bali bhāvanā*

Oṃ hriṃ ācamanaṃ praticcha svāhā

OṂ HṚIM accept this water SVĀHĀ
Water for the spirits is offered.

prathamaṃ śunyatānantaraṃ tato yaṃkāreṇa vāyumaṇḍalaṃ tadupari raṃkāreṇa agnimaṇḍalaṃ laṃkāreṇa āpamaṇḍalaṃ tadupari āḥkāreṇa muṇḍa tritaya curiko pariśuklapadmabhāñjanaṃ tatra bhaktārī paripuritaṃ būm̐ ām̐ jiṃ kham̐ hūm̐ lām̐ mām̐ pām̐ tām̐ vam̐ vam̐kārajātaṃ dadhiṣṭita pañcāmṛtapañcapradiparūpena niṣpādya

prathamaṃ śunyatānantaraṃ

First, the voidness within emptiness is imagined.

tato yaṃkāreṇa vāyumaṇḍalaṃ

From that voidness a YAṂ syllable is imagined coming into being, and a wind maṇḍala arises from that YAṂ syllable.

tadupari raṃkāreṇa agnimaṇḍalaṃ

Then, on top of that wind maṇḍala, a RAṂ syllable arises, on top of which a fire maṇḍala arises.

laṃkāreṇa āpamaṇḍalaṃ

A water maṇḍala arises from the LAṂ syllable. From that water maṇḍala arises a great turtle. From that great turtle arises the earth maṇḍala (*pṛthvīmaṇḍala*). It is well known that there are nine planets that one could ostensibly label "world" (*pṛthvī*), but in this case "Pṛthvī" (the Earth) refers to our world. In the midst of that earth maṇḍala arises a SUṂ syllable, from which arises the mountain Sumeru.

tadupari āḥkāreṇa muṇḍa tritaya curiko pariśuklapadmabhāñjanaṃ

He establishes a vessel made from a lotus.

tatra bhaktārī paripuritaṃ

The vessel is filled with a purifying mantra.

būm̊ ām̊ jiṃ kham̊ hūm̊ lām̊ mām̊ pām̊ tām̊ vam̊

This ten-syllable mantra ending with VAṂ purifies.

vam̊kārajātaṃ dadhiṣṭita pañcāmṛtapañcapradiparūpena niṣpādya

Having purified by means of the ten-syllable mantra ending with VAṂ, he visualizes the form of the five nectars.

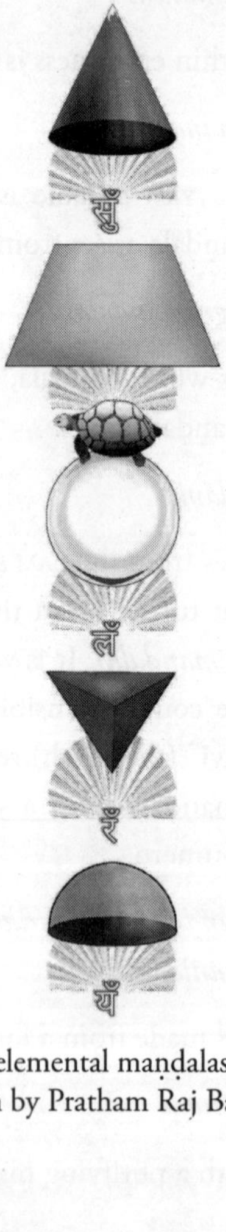

Generation of the elemental maṇḍalas and seed syllables.
Illustration by Pratham Raj Bajracharya.

indrādi lokapālebhyo pādyāghacamanaṃ praticcha svāhā

He implores the lords of the directions, beginning with Indra, to accept the offering in the form of a washing of their feet.

oṃ āḥ hūṁ
garuḍa mudrāyāṃ darśayet

He should display the Garuḍa *mudrā.*

lokapālamudrāyāṃ darśayat

He should display the Lokapāla *mudrā.*

oṃ ja hūṁ va ho[16]

8.1 The Spirit Offering Maṇḍala

oṃ indrāya svāhā

At the eastern direction is King Indra, lord of the gods.

oṃ yamāya svāhā

The lord of the southern direction is King Yama, lord of the *pitṛ*s.

oṃ varuṇāya svāhā

At the western direction is King Varuṇa, the lord of *nāga*s.

oṃ kuberāya svāhā

At the northern direction is King Kubera, the lord of *yakṣa*s.

---

[16] The instructions concerning these syllables are too esoteric to print, and the original Newar records only the syllables as we have them here.

oṃ agneya svāhā

At the southwestern direction is the god Agni, lord of fire.

oṃ nairṭya svāhā

At the northwestern direction if the god Nairṭya, lord of the demons (*rākṣasa*).

oṃ vāyuve svāhā

At the northeastern direction is the god Vāyu, lord of the wind.

oṃ iśānāya svāhā

At the southeastern direction is Mahādeva, lord of ghosts and ghouls (*bhūta*).

oṃ arddhabramhane svāhā

Nārāyaṇa is the master of the lower region.

oṃ ūrddhvabramhane svāhā

Brahmā is the master of the upper region.

oṃ sūrya grahādhipataye svāhā

At the right side is the Sun, the lord of the planets.

oṃ candra nakṣatrādhipataye svāhā

At the left side is the Moon, lord of the constellations (*nakṣatra*, lit. lunar stations).

oṃ nāgebhyaḥ svāhā

All the *nāgas*.

oṃ yakṣebhyaḥ svāhā

All the *yakṣas*.

oṃ asurebhyaḥ svāhā

All the demons (*daitya*).

oṃ sarvadigvidigdaśadiglokapālebhyaḥ svāhā

All the *lokapāla*s of all the directions, meaning the ten directions.

8.2 Offerings made to the spirit | *balisa pañcopacāra pūjā*

vajrapuṣpa, vajradhūpa, vajragandha, vajradīpa, vajranaivedya

[Accept this] *vajra* flower, *vajra* incense, *vajra* unguent, *vajra* light and *vajra* food.

indrādayo mahāvīrā lokapālā maharddhikā kilayantu daśakrodha vighnahantān namastu te

One makes homage to the lords of the directions (those just named, Indra and so forth), who are now enthroned at the ten directions.

Water offering (tarpaṇa)
oṁ̐ ha ho hiṃ khaṁ̐ svāhā

oṃ vibhrāṇāṃ buddhabimbaṃ divasakarodharadhararāsapāsa-bindurekhamaitrīyacārarūpaṃ śivaśi vapuṣaṃ mañjughoṣaṃ ca gātraṃ padmoṣṭaṃ dvandarūpaṃ kulita bhūṣaṇa vajrī naṃ bhīmanādaṃ vijñānajñānarūpaṃ nihita bhava bhayaṃ pañcamūrtiḥ praṇamya .

While uttering the recitation (the passage being described), the practitioner's cupped left hand is filled with water and drops are sprinkled upon the image of the buddha [that is the maṇḍala itself]; while a mind of compassion is developed, the practitioner grows liberating knowledge as he or she pays respect to the *pañcamūrti*.

8.3 Ordering the spirits | *bali biya*

oṃ indrādivajrīsahadevasaṃghai nimañ ca gṛhantu baliviśuddha agnir yamo nairṭya bhūpatiś ca āpāpatir vāyu dhanādhipaś ca iśāna bhūtādhipatiś ca deva urdhvārddha candrāvaka pitāmahaś ca devā samastā bhuvicaya nāgā dharodharāmai agnis samastā prati prati tvekanivedayañ ca svakasvakā caiva thasā suputrā gṛnhantu duṣṭāsa varāra sainyāsa saputradārā sahabhṛtya saṃghai puṣpaṃ balidhūpaṃ balilepanaṃ ca gṛnhantu bhujantu jighrantu pibantu cedaṃ idaṃ ca karmasaphalaṃ bhavantu svāhā

oṃ indrādivajrīsahadevasaṃghai

This commences the recitation to the group of *vajra*-bearing lords beginning with Indra.

nimañ ca gṛhantu baliviśuddha

This is a statement in the imperative, instructing the lords to accept the *bali* offering of the five *vajra* offerings.

agnir yamo nairṭya bhūpatiś ca

Now named lords of the direction are invoked: Yama the lord of the southern direction, the god Agni of the southwestern direction, and the lord of demons.

āpāpatir vāyu dhanādhipaś ca

More gods are invoked: the god Varuṇa (*āpāpati*, lord of the waters), lord of the western direction, the god Vāyu in the northeastern direction, the god Kubera in the north.

iśāna bhūtādhipatiś ca deva

At the southeast is Mahādeva, lord of ghosts and ghouls.

urdhvārddha candrāvaka pitāmahaś ca devā

The realm of all the gods (*deva loka*), Brahmā and the moon are above.

samastā bhuvicaya nāgā

Below, in the ground, is the realm of the *nāga*s and mother earth, and the mother goddesses.

dharodharāmai agnis samastā prati prati tvekanivedayañ ca

This line finishes up the remainder of the kinds to spirits to be worshiped.

svakasvakā caiva thasā suputrā

The lords of the directions come into the space, as if they are his own son [i.e., they respond as if commanded by a parent].

gṛnhantu duṣṭāsa varāra sainyāsa

This begins a section of the offering recitation where the ritualist elucidates the offerings that will be given in the spirit worship.

saputradārā sahabhṛtya saṃghai

The groups [offered] consist of sons, daughters, wives, and male and female servants.

puṣpaṃ balidhūpaṃ balilepanaṃ ca

The fivefold offering is given, which consists of flower, incense, light, aromatic tika and food.

gṛnhantu bhujantu jighrantu pibantu cedaṃ

This is in the imperative, instructing the spirits to be pleased and to consume the offering.

idaṃ ca karmasaphalaṃ bhavantu svāhā

This completes the recitation, and states that the offering will be successful.

oṃ namo ratnatrayāya candravajrapāṇāya vajramahākrodhāya mahādraṣṭotkaṭa bhairavāya. oṃ asimuśalaparaśupāśagṛhitahastāya amṛtakuṇḍalī. oṃ kha kha khāhi khāhi tiṣṭa tiṣṭa baṃdha baṃdha hana hana daha daha paca paca garja garjja visphoṭaya visphoṭaya sarvavighnavināyakānāṃ mahāgaṇapatijivitāṃdhakārāya vapuṣāya hā hā phaṭ phaṭ svāhā.

oṃ namo ratnatrayāya caṇḍavajrapāṇāya vajramahākrodhāya

This refers to a fiercely angry image of a deity who is named Caṇḍavajrapāṇi.

mahādraṣṭotkaṭa bhairavāya

He is terrifying when he appears.

oṃ asimuśalaparaśupāśagṛhitahastāya amṛtakuṇḍalī

He has the power of Amṛtakuṇḍalī and he possesses a noose, a club, an axe and a sword.

oṃ kha kha khāhi khāhi tiṣṭa tiṣṭa baṃdha baṃdha hana hana daha daha paca paca garja garjja visphoṭaya visphoṭaya sarvavighnavināyakānāṃ

These are various words instructing the fierce vajra-holder to capture, bind, enclose, and destroy.

mahāgaṇapatijivitāṃdhakārāya vapuṣāya hā hā phaṭ phaṭ svāhā

He is the great lord of the ghouls and his body is dark. This spirit offering is necessary for the overall pūjā to be successful.

vajrapuṣpa, vajradhūpa, vajragandha, vajradīpa, vajranaivedya

[Accept this] *vajra* flower, *vajra* incense, *vajra* unguent, *vajra* light and *vajra* food.

9. Closing Rites

9.1 Verses on Dependent Arising | *pratītyasamutpāda gāthā*

ye dharmā hetuprabhāvā hetuṃ teṣāṃ tathāgato hy avadat teṣāṃ ca yo nirodha evaṃ vādī mahāśramaṇaḥ

ye dharmā hetuprabhāvā

All existents are called "*dharmas*", and all *dharmas* in *saṃsāra* arise as the effects of causes.

hetuṃ teṣāṃ tathāgato hy avadat

Such effects include the arising of birth in *saṃsāra*. According to the Buddha, this effect, birth, is the cause giving rise to death.

teṣāṃ ca yo nirodha

He also stated that those *dharmas* arising in the wheel of *saṃsāra* will all eventually be destroyed. This refers to the path leading to liberation.

evaṃ vādī mahāśramaṇaḥ

This was stated by the Buddha in the scriptures of the Śrāvakayāna.

9.2 The 100-syllable mantra of Vajrasattva | *śatākṣara*

oṃ vajrasattva samayam anupālaya vajrasattva tvenopatiṣṭha dṛḍho me bhava sutuṣyo me bhava supuṣyo me bhava anurakto me bhava sarvasiddhim me prayaccha sarvakarmāsu ca me cittaṃ śrīyaṃ kuru hūṁ ha ha ha ha ho bhagavān sarvatathāgata vajra mā me muñca vajri bhava mahāsamayasattva āḥ oṃ vajrasattva samayam anupālaya

OṂ Protect my *samaya* Vajrasattva.

vajrasattva tvenopatiṣṭha

Be firm like the *vajra.*

dṛḍho me bhava

Become firmly established in front of me.

sutusyo me bhava

He must be pleased.

supuṣyo me bhava

He must be clearly (*spaṣṭa*) established for me.

anurakto me bhava

He is compelled to protect me.

sarvasiddhim me prayaccha

He must bestow all *siddhis*.

sarvakarmāsu ca me cittaṃ śrīyaṃ kuru

He is compelled to make my mind and all my actions virtuous.

hūṃ ha ha ha ha ho bhagavān

This is a vocative-"hey *bhagavān* vajrasattva"-made by the practitioner in order to direct Vajrasattva to act for the sake of all beings.

sarvatathāgata vajra mā me muñca vajri bhava

All you *tathāgatas* who are like the *vajra*, please do not abandon me.

mahāsamayasattva āḥ

Oh Lord Vajrasattva, the best guru, protect my body, speech and mind until the destruction of the world and the end of time.

9.3 Final Dismissal | *visarjana*

kṛtova sarvasatvārtha siddhiṃ yatvā yathānugā gacchaś ca buddhaviṣayaṃ punarāya gamanāya ca punar vāda oṃ āḥ hūṁ gaccha maṇḍale visarjana

kṛtova sarvasatvārtha

I have acted for the sake of those in *saṃsāra.*

siddhiṃ yatvā yathānugā

Having come to this realm and accomplished the goal

gacchaś ca buddhaviṣayaṃ

Thus, you are returned to the realm of the buddhas.

punarāya gamanāya ca punar vāda

You must come when I summon you.

oṃ āḥ hūṁ gaccha maṇḍale visarjana

Hey lord Vajrasattva, the true guru, go HŪṂ go HŪṂ!
He dismisses him from the maṇḍala with the HŪṂ syllable. This dismissal is done after the 100-syllable mantra of Vajrasattva. He visualizes that all the deities are sent into the atmosphere.[17]

---

[17] Yagyaman Pati includes a second, alternative dismissal recitation, which we have removed to increase readability. We include it here. "*kṛtova sarvasatvārthasiddhiṃ dattvājathānugā*

He has completed this ritual, performed for the benefit of all beings. *gachaś ca buddhaviṣayaṃ pūrṇāgamanāya ca oṃ āḥ hūṁ vajramaṇḍalam*

Closing recitation

The day this was completed was the 14th of Vaiśākh in 2060 (April 27, 2003).[18]

śuddho vā aśuddho vā mama doṣa na dīyate

Whether good or bad, may my faults not be offered.
Śubham.[19]

---

i. What is recorded in my handwritten manuscript (thyāḥsaphū) collection authored by Ṣadānanda of Makhaṃ Bahāḥ and Machelāla of Nhūghaḥ Bahāḥ supports what is printed in the later books. Thus special effort is made to clearly lay out the procedure according to the position of Ṣadānanda.

ii. This is also in the White Kurukullā sādhana (pp. 364).

Through visualizing the HŪṂ, he is summoned to sit on the buddha's throne of the Vajramaṇḍala and fills it completely."

[18] There is nothing particularly special about April 27, 2003. This just happens to be the day that Yagyaman Pati wrote this section. The day that a person says at this point in the performance of the gurumaṇḍala rite should be the day on which the person is performing the rite.

[19] *Śubham* means "good" and/or "auspicious." It closes the rite, similar in sentiment to closing a prayer with "Amen."

9.

The Occasion to Undertake the Guru Maṇḍala | *Guru Maṇḍala chyalegu avasarat*

Foundation | *pṛṣṭhabhūmi*

In Vajrayāna, there must be an understanding of the reasons for the performance of the Guru Maṇḍala rite. The subject of the Guru Maṇḍala is a critical one. Tantric practice is insufficient without an understanding and performance of this ritual. Failure to adhere to this necessary Guru Maṇḍala rite is simply not done. Any *pūjā* done includes the Guru Maṇḍala rite, whether that be empowering items to be used in a larger *pūjā*, *kalaś pūjā*, rites of establishment (*sthāpanā*) of a deity and/or a geographic location, *svanā pūjā*, etc. It is written in the various rituals that each of these rites includes the performance of the Guru Maṇḍala.

Importance | *viśeṣatā*

Vajrācārya gurus must perform *pūjā* once every day, either at his own home or at the place of a ritual client. Every *pūjā* must include the Guru Maṇḍala rite. It is part of Newar Buddhist tradition that in the undertaking of one's assorted daily responsibilities (New. *chathi nithi*) whenever there is *pūjā* to be done, the Guru Maṇḍala rite is done. It is also, therefore, one's heritage. It is not only *vajrācārya* gurus that do the Guru Maṇḍala at the commencement of their service, performing *pūjā* for ritual clients. Performing the *Guru Maṇḍala* is the responsibility (New. *pālanā*) of all Buddhists.

Daily worship | *nityapūjā*

Those individuals who have completed the baseline initiation (*cūḍākarma*) must perform the daily Buddhist *pūjā*. This daily *pūjā* has been done in a family's shrine room, passed from one person to the next in lineage. This observance was established long ago.

Performing the Guru Maṇḍala with a ritual client | *jajamānaṃ Guru Maṇḍala vidhi yāïgu*

Only *vajrācārya* gurus are allowed to perform the Guru Maṇḍala for ritual clients. The rite, when done for a ritual client, must be done through a *bhāvanā* of an abbreviated version of the Guru Maṇḍala at the *samādhi* stage of the *pūjā*. The rite of the Guru Maṇḍala itself always stays the same during the performance of a variety of different *pūjā* types.

Undertaking the rite that entails fasting | *dhalaṃ danegu*

Undertaking the rite that entails fasting is explained as performing a ritual, a particular rite. It is also taught that to complete the Guru Maṇḍala, one undertakes the fast. The hereditary rituals given at particular moments in the life of a practicing Newar Buddhist (*daśakarmayā saṃskār*) are among the litany of rituals that involve performing this Guru Maṇḍala rite along with a fast. It is compulsory in the following hereditary rites:

1. In the prenatal birth-purification ceremony (*jātābhiṣeka kriyā*), the parent welcomes the child and performs the Guru Maṇḍala rite along with fasting.[1]
2. The parents are also to do the Guru Maṇḍala rite along with a fast for the baby in performing the first rice-feeding ceremony (*annaprāśanābhiṣeka*).
3. The young girl is to do the Guru Maṇḍala rite along with a fast during the undertaking of the initiation rite of a young girl in which she is married to a deity (*ihī*).
4. In the rite of confinement (New. *bāhāḥ*, var. *bādhā*, *bārāy*) for a girl on the occasion of her first menstruation, the girl is to do the Guru Maṇḍala rite along with a fast when she ends the confinement period.
5. During the course of the procedure of the ritualized abandonment of the householder life in favor of the monastic life and the ritualized tonsuring (*cūḍākarma*), every single

---

[1] For a detailed description of the following rites see the corresponding page numbers in Vajracharya, Asha Kaji. *The Daśakarma Vidhi: Fundamental Knowledge on Traditional Customs of Ten Rites of Passage Amongst the Buddhist Newars.* Mandala Book Point, 2010. For the prenatal birth-purification ceremony (*jātābhiṣeka kriyā*) see pp. 31-33. For the first rice-feeding ceremony (*annaprāśanābhiṣeka*) see pp. 37-34. For the initiation rite of a young girl in which she is married to a deity (*ihī*) see pp. 109-115. For the rite of confinement (*bāhāḥ*, var. *bādhā*, *bārāy*) for a girl on the occasion of her first menstruation see pp. 117-121. For the hair-tonsuring rite (*cūḍākarma*) see pp. 41-85. For the *vajrācārya* initiation (ācāryābhiṣeka, ācāḥ luyegu) see pp. 87-108. For the Newar Buddhist wedding ceremony see pp. 123-135. For old-age Newar Buddhist rites see pp. 179-182.

participant, both the children and their parents, must fast/do the Guru Maṇḍala rite along with a fast.

6. In the *vajrācārya* initiation (S. *ācāryābhiṣeka*, New. *ācāḥ luyegu*), the disciples that are being initiated must have already done the Guru Maṇḍala rite along with a fast in preparation for the rite.
7. After the taking of membership by the new members of the religious organization called *guthis*, they also undertake and complete the Guru Maṇḍala rite. Regarding the Kathmandu Ācārya Guthi, during the dark half of Phalgun, the honorable new members perform the Guru Maṇḍala at the peak of the Svayambhū *mahācaitya* hill. The custom is that a share of each in the middle and at the top of the hill must complete the rite observing the Guru Maṇḍala. Nowadays, such a tradition is extinct.
8. The wedding ritual (*pāṇīgrahaṇa*) in a marriage ceremony—during the fire sacrifice that occurs in the course of the wedding, the betrothed are to perform the Guru Maṇḍala. They fast until the five-colored strings and braids are fully pulled from the bride's pulled-back hair.[2]

[2] This refers to a point in the wedding ceremony where the bridegroom braids the bride's hair, worships the braids, and then eventually undoes the braids. "Then the bridegroom unties the hair of the bride which is sprinkled with śaṅkha water by the *purohit*. Then the groom parts the hair into five strands and ties them with *kumbha kā* (thread) in the shape of a small *caitya* with the help of a pointed instrument. He then puts some scented flowers and *abhir* on her head and red tika on her forehead. The groom performs *pūjā* to those five bundles of hair as symbolic representatives of the five Tārās. He shows burning incense to them and puts red powder in the parting of the hair. The purohit reads aloud the sutra while ringing his bell. The bride is regarded as Kumārī or Vajradevī. The groom pours fruit from a brass pot, and pays reverence to the bride by reciting [a mantra to the five goddesses represented by the five braids of hair]. The first bundle of hair

9. Tantric initiation (New. *dekhā*)—the disciples being initiated will observe the Guru Maṇḍala along with a fast in each required step of the tantric initiation ritual, giving each successive offering accompanied by the recitation of mantras.
10. The consecration of a monastery elder—the honorable elder performs the Guru Maṇḍala at the seat of the elder prior to the procedure that is consecrating a monastery elder with water (New. *thāypā luyegu*).
11. The Guru Maṇḍala, along with a fast, is also to be performed on the occasion of the life-cycle rite for elders called *bhīmaratha* that marks the life of someone who has lived 77 years, 7 months and 7 days; that is, someone who has seen 950 full moons.
12. At the end of a person's life, the Guru Maṇḍala rite, along with a fast, is to be performed as a part of the funeral ceremony.[3]

---

denotes the union of Vairocana with Tara Rocani, the second of Aksobhya with Tārā Māmaki the third of Ratnasambhava with Tārā Pandara, the fourth of Amitabha with Āryā Tārā and the fifth of Amoghasiddhi with Tārā Kamalā. The *purohit Vajrācārya* wears his *mukuta* [crown] with the five images of *Tathāgata*s and Five Tārās, while holding his *vajra* in right hand and *ghaṇṭā* in left hand and wearing beads (*mālā*) around his neck. These five unions are collectively known as *prajñopāya jñāna mūrti*-the five colours merging into one denoting emptiness or the void (*śunyatā*)." (Asha Kaji Vajracharya, 2010: 130-131).

[3] For the an analysis of the Newar Buddhist funeral rites see Gellner, David N. Monk, *Householder, Tantric Priest: Newar Buddhism and Its Hierarchy of Ritual.* New Delhi: Cambridge University Press, 1992. pp. 246-247. and Anderson, Kris L. *Raising the Dead and Saving Them: Transformations in Funerary Manuals of the Sarvadurgatipariśodhana Tantra.* PhD Dissertation. University of California, Berkeley, 2022. pp 29-33.

The undertaking of the rite that entails fasting by ritual clients | *jajamānapisaṃ danegu dhalaṃ*

Only *vajrācārya* gurus may perform the Guru Maṇḍala for ritual clients, which is also the rite performed by those same ritual clients. The ritual clients perform the rite in the following rituals along with a fast under the supervision of a *vajrācārya* guru:

1. To complete any *pūjā* he performs for a ritual client, the honorable *vajrācārya* guru (who does the rite as a visualization in *samādhi*) will do an abbreviated form of the Guru Maṇḍala for the ritual client.
2. During the funerary rites, the Guru Maṇḍala is done for the son or daughter of the deceased taking part in the ritual in the course of performing the ghost feeding (ritualized feeding) in front of the body of the deceased that is cremated.
3. For the ten rice-ball offering observance rite (*daśapiṇḍa vidhāna*), the Guru Maṇḍala is done by the ritual client during the food offering on the tenth day of this ritual, which is performed daily over a ten-day period.
4. The Guru Maṇḍala is to be done by the ritual client when he has bad luck (New. *kvajīkegu avasaray*), meaning that suffering is dispersed.
5. Monthly ancestor worship (*māsika śrāddha*)—the life-cycle rite to do the ancestor worship involves making offerings at a *tīrtha* in each and every month. The rite of the Guru Maṇḍala is performed by the ritual client under the supervision of a *vajrācārya* guru in the course of the ancestor worship.
6. In the same way the ritual client performs the Guru Maṇḍala in the course of performing the ancestor worship on the 45th day after the death of a parent (*latyā*), three months after

death (*svalā*), six months after death (*khulā*) one year after death (*dakilā*) and two years after death (*nidaṃyā tithi*).[4]

7. Annual food offering (*varṣa piṇḍa*)—the Guru Maṇḍala is performed by a ritual client on the occasion of the annual ancestor worship; this is done once a year.
8. While taking *dīkṣā* with the honorable *bodhisattva* guru, he is to offer the Ratna Maṇḍala, the best and rarest thing in the world, when the visualized form (*bhāvanā anurupa*) of the Guru Maṇḍala rite is generated.
9. During the *Saptavidhānottara pūjā*[5] the Ratna Maṇḍala form is generated in a visualized (*bhāvanā*) Guru Maṇḍala rite. A small amount of uncooked rice is placed on the offering space made of smeared clay.

---

[4] See Gellner, David N. *Monk, Householder, Tantric Priest: Newar Buddhism and Its Hierarchy of Ritual.* New Delhi: Cambridge University Press, 1992. pp. 211. and Lewis, Todd. T. "Buddhist Merchants in Kathmandu: The Asan Twāḥ Market and Urāy Social Organization." In *Contested Hierarchies: A Collaborative Ethnography of Caste in the Kathmandu Valley, Nepal,* edited by David N. Gellner and Declan Quigley, 38–79. Oxford: Oxford University Press, 1995. pp. 19.

[5] "This 'seven Element Ritual' is a very popular Newar householder practice, one that conjoins meditation and ritual offerings. It is performed for any Buddhist deity, but is most popularly directed to *caityas*, and bodhisattva images such as Avalokiteśvara or Tārā. [...] The central ritual focuses on the water jar (*kalaśa*) surrounded by eight auspicious symbols (*aṣṭamaṅgala*) that symbolize the eight bodhisattvas. The purpose of this *pujā* [sic.] is to take refuge in Triple gems [sic.], offer sensory objects, confess misdeeds with vows not to commit them again, rejoicing in the good deeds of the śrāvakas, bodhisattvas, and Buddhas, and finally, requesting that the latter not enter *nirvāṇa* [italics added], but remain in *saṃsāra* for the welfare of living beings. Those doing the ritual then take a bodhisattva vow to seek Buddhahood in the future; the *Saptavidhanuttara pūjā* reaching completion after all are given the bodhisattva initiation (*abhiṣeka*)." Lewis & Bajracharya 2016: 146-147.

10. The undertaking of the Guru Maṇḍala is also performed in the case of a few critical rites: the *aṣṭamīvrat*, the full moon *vrat* (New. *punhiyā vrat*, S. *pūrṇimā pūjā*) and the *tilā vrat*.

In the first part of this chapter, it was an abbreviated form of the Guru Maṇḍala that was discussed. Next is the entire, full Guru Maṇḍala form. Only all those ritual clients who are actively participating in a rite should perform the undertaking of the full Guru Maṇḍala. In this case, the *vajrācārya* guru is helping the ritual clients, and the participating *vajrācārya* guru alone is reciting the spoken portions of the rite. This means that in a different *pūjā*, the *vajrācārya* guru himself must not do the Guru Maṇḍala rite. Each ritual client performs according to his or her respective caste. Upper caste members, *thakuri*, [who are not themselves *vajrācārya*], are not allowed to perform for other similar [high] castes (New. *ajāḥgu*). Therefore, *vajrācārya* gurus alone perform the rite for other castes. The Guru Maṇḍala, part of the procedure of whatever *pūjā* is being performed, is successfully performed by those who understand. The guru priest (*guru purohita*) and the ritual clients do the rite, the Guru Maṇḍala, in cooperation.

The undertaking of the Guru Maṇḍala by both male and female lay Buddhists | *upāsaka-upāsikāpisaṃ danegu gurumaṇḍala*

The *upoṣadha vrat*: the custom is that the occasion to perform the ritual is on the eighth day following the full moon. This rite, accompanied by a fast, is always undertaken on the grounds of a *tīrtha*. The *tilā vrat*: the rite accompanied by a fast that is undertaken for Vasudharā. It is done the same way and according to the same procedure for both the male and female lay Buddhists. They come together as a group of hundreds. On such an occasion of a group *upoṣadha vrat*, the leader (New. *mūmha*) worships the deity while the male and female lay Buddhists must perform the Guru Maṇḍala procedure. They must also perform the rite of the Guru Maṇḍala when the nine planet *pūjā* is done on the occasion of a birthday by a *vajrācārya*.

Regarding the rite of *śrāddha*, it is done by male and female lay Buddhists differently according to each respective caste. So, each of the ranks (N. *starayā*) is able to perform. Their Guru Maṇḍala is completed accordingly when the ritual calls for it. There is not a particular Guru Maṇḍala done by *vajrācārya* gurus, a particular Guru Maṇḍala done for the ritual clients for the *śrāddha* performance, nor another Guru Maṇḍala to succeed in the case of performing the *upoṣadha vrat*. The Guru Maṇḍala does not vary according to each respective caste. The Guru Maṇḍala is the same for everybody.

Therefore, it is not only *vajrācārya* gurus that are permitted to perform the entirety of the Guru Maṇḍala. Ritual clients are also able to do the Guru Maṇḍala rite. The honorable *vajrācārya* guru himself does not perform the Guru Maṇḍala at the time of the *śrāddha* commencement. Rather, the ritual client performs the rite of the Guru Maṇḍala according to the instructions (*nirdeśana*) of the *vajrācārya* guru. The *upoṣadha vrat* is also performed by ritual clients according to the instruction of a *vajrācārya* guru, just like the rite of the Guru Maṇḍala is completed according to his instruction.

Since the rite of the Guru Maṇḍala is not only done by the *vajrācārya* guru, and must also be performed by the ritual clients, the *vajrācārya* gurus must, therefore, plainly explain the rite of the Guru Maṇḍala and the ritual clients must listen to the explanation. By having faith in that explanation, the knowledge regarding the Guru Maṇḍala rite will necessarily be ascertained by the clients.

Aim | *uddeśya*

The rite done by anyone is performed according to the form of the established Guru Maṇḍala rite procedure. Now, reasons for performing it are given:

1. It is done to develop devotion for the guru.
2. It is not done without the permission (lit. speech, *vacana*) of the guru.
3. The task is accomplished without any hindrance.
4. It is done in the expectation of the favor/boon/grace (*prasāda*) of the guru.

Brief discourse regarding the procedure of the Guru Maṇḍala | *gurumaṇḍala daneguyā saṃkṣipta khaṃ*

Each respective step within the Guru Mandala is given below. To succeed at the Guru Maṇḍala, each procedure and its purpose is understood as they arise during the course of the ritual. Each step in brief:

1. Purifying the body, speech and mind | *kāya, vāk, citta śuddha yāyegu*

The first of all the steps is to purify the body, speech and mind. The body, speech and mind are, therefore, purified in the performance of every single act throughout the ritual. The activity and speech never go astray on account of purifying them prior to doing anything else.

2. Arranging for the protection of the space | *surakṣāyā vyavasthā*

In the performance of any action, this act will also be done in the course of the rite.

3. Recitation that strengthens the Six Perfections | *ṣaṭpārmitāyā bala prayog*

Generosity (*dāna*), discipline (*śīla*), patience (*kṣānti*), vigor (*vīrya*), meditation (*dhyāna*) and wisdom (*prajñā*) are the six to be strengthened. Such are the Six Perfections. A recitation involving all six of these is performed.

4. Maṇḍala Practice | *maṇḍalādhiṣṭhān*

Then there will be the construction of the maṇḍala. It is fixed through both visualization (*bhāvanā*) and the material form, which contains the ten directions within the maṇḍala. Through *bhāvanā*, the splendid form of Vajrasattva, the lord of the maṇḍala, is visualized as filling the middle of the maṇḍala.

5. Performing *pūjā* | *pūjā yāyegu*

In performing *pūjā*, the basic constituents consist of the five offerings (*pañcopacāra*)—flower, incense, light, smell and colored unguent (*rasa*). The Ratna Maṇḍala is dedicated/offered by disciples, ritual clients and male and female lay Buddhists since it is exceedingly rare to be born in *saṃsāra* as a human. The reason for offering the Ratna Maṇḍala is to offer it for the guru, namely the guru Vajrasattva.

6. Honoring the guru | *guru vandanā*

One does the *guru darśan*, that is to say, *darśan* of Vajrasattva. This involves giving the fee and water for the *darśan* of the guru, reciting praise hymns, offering incense and the *Ratna Maṇḍala* made and offered to the guru. This is how honoring the guru is done.

7. Confession of sin | *pāpadeśanā*

While ringing the bell, the practitioner makes a promise in the presence of the guru that not even the smallest sinful actions are to be concealed and that he or she will not commit such even up until death. So an explicit act is undertaken to acknowledge the sins committed by oneself. Serious errors occur all the time and are made into sins when they are concealed.

8. Delighting in merit | *puṇyānumodanā*

Whether the solitary wise people (*pratyeka jñānī guṇītaysaṃ*) undertaking extremely difficult auspicious actions, bodhisattvas performing actions for the sake of the virtue (*kalyāṇayā*) of the world, or buddhas who are mentally gleeful (*ullāsa*) in their own minds as regards what is seen, heard or thought about; they always delight in such action.

9. Undertaking of the Bodhisattva Vow | *praṇidhāna*

Becoming awakened is not done for the sake of glory. The undertaking of the path leading to buddhahood is not for oneself; it is done for the benefit of the world. The bodhisattva bears the experience of suffering everywhere for the sake of benefiting the world. The arising of pleasure (*sukha*) is not experienced in this suffering. Suffering is to be observed; through *bhāvanā*, one is to confront it little by little and not to retreat from it.

10. The Mental Generation of Amṛtakuṇḍalī | *amṛtakuṇḍalīyā bhāvanā*

Knowledge and nectar of immortality (*amṛta*) are the same when the collection of body, speech and mind comes together. There is a very large store of *amṛta* at the place where body, speech and mind are united. This confluence is also called the *amṛtakuṇḍalī*.[6] Bearing all this in mind, the generation of *amṛtakuṇḍalī* is done through visualization. During the *bhāvanā* one should give him the requisite offerings, satiate him with liquor and feed him meat. Such is the *pūjā*.

11. Dismissal | *visarjana*

This is the sending away of the god/lord (*pāla*). The procedure of the dismissal is a solicitation for aid in the future when the invocation is made again. The Guru Maṇḍala procedure is now finished.

In brief, the stages of delighting in merit, undertaking the bodhisattva vow, the *bhāvanā* of Amṛtakuṇḍalī, protecting the area from molestation by nefarious spirits (*tāraṇa*), the *bhāvanā* of the ten directions, libations offered to the dead, praise, etc. were explained.

Everyone needs a guru. One is necessary at all times. The ritual *pūjā* performance done in the midst of the maṇḍala for the guru was explained. The discourse, consisting of directions concerning the core Guru Maṇḍala ritual, is completed. This discourse, that serves as an introduction to the subject of the guru, is to be kept in mind, and it is intended for those individuals who have not received training. Therefore, they may learn the ritual.

---

[6] Amṛtakuṇḍalin is a world protector (*lokapāla*) in Mahāyāna Buddhism. However, in the context of the internalized practice Yagyaman Pati details, *amṛtakuṇḍalī* is a part of the subtle human anatomy.

10.

The History and Importance of the Guru Maṇḍala | *Guru Maṇḍalayā aitihāsik pakṣa va viśeṣatā*

It can be seen that the Guru Maṇḍala underwent a gradual development and expansion. The Guru Maṇḍala was not the product of one single event. The maturity of the Guru Maṇḍala can be seen to have been gradual. Bringing the Guru Maṇḍala to maturity was not the work of only a single accomplished person. It is the product of the teachings on meditation and ritual procedures of various *ācāryas* at various times. In this regard, we shall look into it by considering multiple periods.

Initial Period

Since the guru is the epitome of knowledge, humans created the establishment of the guru. In Vajrayāna, we can also observe the importance of the guru from the initial period. This can be seen to have come to its fullness with the passage on guru *darśan*, which comes to be to honor the Lord Bhāṣkara (light-maker)—meaning, the sun—the incomparable guru. That is as follows:

> *oṃ āḥ hūṁ śrīmat vajrasattvaguruvaracaraṇakamalāya*
> *śūṇyatāṃ jñānavajrabhāṣkarāya namostute namo*
> *bhagavatyāṃ tvaṃ namasyāmi śrī gurunāthaṃ*
> *prasiddha me* |

> OṂ ĀḤ HŪṀ! Homage to the lotus-like feet of the supreme guru, Vajrasattva, the sun of vajra-like knowledge of emptiness! Homage to the Bhagavatī! I pay homage to the Noble Lord Guru! Make me accomplished!

Vajrasattva, the "sun" (light-maker), the Lord/Bhagavān, the teacher, and all *tathāgata*s are there. Vajrasattva, the sun, and all *tathāgata*s are one. Therefore, we have come to see that we first respect the guru.

In this initial period, while the guru was essential, its outward expression was not in the *pūjā* of giving the Guru Maṇḍala that we have today. One needed to pay respect to the guru. It was a period in which one's expression of respect to the guru was treating the guru's instructions as mandatory.

The Respectable Period

In this period, if there was to be respect for the guru, then it is not that he is to be worshiped. This is written in Āryadeva's work, called *Svādhiṣṭhānaprabheda*. The meaning of *svādhiṣṭhāna* is "one's own body" or the establishment in the body of the true form of the *deva* to be propitiated. Having finished the sequence of such a *svādhiṣṭhāna*, to attain buddhahood, one performs other tasks in meditation, which means, to perform it, one needs initiation. Such is the main subject of his book. It is worth considering his words here, which are akin to the bell (*ghaṇṭā*) and *vajra* (in their power). According to his words, in the ordering of initiations, the first must be the guru's initiation. One does not need to practice a sādhanā to perform a guru's initiation. One also doesn't need to perform meditation. *Pūjā* is also not required. One only needs to devote to the guru and not disobey the guru's instructions. Having performed devotion in one's conduct thus, one will create in oneself, by oneself, the qualities of a guru.[i]

Guhyasamājatantra

The first Vajrayāna scripture is the *Guhyasamājatantra*. Therein, there is a praise of the guru. It is said that the guru is everything. However, we do not see an explanation of the *pūjā*-procedure for the Guru Maṇḍala. So, the system of the Guru Maṇḍala *pūjā* procedure does not come from the *Guhyasamājatantra*. The *Guhyasamājatantra* is said to have been composed by the famous yogi called Asaṅga in the third century.

Hevajratantra

After the *Guhyasamājatantra*, the *Hevajra Tantra*'s place in Vajrayāna is prominent. Just like the *Guhyasamāja*, the *Hevajratantra* is a king of tantras. Padmavajra and Kambalapāda drew out the significant aspects of this tantra. Bhattacharyya writes, "According to Tāranath he [Padmavajra] was the first to introduce the *Hevajratantra* in Vajrayāna, which he did along with his collaborator, Kambalapāda."[ii] In this way, the *Hevajratantra* is in accordance with the teaching and practice of Vajrayāna. Therein, the guru is said to be the same as a "*vajrācārya*." Still, a complete *pūjā* procedure for the Guru Maṇḍala is not written therein.

Cakrasaṃvaratantra

In the *Cakrasaṃvaratantra*, a *pūjā* for the guru is written about. The *Cakrasaṃvaratantra* is also a vital tantra scripture in Vajrayāna. If we consider it in terms of its time of development, it is not of low quality. This tantra's commentator was Bhavabhaṭṭa. Sometimes, we don't see the name Bhavabhaṭṭa associated with it, but rather Bhavabhadra. But this is just Bhavabhaṭṭa, as explained by the commentator Janārdana in his introduction. Bhavabhadra is also said to be one of the 12 tantric *ācārya*s of Vikramaśīla Mahāvihāra. Līlāvajra (741 CE) himself, as well as Bhavyakīrti, also refer to him as Bhavabhadra. This tantric scripture must also be that old if this is the case. In this tantra, the third section is called "The Ritual Donation and Consecration" (*dakṣiṇābhiṣeka*). In this chapter, one must first perform *pūjā* to the guru. It is written in this tantra's commentary that "Since there is no accomplishment (*siddhi*) without the instruction of an *ācārya*, one should therefore worship the guru." It also explains that "After that is the creation of the maṇḍala" and "one should perform *pūjā* there for the sake of entering, etc." In this way, it explains that one must also perform *pūjā* for the maṇḍala to enter it.[iii] Still, we do not see a clear explanation of how to draw the Guru Maṇḍala. We also do not yet have a ritual manual for the Guru Maṇḍala.

Here, the following *śloka* is written in the *Cakrasaṃvaratantra*:

ācāryaṃ toṣayet pūrvaṃ sarvabhāvena sādhakaḥ |
yathāśaktyā pūjayed guruṃ siddhikāmaḥ susamāhitaḥ ||

The aspirant should first please the *ācārya* with all of his being,
One well-composed and desiring accomplishment should worship the guru as much as possible.

Guhyasiddhi

The guru is worthy of worship. One must perform *pūjās* for the guru. There is a middle-length *pūjā* for practicing guru devotion. It is seen that having performed such a *pūjā*, it gradually developed. We can see a remark on this topic in Padamavajra's *Guhyasiddhi*. He describes the complete *pūjā* as including vestments, ornaments, *mudrās*, and so forth. Yet, we still do not see a ritual manual for the Guru Maṇḍala. Padmavajra is the creator of the *Guhyāsiddhi*. Padmavajra comes from the tradition of the *Hevajratantra*. It was written around 693 CE. A *śloka* in the *Guhyasiddhi* goes as follows:

vastrālaṅkāra bhogādyair pūṣayitvā samarpayet |
svamudrāṃ gurupūjārtha buddhasiddhiprasiddhaye ||[iv]

Having offered vestments, ornaments, food, and so forth to the guru, he should offer
His own *mudrā* for the sake of the accomplishment of the attainments of a buddha.

In this one type of *pūjā* manual, devotion is shown by performing a dance with various kinds of *mudrās* and singing songs freely with the throat.

For instance:

tasmāt sarvaprayatyena gurubhaktyā prapūjayet |
svamūdrāpadmapūjādyais tatkaṇṭhedbhūtagītibhiḥ ||[v]

Therefore, with all effort and devotion for the guru, one should worship him
With one's own *mudrā*, lotus-like *pūjā*, and so forth, and by singing songs with the throat.

Having prepared ornaments, clothing, dance, and songs, various kinds of good things to eat and drink are described as needing to be prepared. First, fish and other small foods must be presented. This matter is written.

For instance:

pakvānnair vividhākāraiḥ pūpikāśuṣkadalluraiḥ |
śīdhumatsyādibhir divyair vividhais tatra coditaiḥ ||[vi]

With cooked-goods and various kinds of sweet cakes and dried fruits,
Various other divine liquors and fish are prepared there.

Kriyāsaṃgraha

All the rituals in Vajrayāna are gathered into the *Kriyāsaṃgraha*, which is like a kind of encyclopedia for *vajrācāryas*. Kuladatta wrote this book. Kuladatta wrote it in around 1100 CE.[vii] Even in this book, one does not see a ritual manual for the Guru Maṇḍala. However, it includes everything about the selection of the guru, the investigation of the disciple, the entry into the maṇḍala for the disciple, and so forth. On the topic of the *Kriyāsaṃgraha*, the *Blue Annals* feature a discussion on page 974 of de Roerich's translation. One of the main things that this *Kriyāsaṃgraha* emphasizes is that initiation is necessary for these practices.

Vajrāvali

The *Vajrāvali* is a book related to the *Kriyāsaṃgraha*. In this book also, like in the *Kriyāsaṃgraha*, each different ritual procedure for *pūjās* is collected. It was written by Abhayakaragupta, the Kashmiri paṇḍit of Vikramaśīla Mahāvihāra, who wrote the *Nispannayogāvalī* and served as a lecturer in the court of King

Rāmapāla. He wrote it around 1105 CE. We also do not see a ritual procedure for the Guru Maṇḍala in his *Vajrāvali*.

Niṣpannayogāvalī

Abhayakaragupta knew how to create and explain various kinds of maṇḍalas. He collected and explained 26 different types of detailed maṇḍalas in a high-quality work. That book was the *Niṣpannayogāvalī*. There is still not a Guru Maṇḍala even in this book. If there were already a ritual procedure for the Guru Maṇḍala, then of course, it would have to be in such a high-quality work as the *Niṣpannayogāvalī*.

Guru Maṇḍala: *Kriyāsamuccaya*

Another related book, similar to the *Kriyāsaṃgraha* and the *Vajrāvali*, is the *Kriyāsamuccaya*. The *Kriyāsamuccaya* and the *Kriyāsaṃgraha* share many subjects in common. However, they also have several differences. The author of the *Kriyāsamuccaya* was Jagaddarpaṇa. His precise dates are not known. However, when he was elderly, his milk teeth came out again, like a child. So, it's said that Jagaddarpaṇa Ācārya's milk teeth came out 20 times. It is worth speculating on his dates from inference. It is written that he lived to 1200 years. But if Jagaddarpaṇa is later than Kuladatta (around 1100), there may seem to be little need for his text. Therefore, we cannot be confident about this matter. The way of counting years could also have been different. For instance, the calculation would differ if one season were counted as one year. On other planets of the solar system, 24 hours do not make a day, which is worth considering. In this book, there is a ritual procedure for a Guru Maṇḍala. The Guru Maṇḍala's ritual procedure, as seen in this book, is a developed form when compared to the Guru Maṇḍala of that time. In this book, a ritual procedure for the Guru Maṇḍala is written. But there is no *amṛtakuṇḍalī* cultivation, as there is in the Guru Maṇḍala of today.

It is written that before coming to *amṛtakuṇḍalī* cultivation, one performs "viewing the Guru" (*guru darśan*), fast day observance (*upoṣadha*), the three refuges, confession of transgressions, rejoicing in merits, devotion to the Noble Eightfold Path, and vowing with a declaration (*saṃkalpa*) that one's work is performed for the benefit of the world. But it does not have the passage for the declaration of the Ratna Maṇḍala: "Meru, made of four jewels, is the complete Ratna Mandala." We also don't see the flower offering ending in "CAṂ! Homage to Candra! SŪṂ! Homage to Sūrya!" and "Homage to the Guru Vajrasattva!" Other things than that are also lacking. [Now], only after these three things, is [the maṇḍala] offered. Therefore, the *Kriyāsamuccaya* presents an earlier form of the more refined Guru Maṇḍala of today.

Later, Gö Lotsāwa wrote about the *Kriyāsamuccaya* in his *Blue Annals*. The *Kriyāsamuccaya* also has a guru lineage. Those to whom Darpaṇa Ācārya (i.e. Jagaddarpaṇa) initiated into this book received the suffix "*bhadra*" (Good) to their names.

That lineage spans from our own Vajradhara down to Dharmasvāmin. The *Kiryāsamuccaya* was also taken from Nepāl to Tibet. Gö Lotsāwa wrote around 1476. Therefore, the *Kriyāsamuccaya*, after Kuladatta (1100), was still well-regarded over three centuries later in 1476. The *Blue Annals* writes on the topic of the *Kriyāsamuccaya*. We see it written about in the *Blue Annals* in a section on the Guru-Disciple Lineage.

1. The Ritual Procedure of the Guru Maṇḍala is thus Perfected through Refinement

Regarding the ritual procedure for the Guru Maṇḍala, it was heard of before Advayavajra. However, no one was able to write about it at length. Advayavajra's dates are 978-1030, according to

Bhattacharyya.[xviii] When we look at his work, we can see that it is earlier than the *Kriyāsaṃgraha* and *Kriyāsamuccaya*. The Guru Maṇḍala comes out in the *Kriyāsamuccaya*. That is also still just in an unrefined form. Nowadays, if there is no *bali* cultivation or *amṛtakuṇḍalī*, then it is not a Guru Maṇḍala. Therefore, looking at it from the time of Kuladatta, or even his predecessor Advayavajra, it has been [gradually] polished, meaning that we won't find explanations of [today's] Guru Maṇḍala in their works.

This is because, if we were to seek an explanation of the Guru Maṇḍala of today in Advayavajra's works, we would need to look at what his successor Kuladatta wrote in the *Kriyāsaṃgraha* on the Guru Maṇḍala. If we rely on Kuladatta's *Kriyasaṃgraha*, however, even in Nāgārjunapāda's *Kriyāsaṃgrahakārika* (verse commentary), there still is no Guru Maṇḍala. The homage in the polished Guru Maṇḍala of today even includes the ritual procedure of the sixteenfold dance rite (*ṣoḍasalāsyā vidhi*). The sixteenfold dance rite isn't even in Kuladatta's *Kriyasaṅgraha*. In place of the sixteenfold dance rite, in the *Kriyasaṃgraha*, there is only an eightfold dance rite. Perhaps at the time of the emergence of the *Kriyāsamuccaya*, it only reached up to the eightfold dance rite.

The Guru Maṇḍala that emerges in the *Kriyāsamuccaya* is still only an unrefined form. As for the *Advayavajrasaṃgraha*, having considered the *Kriyāsamuccaya*, it must be earlier. This is because:

1. The *Advayavajrasaṃgraha* does not mention the Guru Maṇḍala. It is not until the *Kriyāsamuccaya* that we see a Guru Maṇḍala ritual procedure.
2. Some of the sentences included in the *Advayavajrasaṃgraha* are included in the sentences of the Guru Maṇḍala in Darpaṇa Ācārya's *Kriyāsamuccaya*. When we look at these, it appears that Advayavajra is earlier than Jagaddarpaṇa Ācārya.[ix]

Regarding those sentences in the Guru Maṇḍala that are seen in the *Advayavajrasaṃgraha*, they are as follows:

1. The following words appear in the "Kudṛṣṭinirghātana," a section of the *Advayavajrasaṅgraha*: *namo buddhāya gurave namo dharmmāya ... āryyāṣṭaṅgikapoṣadham* ||[x] "Homage to the Buddha, the Guru! Homage to the Dharma! ... The Noble Eightfold Fast..."

   As well as: *ratnatrayaṃ me śaraṇaṃ ... buddhabodhau dadhe manaḥ* ||[xi] "I go for refuge to the Triple Gem... I set my mind on the awakening of the buddhas."

   This also appears in the *Kalpoktatāra-udbhava-kurukulla Sādhana*.

   In the same way, these words: *utpādayāmi varabodhicittaṃ ... buddho bhaveyaṃ jagato hitāya* || "I arouse [the excellent *bodhicitta*]... I will become a buddha for the benefit of the world," are also read in both the "Kudṛṣṭinirghātana," and the *Six-armed Kurukullā Bhaṭṭārikā Sādhana*. This verse is also used in *Pañcarakṣā* scriptures as the heart mantra of Noble Pratisarā.[xii]

2. In the same way, [a couple of verses, from] *dānaṃ gomayamambunā* "Generosity with cow dung..." up to *sugatavaragṛhe'smin kāyakarmmāṇi kṛtvā* "Having performed bodily actions in this world, he [is born] in the excellent house of the *sugatas*," are [also found in both the "Kudṛṣṭinirghātana" and the *Kriyāsamuccaya*].[xiii]

3. Moreover, in Advayavajra's "Kudṛṣṭinirghātana", we see the passage:

yathā te tathāgatā arhantaḥ samyaksambuddhā buddhajñānena buddhacakṣuṣā jānanti paśyanti tatkuśalamūlaṃ yajjātikaṃ yannikāyaṃ yādṛśaṃ yallakṣaṇaṃ yatsvabhāvaṃ yayā dharmmatayā sambidyate tathā anumode tatkuśalamūlam | yathā ca te tathāgatā arhantaḥ samyaksambuddhā abhyanujānanti pariṇāmyamānaṃ tatkuśalamūlamauttarāyāṃ samyaksambodhau tathāhaṃ pariṇāmayāmi iti |[xiv]

Just as the *tathāgatas*, arhats, perfectly and completely awakened buddhas know and see that root of the wholesome with their buddha-knowledge and buddha-eye, in whatever class, category, kind, mark, nature, and with whatever dharma it is connected, in just that way I rejoice in that root of the wholesome. And just as the *tathāgatas*, arhats, perfectly and completely awakened buddhas allow that root of the wholesome to be dedicated to *anuttara-saṃyak-sambodhi*, in just that way, I dedicate it.

This is also in Advayavajra's *Vajravārāhī Sādhana*. The concept of "*ya ra la va*," which occurs in the Guru Maṇḍala, is also written about by him. For instance:

samādhercyūtthāya ākāśe yaṁ raṁ laṁ vaṁ pariṇatāni dhanustrikoṇavartulacaturasrāṇi harinīlaraktasvetāni caturmahābhūta maṇḍalāni uparyupari paśyeta |

Having arisen from *samādhi*, one should visualize in the sky above transformed from YAṀ RAṀ VAṀ and LAṀ, the maṇḍalas of the four great elements, being yellow, blue, red, and white, and in the shape of a bow, triangle, circle, and square.

In this *sādhana*, there is also the idea of the eight peaks. For instance:

> *tadupari suṃkārasambhavaṃ sumeruṃ caturasraṃ ca catūratnamayaṃ aṣṭaśṛṅgopaśobhitaṃ vicintya tadupari* |

> Above that, born from the letter SUṂ, the square Sumeru is visualized, which is made of the four jewels and adorned with eight peaks.

However, in this manual for performing the *Vajravārāhī Sādhana*, Advayavajra does not present the matter as going so far as the offering of a Guru Maṇḍala. In addition to these, this Advayavajra also wrote the *Saptākṣara Sādhana*, as well as the *Siṃhanāda Sādhana*. In each of these sādhanas, a Guru Maṇḍala is nowhere to be found. In these texts, it is written that there is a *pūjā* involving the visualization of the establishment of gurus in space, the confession of transgressions, and that one must cultivate the four *brahmavihāras*. So, while one must engage in a kind of Guru Maṇḍala worship, it is nowhere written that this is "Guru Maṇḍala worship."

When we look at the above description of we see it is related to the description in the Guru Maṇḍala practice, which involves the eight directions and intermediate directions. However, Advayavajra does not appear to present the eight directions and intermediate directions. The passages explaining Sumeru, Madhyameru, the Wind Maṇḍala, Fire Maṇḍala, and so forth are written about in lines 50-55 in Vasubandhu's chapter on the "Exposition of the World" in the *Abhidharmakośa*.[xv] Vasubandhu lived around the year 400 CE. He is considerably earlier than Advayavajra.

When we consider this matter, those sentences written in the *Kriyāsamuccaya* appear to be selected from the work of Advayavajra. Therefore, it seems that Advayavajra did not complete the work of refining the Guru Maṇḍala. That appears to be the *Kriyāsamuccaya*, which contains the Guru Maṇḍala. Concerning its contents, the sixteenfold dance rite, the *amṛtakuṇḍalī* cultivation, *mudrās*, and so forth, were only developed later. Guru Maṇḍala worship, as it has been modified today, includes ritual instructions that include the sixteenfold dance rite. The sixteenfold dance rite isn't in Kuladatta's *Kriyasaṃgraha*; instead, in the *Kriyāsamgraha*, there is only the eightfold dance rite. Perhaps when the *Kriyasaṃgraha* emerged, it was only at the stage of the eightfold dance rite.

A Summary Review of the Guru Maṇḍala | *gurumaṇḍalayā sārāṃśa samīkṣā*

1. The Place of the Internal Guru | *ādhyātmika guruyā thāy*

In the Guru Mandala, the guru does not take on a material form. As an internal guru, the guru is thought to embody the initiation of training and words of wisdom for all. And the ultimate guru is believed to be Vajrasattva.

2. The Eight Directions | *cyāgū diśā*

The eight directions surround the Guru Maṇḍala. We can see the places in the eight directions for the cultivation of the Guru Maṇḍala. If we cannot see the eight directions, then there is nowhere. They [represent] everywhere. Therefore, the Guru Maṇḍala implies wisdom reaching in every direction.

3. Twofold Division | *nigū pūṭa*

The Guru Maṇḍala has a twofold division. One division is the four directions, and the other is the four intermediate directions. So, in these separate divisions, there are eight signs.

4. Eight Signs | *cyāgū pratīka*

In different maṇḍalas, images of deities surround in various directions. That is not the case with the Guru Maṇḍala. Within the eight directions, the ground colors are in the four directions and intermediate directions. There are symbols in the eight directions, such as the elephant treasure.

5. Eight-sided Maṇḍala | *cyācyaḥyā maṇḍala*

The Guru Maṇḍala is not a four-sided maṇḍala. It has eight sides. In addition to this eight-sided maṇḍala, there are other kinds of maṇḍalas, such as four-sided, triangular, or bow-shaped maṇḍalas.

6. Includes Natural Objects | *prākṛtik vastuta duthyāḥ*

It is a land that includes natural things, such as mountains, oceans, flora, and ground. It encompasses water, fire, wind, and space.

7. Unlimited Scope | *asīmita vyāpakatā*

The Guru Maṇḍala does not apply to a specific class or type of person. It applies to everyone. Guru priest, *vajrācārya*, ritual patron, lay male and female devotee: it unites all.

8. YA RA LA VA | *ya ra la va*

In Vajrayāna, the syllabary is categorized into the five *tathāgata*s, Vajrasattva, and Uṣmāṇī. For instance, under the category of KA (gutturals) comes Vairocana, CA (palatals) is Akṣobhya, ṬA (retroflexes) is Ratnasaṃbhava, TA (dentals) is Amitābha, PA (labials) is Amoghasiddhi, YA (semivowels) is YA RA LA VA, which is Vajrasattva, and HA is Uṣmāni. One must produce these sounds with the tongue and the top and bottom lips, or the sound won't come out, but the letters that come out independent of these are the four YA RA LA VA. These four letters of Vajrasattva encircle the Guru Maṇḍala. These four letters are in the Vajrasattva category.

9. An Ancient Method | *pūrvāga vidhi*

Whatever the prior and primordial form of the Guru Maṇḍala was in the past, that has finished, and it has come to be a helpful device.

10. The Highest of All Things | *sarvottama vastu*

The Guru Maṇḍala has taken on the form of the Ratna Maṇḍala. As for an explanation of the Ratna Maṇḍala, it is the greatest thing of all in the world. It is one of a kind.

---

i. Janardan Shastri Pandey, *Collected Short Buddhist Texts: Brief Introductory Section* [*Bauddha Laghugrantha Saṃgraha: Saṃkṣipta Paricaya Khaṇḍa*], Rare Buddhist Texts Research Team [Durlabha Bauddhagrantha Śodhayojanā], Varanasi, 1997, p. xv.

ii. Ed. Benoytosh Bhattacharya, *Sādhanamālā* vol. II, Oriental Institute Baroda, 1968.

iii. Janardan Shastri Pandey, Śrī Herkuābhidhāna *Cakrasaṃvaratantra with Commentary by Bhavabhaṭṭa*, Part I, Rare Buddhist Texts Research Team, Varanasi, 2002, p. 37.

iv. *Guhyādi-Aṣṭasiddhisaṃgraha*, "Guhyasiddhi," Rare Buddhist Texts Research Team, Varanasi, 1987 p. 59, paragraph 9, verse no. 13.

v. *Guhyādi-Aṣṭasiddhisaṃgraha*, "Guhyasiddhi," Rare Buddhist Texts Research Team, Varanasi, 1987 p. 59, paragraph 9, verse no. 16.

vi. *Guhyādi-Aṣṭasiddhisaṃgraha*, "Guhyasiddhi," Rare Buddhist Texts Research Team, Varanasi, 1987 p. 59, paragraph 9, verse no. 19.

vii. Ed. Benoytosh Bhattacharya, *Sādhanamālā* vol. II, Oriental Institute Baroda, 1968. Preface, clii.

viii. Benoytosh Bhattacharya, *Sādhanamālā* vol. II, Oriental Institute Baroda, 1968. Preface, xci.

ix. Jaggadarpaṇa Ācārya's brief biography is given in the *Blue Annals*. When he became old, his teeth came in again, then went out, and his milk teeth came in again. In this way, he grew to be 1200 years old. It is said he died at 1200 years of age, and here, this matter is worth considering. Advayavajra's dates are 978-1030. If Jagaddarpaṇa's years of life were counted from that time, he would still be around today. But that is not the case. When the *Blue Annals* says that he lived to 1200 years, then at that time, it is reported as if his death has already occurred. Regarding the dating of the *Blue Annals*, according to the introduction in Roerich's translation, it appeared about a century before the work of Lama Tārānātha: "Composed by the well-known scholar and translator [Gö Lotsawa Zhönnu-pel] (1392-1481 A.D.) between 1476 A.D. and 1478 A.D., the "BLUE ANNALS" share with the "History of Buddhism" by Butön Rinpoche (composed in 1322 A.D.)...".

x. Ed. Benoytosh Bhattacharya, *Advayavajrasaṃgraha*, Oriental Institute Baroda, 1927. p. 5.

xi. Ed. Benoytosh Bhattacharya, *Sādhanamālā* vol. II, Oriental Institute Baroda, 1968. p. 344 & 347.

xii. *Ibid.* p. 379.

xiii. Ed. Benoytosh Bhattacharya, *Advayavajrasaṃgraha*, Oriental Institute Baroda, 1927. p. 6.

xiv. *Ibid.* pp. 9.

xv. Trans. Ācārya Narendra Deva, *The Abhidharmakośa* by Ācārya Vasubandhu, Hindustānī Academy, Uttar Pradesh, Allahabad, 1958, p. 365-369.

Appendix A

The Guru Maṇḍala Procedure in the *Kriyāsamuccaya*

These days, the current method of practicing the Guru Maṇḍala is not exactly the same as the Guru Maṇḍala as written in the *Kriyāsamuccaya*. But it is important to practice the Guru Maṇḍala as it is in the *Kriyāsamuccaya*. Therefore, I present it here:[1]

---

[1] The original volume reproduces the Sanskrit text in toto. Nepalese readers will get a general idea of the contents of the Sanskrit text due to the shared vocabulary that Sanskrit has with Nepali and Newar. For English readers, Sanskrit sentences and homages are translated. Mantras are transliterated with a gloss in the notes—seed syllables are not translated.

There are many variants of these mantras and verses, which can be reviewed in the below publications. In principle, this translation represents the version presented and taught by Yagyaman Pati Bajracharya. But where necessary for clarity, comparison will be made to other readings. Manik Bajracharya, *Gurumaṇḍala Pūjā*, Nagoya: Aichi Gakuin University, n.d.

David N. Gellner, "Ritualized Devotion, Altruism, and Meditation: The Offering of the 'Gurumaṇḍala' in Newar Buddhism," *Indo-Iranian Journal* 34 (3), 1991, 161-197.

After abandoning the ten unwholesome actions, one becomes an *upāska*,[2] There, having initially created the Guru Maṇḍala, proceed in this sequence:

1. *OṀ vajrodake HUṀ SVĀHĀ!* This is the water purification.
2. Just as all *tathāgatas* are bathed immediately upon birth, so shall I bathe and purify with divine water. *OṀ sarvatathāgatābhiṣekasamayaśriye HŪṀ!* With this is the bathing.
3. *OṀ HRIḤṀ SVĀHĀ!* The mantra for cleansing the hands and feet.
4. *OṀ namo bhagavate puṣpaketurājāyā tathāgatāyārhate samyaksaṃbuddhāya! tadyathā: OṀ puṣpe supuṣpe puṣpodbhave puṣpa saṃbhave puṣpāvakiraṇe SVĀHĀ!* This is the flower purification.
5. *OṀ vajrabhūme HŪṀ PHAṬ SVĀHĀ!* With this, sprinkling water on the ground.
6. *OṀ vajrasattva sarvavighnānutsāraya HŪṀ PHAṬ!* With this, ground purification.
7. [3]Generosity: cow dung together with water. Morality: cleansing.
   Patience: removing small ants.
   Effort: instigating the ritual action.
   Meditation: the making of single-mindedness immediately.
   Prajñā: blazing light rays.

---

[2] A lay devotee. Prior to this section in the *Kriyāsamuccaya*, the disciple takes the eight precepts in a poṣadha fast.

[3] The metre of the lines is not perfect, but bears some traces of *śārdūlavikrīḍitam*. It has thus been arranged into *padas* accordingly.

These six pāramitās are indeed obtained having made the maṇḍala of the sage.

One [then] becomes golden in colour, free from all illnesses, Distinguished among gods and humans, with brilliance shining like the moon. One is born in the prosperity of riches and gold, in a royal lineage, In the best house of the Sugata, having performed one's duties [in making the maṇḍala].

This is the maṇḍala creation.

8. *OM̐ surekhe vajrarekhe adhitiṣṭhantu sarvatathāgatāḥ SVĀHĀ!* With this, draw an eight-petaled lotus in the centre of the maṇḍala.
9. *OM̐ candrārkavimale SVĀHĀ!* With this, put a single flower in the centre of the maṇḍala.
10. *OM̐ ĀḤ HŪM̐!* With this, perform an establishment (*adhiṣṭhāna*) of the body, speech, and mind three times.
11. *OM̐ maṇidharivajriṇī mahāpratisare rakṣa rakṣa māṃ HŪM̐ HŪM̐ PHAṬ PHAṬ SVĀHĀ!* With this, put a single flower on your head.
12. *OM̐ āsanavajre HŪM̐!* With this, put one flower on the seat (*āsana*).
13. *OM̐ SUṂ su[me]rave namaḥ!* With this, put one flower in the middle of the maṇḍala.
14. *OM̐ HAḤ [ūrdhva]merave namaḥ! OM̐ HŪM̐ madhyamerave namaḥ!*
    OM̐ HĀ adho merave namaḥ! With this, offer flowers to the lower, upper, and middle parts of Meru.
15. *OM̐ YAM̐ pūrvavidehāya namaḥ!*
    With this, a flower should be offered to the eastern side of Sumeru.

OM̐ RAM̐ jambudvīpāya namaḥ! To the southern side.
OM̐ LAM̐ aparagodānīyāya namaḥ! To the western side.
OM̐ VAM̐ uttarakurave namaḥ! To the northern side.

16. *OM̐ YĀM̐ upadvīpāya namaḥ!*
OM̐ RĀM̐ upadvīpāya namaḥ!
OM̐ LĀM̐ upadvīpāya namaḥ!
OM̐ VĀM̐ upadvīpāya namaḥ! With this, a flower should be offered to the south-eastern corner and so forth.

17. *OM̐ YAM̐ gajaratnāya namaḥ!*
OM̐ RAM̐ aśvaratnāya namaḥ!
OM̐ LAM̐ puruṣaratnāya namaḥ!
OM̐ VAM̐ strīratnāya namaḥ! A flower should be given to the womb (*garbha* [i.e., the interior]) of Pūrvavideha and so forth.

18. *OM̐ YĀM̐ cakraratnāya namaḥ!*
OM̐ RĀM̐ khaḍgaratnāya namaḥ!
OM̐ LĀM̐ maṇiratnāya namaḥ!
OM̐ VĀM̐ sarvanidhānebhyo namaḥ! A flower should be given to the womb of the [island in the] south-eastern [corner] and so forth.

19. *OM̐ ĀḤ vajragurave idaṃ vajrapuṣpaṃ pratīccha HŪM̐ SVĀHĀ!* With this, having meditated on the guru Vajrasattva upon a moon on a universal lotus (*viśvābja*)[4] in the pavilion (*kūṭāgāra*) on the middle part of Meru (*madhyameru*), a threefold presentation of flowers (*puṣpāñjali*) should be given to the head.

20. *OM̐ ĀḤ vajragurave vajradhūpe HŪM̐!*
OM̐ ĀḤ vajragurave vajradīpe HŪM̐!
OM̐ ĀḤ vajragurave vajragandhe HŪM̐!

---

[4] This may refer to a four-pointed lotus, like how a *viśvavajra* is a four-pointed *vajra* (crossed *vajra*).

OM̐ ĀḤ vajragurave vajranaivedye HŪM̐! Whatever else there is, it should be given in this order. Again, taking a floral offering to the head.

21. Homage to the Buddha, the Guru! Homage to the Dharma, the deliverer! Homage to the great Saṃgha! Constant homage to the three!
The Triple Gem is my refuge; I confess all my faults (*agha*).
I rejoice in the merit of the world; I dedicate my mind to the awakening of a buddha.
I go for refuge, until awakening, in the Buddha, the Dharma, and the highest Assembly.
I make the aspiration for awakening, which is for the accomplishment of both self and others.
I arouse the best aspiration for awakening, I summon all the many beings,
And as they wish, I shall practice the best conduct for awakening (*bodhicārikā*);
May I become a buddha for the benefit of the world.
I confess all my faults and rejoice in the merits [of others].
I will practice the *upoṣadha* fast and the noble eight precepts.
With this verse, may the guru, who embodies the Triple Gem, be the refuge.[5]
I present, with affection, the complete Ratna Maṇḍala,[6]
To the gurus, the bodhisattvas, and the foremost omniscient ones of the world,
Which is adorned with Meru, furnished with eight peaks, and the continents and islands,

---

[5] This is questionable, Yagyaman Pati's MS has "*ratnatrayaṃ rūpiṇāṃ* [*rūpiṇaṃ*] *guruṃstusrayāta* [possibly *guruṃ astu śrayātam*]."

[6] Yagyaman Pati's MS: "*saṃpūrṇa ratnamaṇḍalaḥ,*" emended to "*saṃpūrṇaratnamaṇḍalam.*"

And equipped with the eight gems; I give it to the supreme giver. Thus, one should give.

[7] He is one with a shining true nature—by whose light of grace those in darkness had it dispelled by the aid of his jewel-like light,

[Whereupon] they see with unobscured vision[8] playfully and loftily.[9] This *namaskāra* is for that one: the sun-like Guru (*gurubhāskara*).

Then, having thrown a flower, perform *namaskāra*.

\+ The manuscript reads *kumta*, but most manuscripts these days have "*kṣudra*" [i.e. small].

i. In some books the order of these two, *aśvaratna* and *puruṣaratna*, is reversed.

---

[7] The following two verses are in Vasantatilakā meter in Sanskrit.

[8] Yagyaman Pati's MS has "*anāvila dṛśaḥ*;" this must be amended to "*anāviladṛśaiḥ*."

[9] Taking both *savilāsam* and *uccaiḥ* in their adverbial senses.

Appendix B

The Offering of the Ratna Maṇḍala | *ratnamaṇḍala dohalapegu*

A guru is essential in the life of humans. Without a guru, a human must undergo many kinds of suffering in their life. To a guru who gives one deliverance across the sea of the sorrowful existence of life, it is inconsequential if one were to offer great wealth. So, what is essential for a guru? In this case, cultivation is necessary. For this reason, the tradition of offering the Ratna Maṇḍala to the guru has developed. Having seen the Ratna Maṇḍala, one knows nothing is greater in the world. Thus, of all things in the world, the greatest respect to the guru is to offer the Ratna Maṇḍala. Here, it is worth considering the importance of the Ratna Maṇḍala. Offering the Ratna Maṇḍala is essential. It is done for the benefit of all beings in *saṃsāra*. They are:

A. Jewel (*ratnapudgala*)

B. Blue Lotus

C. White Lotus (*puṇḍarīka*)

D. Red Lotus (*padma*)

E. Sandalwood

Among these, the jewel is the very best.[i] In the commentary of the *Guhyasamājatantra* called *Pradīpodyotana*, the author Candrakīrti confirms this fivefold classification. This fivefold classification is in his Seven ornamentation (*saptālaṃkāra*) organization as well. Specifically, these types are in the sixth ornament. The seventh decoration concerns effects ("*kārya* (*phalatantra*)") related to effect tantras (*phalatantra*). It lists the possible ultimate attainment dependent upon what kind of person someone is. This seventh decoration, the classification within the effect tantras, is further subdivided into two parts. There is the ordinary (*sāmānya*) type of person. This includes 1. Blue Lotus, 2. White Lotus (*puṇḍarīka*), 3. Red Lotus (*padma*), and 4. Sandalwood. The other kind is the extraordinary (*asādhāraṇa*) person. This extraordinary category includes the jewel-type person. This also applies to the Ratna Maṇḍala offering, which is not of the ordinary kind but is rather said to be of the extraordinary kind.

Just anything could potentially be given. However, not just anything should be given by you. Such a position is considered to be (*siddhānta*) something of the ordinary kind. It is demonstrated that what is called "jewel-type" may refer to the Ratna Maṇḍala offering. Therefore, it is the case that whoever offers the ratnamaṇḍala creates the jewel-type. Or it is A. Blue lotus, B. White lotus, C. Red lotus, D. Sandalwood; this is the organization given. This is the concept (*upaladbhi*) of the effect tantra.

Now, [regarding the Ratna Maṇḍala] there are the formulae of that which are called the "four gems," which are:

A) the Man Gem, B) the Woman Gem, C) the Elephant Gem, and D) the Horse Gem.

There are also A) the Wheel Gem, B) the Sword Gem, C) the Wish-Fulfilling Jewel Gem, and D) the Receptacle of All Gem.

The cultivation of the Ratna Maṇḍalas and the cultivation of the Guru Maṇḍala are both thus. The Bhagavān told Mañjuśrī that it is essential to study the explanations of the Ratna Maṇḍala. That was as follows:⁺

oṃ namo ratnatrayāya
idāniṃ sattvāsayevaśena lokadhātumānaṃ bhāgavatāt taḥ
paramādibuddhan mañjuśtrīyā saṅgītikāreṇa |
daśamādivṛtai saṅgītaṃ tad eva vitanām iti ||

OṂ homage to the three jewels!
Now, in the abode of beings, in this world system, with authorisation from the Bhagavān, and with the singing of the song of Mañjuśrī, the highest Ādi Buddha,
I let his song resound throughout the ten directions.

O Disciples! This Ratna Maṇḍala is the world with its Sumeru, for so it was said by the Śrī Bhagavān to Mañjuśrī.

First is the coming to be of the sky.

yaṃkāreṇa vāyumaṇḍalaṃ: With the arising of the letter YAṀ, there is the Wind Maṇḍala. If it is asked how this Wind Maṇḍala is—*dhanvābhaṃ*—it comes to be in the shape of a bow. *pañcāsatsahasrayojana*: It is five-hundred-thousand *yojana*s in thickness. *dvādaśalakṣayojanavṛtamāna*: Its circumference is one-million-two-hundred-thousand *yojana*s. Such is the coming to be of the Wind Maṇḍala.

raṃkāreṇa agnimaṇḍalaṃ: With the arising of the letter RAṀ, there is the Fire Maṇḍala. If it is asked how this Fire Maṇḍala is, it is a triangular. *pañcāsahasrayojana uchuya*: It is five-hundred-thousand *yojana*s in thickness. *navalakṣayojanavṛtamāna*: It is nine-hundred-thousand *yojana*s in circumference. Such is the coming to be of the Fire Maṇḍala.

vaṃkāreṇa varuṇamaṇḍalaṃ: With the arising of the letter VAṀ is the arising of the Water Maṇḍala, called the "Varuṇa Maṇḍala." If it is asked how this Water Maṇḍala is—*vartula*—that is, it is round. *pañcāsahasrayojana uchuya*: It is five-hundred-thousand *yojana*s in thickness. *ṣaṭlakṣayojanavṛtamāna*: It is six-hundred-thousand *yojana*s in circumference. Such is the coming to be of the Water Maṇḍala.

laṃkāreṇa pṛthvīmaṇḍalaṃ: With the arising of the letter LAṀ is the arising of the Earth Maṇḍala. If it is asked how this Earth Maṇḍala is—*caturaśra*—it is square. *pañcāsahasrayojana uchuya*: It is five-hundred-thousand *yojana*s in thickness. *trilakṣayojanavṛtamāna:* It is three-hundred-thousand *yojana*s in circumference. Such is the coming to be of the Earth Maṇḍala.

suṃkāreṇa sumerumaṇḍalaṃ: With the arising of the letter SUṀ, there is Mount Sumeru. If it is asked how this Sumeru is, it is furnished with thirteen abodes. *Dvilakṣayojana uchuya*: It is two-hundred-thousand *yojana*s in thickness in the middle [i.e. at the tallest point]. *bhūmitalātamerulakṣayojana*: It is a hundred thousand *yojana*s on the ground [in diameter, i.e., the platform at the top]. *merulakṣayojana uchuya:* All the gods and goddesses dwell on that surface, which has one-hundred-thousand abodes. Śrī Vajrasattva Guru dwells there. Such is the exterior of Mount Sumeru.

It is connected to seven seas. If it is asked what are the seven seas: *tasya bāhye sālavaṅkṣāramadhughṛtadadhikṣirajalasāgaroyaṃ sobhaṃtipramaṃ tathā* |

1. First is the salty sea called "Saline."
2. Outside that is the "Acrid Sea."
3. Outside that is the sweet ocean called the "Honey Sea."
4. Outside that is the "Ghee Sea."

5. Outside that is the "Curds Sea."
6. Outside that is the "Milk Sea."
7. Outside that is the "Water Sea."

In total, the seven seas make up one whole sea of many hundreds of thousands of *yojanas*. Such are the circulating seven seas. Outside those seas, seven continents circulate. If it is asked what the continents are:

dvīpaṃ candrasitāmravaraparamakuśakinnaraṃ bhogabhūmau |
kraumcaraudrajambunivasatimanujaḥ saptamaṃ karmabhūmau |

1. The Moon Continent.
2. The Tāmra Continent.
3. The Kuśa Continent.
4. The Kinnara Continent.
5. The Kraumca Continent.
6. The Raudra Continent.
7. The Jambu Continent.

Each of these continents is sixteen thousand *yojanas* by sixteen thousand *yojanas*, and their positions form a circle. These seven continents are outside the seven mountains that surround Sumeru. If it is asked what those mountains are called:

nimiṃdharo yāgaṃdharaḥ sādharaś ca khadirakaḥ |
sudarśano vinitā ca and Karṇakāṃcanaḥ parbataḥ |

1. Mount Nimiṃdhara.
2. Mount Yāgaṃdhara.

3. Mount Sādhara.[1]
4. Mount Khadiraka.
5. Mount Sudarśana.
6. Mount Vinitā.
7. Mount Karṇakāṃcana.

Outside of these seven mountains are:

In the eastern direction:

yaṃ pūrvavidehāya namaḥ: With the arising of the letter YAṀ, there is the continent called Pūrvavideha. If it is asked how this content is—*dhandābha*—it is shaped like a bow. *ekalakṣaviṃsatasahasrayojanavṛtamāna*: It is one-hundred-and twenty-thousand *yojana*s in circumference. In the middle of Pūrvavideha, there is—*āmravṛksa*—one mango tree. If it is asked how this mango tree is—*satayojanavṛtamāna*—it encompasses a hundred *yojana*s, and its branches are two *yojana*s in length. Such is that one mango tree, called the "Āmravṛkṣa."

On this continent is placed the mantra[2]—*ya gajaratnāya namaḥ*. With the arising of the letter YA, there is the elephant Airāvatī. If it is asked how this elephant is—*śuklavarṇa*—it is white. *ṣattriṃśatadanta*: It has thirty-six teeth and wears a garland of a treasury of gems. It is able to swim across the ocean in one day. Such is that elephant, who is called the Elephant Gem.

---

[1] Yagyaman Pati's note: Numbers 2 and 3 are not written in [the gloss of the *śloka* in] my Newar manuscript. But based on the *śloka*, Yāgaṃdhara and Sādhara are provided here.

[2] "On this continent is placed the mantra—" is an addition made by SG.

In the southern direction:

raṃ jambudvīpāya namaḥ: With the arising of the letter RAṂ, there is Jambudvīpa. If it is asked how this Jambudvīpa is—*trikoṇa*—it is triangular. *unaṃśatasahasayojanavṛtatrimāna*. It is nineteen thousand *yojanas* in circumference. In the middle of that Jambudvīpa, there is a Jambu Tree called "Jambuvṛkṣa." If it is asked how this tree is—*śatayojana ucavṛtamāna*—it is one hundred *yojanas* tall. The branches of that tree—*dviyojanaveṣṭana*—are spread out over two *yojanas*. Such is that Jambu Tree.

On this continent is placed the mantra—*ra aśvaratnāya namaḥ*. With the arising of the letter RA, there is the horse called the "Aśva Ratna." If it is asked how that horse is—*śyāmavarṇa*—it is dark blue in colour. Its neck is like a treasury—i.e., it has a garland of a treasury of gems. It is able to swim the ocean in one day and one night. Such is that horse, who is called the Horse Gem.

In the western direction:

laṃ aparagodāvaye namaḥ With the arising of the letter LAṂ, there is the continent called Aparagodāyanīya. If it is asked how this continent is: It is six thousand *yojanas* in circumference and is a square shape. In the middle of the continent called Aparagodāyanīya is a—*plakṣavṛkṣa*—white fig tree (*Ficus virens*). If it is asked how this tree is—*satayojana ucca vṛtamāna*—it is one hundred *yojanas* tall, and the branches of that tree—*dviyojanaveṣṭana*—are spread out over two *yojanas*. Such is that white fig tree.

On this continent is placed the mantra—*la puruṣaratnāya namaḥ*. With the arising of the letter LA, there is the person called the Man Gem. If it is asked how this person is: He is of golden colour and endowed with the thirty-two marks. Wearing clothes of embroidered cloth, he wears a garland of a treasury of gems. He is able to swim the ocean in one day and night. Such is the one called the Man Gem.

In the northern direction:

vaṃ uttarakurubhye namaḥ: With the arising of the letter VA, there is the continent called Kurubhuvana (i.e. abode of the Kurus). If it is asked how this continent is: It is three thousand *yojana*s in circumference and is a square shape. In the middle of the continent called Kurubhuvana is a—*kadaṃbavṛksa*—burflower tree (*Neolamarckia cadamba*). If it is asked how this burflower tree is—*satayojana ucca vṛtamāna*—it is one hundred *yojana*s tall, and the branches of that tree—*dviyojanaveṣṭana*—are spread out over two *yojana*s. Such is that burflower tree.

On this continent is placed the mantra—*vaṃ strīratnāya namaḥ*. With the arising of the letter VA, there is the woman called the Woman Gem. If it is asked how this woman is, she is of the colour of ghee and endowed with the thirty-two marks. She wears a garland of a treasury of gems. Wearing clothes of embroidered cloth, her front teeth are slightly protruding. Such is that Woman Gem.

In the southeastern direction:

yā upadvīpāya namaḥ: With the arising of the letter YĀ, there is one of [those landmasses] called an "island" [i.e. an *upadvīpa*, as opposed to a continent, *dvīpa*].[3] If it is asked where this island is—*pūrvadakṣiṇasya ardha*—it takes up a *yojana* between the eastern and southern directions. On this island is placed the mantra—[4]*yā khaḍgaratnāya namaḥ*. With the arising of the letter

[3] Less literally, this formula can just be translated: "With the arising of the letter X, there is an island."

[4] "On this island is placed the mantra" is a substitution for "In the middle of this island".

YAṀ, there is the sword Candrahāsa, which cuts the mass of [cognitive] stains, and is called the "Sword Gem."

In the southwestern direction:

rā upadvīpāya namaḥ: With the arising of the letter RĀ, there is one of [those landmasses] called an "island." If it is asked where this island is—*dakṣiṇapaścimasya ardha*—it takes up a *yojana* between the southern and western directions. On this island is placed the mantra—*rā cakraratnāya namaḥ*. With the arising of the letter RĀ, there is the wheel which has eighty-four spokes, which is of red copper, and cuts the mass of faults and stains.

In the northwestern direction:

lā upadvīpāya namaḥ: With the arising of the letter LĀ, there is one of [those landmasses] called an "island." This island—*paścimottarasya ardha*—takes up a *yojana* between the western and northern directions. On this island is placed the mantra—*lā maṇiratnāya naṃaḥ*. With the arising of the letter LĀ, there is the gem called the Jewel (i.e., *maṇi*). If it is asked how this Jewel is: if it is bundled in a red cloth and placed in the ocean, it would turn that whole ocean red. If bundled in a green cloth and placed in the ocean, it would turn that whole ocean green. Whatever colour the cloth is in which it is bundled, if placed in the ocean, it will turn it that colour. Such is the Jewel Gem.

In the northeastern direction:

vā upadvīpāya namaḥ:[5] With the arising of the letter VĀ, there is one of [those landmasses] called an "island." *uttarapūrvasya ardha*—It takes up a *yojana* between the northern and eastern

---

[5] The mantra "*vā upadvīpāya namaḥ*" does not appear in the original, but it obviously belongs here. Instead the mantra "*vā sarvanidhānāya namaḥ*" appears, which we have relocated later in the paragraph to its appropriate place in the description.

directions. On this island is placed the mantra—*vā sarvanidhānāya namaḥ*. With the arising of the letter VĀ, there is the vase, which is the Receptacle of All. If it is asked how this vase is, only one drop of water from this vase can decrease and eliminate the faults committed in one's past lives. Whatever one longs for will be granted. Such is the vase called the Receptacle of All.

Such is the Sumeru Maṇḍala.

Thus concludes the Maṇḍala. Written on the 6th of Āṣaḍha, N.S. 1035 (1914 CE), at Roja 2.

---

i. Alex Wayman, *Yoga of the Guhyasamājatantra*. pp. 113.

+ The following are notes based on what is written in an old manuscript of mine. Since it is not contemporary Newar, it has been simplified.

Appendix C

15 Steps for Summoning and Propitiating a Deity in Guru Maṇḍala

प्यंगू दिशास प्यंगू रत्न

॥ १२॥ ओँ यँ गज रत्नाय नमः ॥ पूर्व द्विपेस गजरत्न।

॥ १३॥ ओँ रँ अश्व रत्नाय नमः ॥ दक्षिण अश्वरत्ने ।

॥ १४॥ ओँ लँ पुरुष रत्नाय नमः ॥ पश्चिमे पुरुषरत्न ।

॥ १५॥ ओँ वँ स्त्री रत्नाय नमः ॥ उत्तरे स्त्रीरत्न ।

प्यंगू कोणस प्यंगू रत्न

॥ १६॥ ओँ या चक्ररत्नाय नमः ॥ अग्नेय उप-द्विपे चक्ररत्न ।

॥ १७॥ ओँ रा खड्गरत्नाय नमः। । नैऋत्य उप-द्विपे खड्गारत्न ।

॥ १८॥ ओँ ला मणिरत्नाय नमः ॥ वायुव्ये उप-द्विपे मणिरत्न।

॥ १९॥ ओँ वा सर्व्वनिधानेभ्यो नमः ॥ इशाने उप- द्विपे सर्व्वनिधान कलशः ।

चन्द्रमा व सूर्य

॥ २०॥ चँ चन्द्राय नमः ॥ जवस चन्द्र मण्डल ।

॥ २१॥ सुँ सूर्याय नमः ॥ खवस सूर्य्य मण्डल ।

वज्रसत्व गुरुयात

ओँ आः हूँ श्री वज्रसत्व गुरुभ्यो नमः ॥ मध्यस गुरु मण्डल ।

४. **पञ्चोपचार पूजा**

१. ओँ वज्र पुष्पे स्वाहा ।

२. ओँ वज्र धूपे स्वाहा ।

३. ओँ वज्र दीपे स्वाहा ।

४. ओँ वज्र गन्धे स्वाहा ।

५. ओँ वज्र नैवेद्य स्वाहा ।

५. **मण्डलयात कथहनं विधिवत् भावना पूजा**

१ **स्वां छफो गुरुमण्डलय् छायेगु**

भगवन श्री गुरुमण्डल पूजानिमित्यर्थ स्वभावशुद्धाः सर्वधर्माः स्वभावशुद्धोऽ हम् शून्यताज्ञानवज्र स्वभावात्मकोऽ हम् ॥

२. **धूं च्याकाः आवाहन यायेगु**
भगवन् श्री रत्नमण्डल सद्वज्रविद्याराजं नमोस्तुते
कर्तुमिच्छामि ते नाथ मण्डलं करुणात्मकम् ॥
शिष्याणामनुकम्पार्थ युष्माकं पूजनाय च
तन्मे भक्तस्य भगवन् प्रसादं कर्तुमर्हसि ॥
समन्वाहरन्तु मां बुद्धा जगदर्थक्रियार्थदाः
फलस्था बोधिसत्वाश्च याश्चान्या मन्त्रदेवताः ॥
देवता लोकपालाश्च भूताः सम्बोधिसाधिताः
शासनाभिरताः सत्वाः ये केचिद् वज्रचक्षुषः ॥
(पूजायाम्हं थःगु नां ब्वने) महावज्रीदयोदयमण्डलम्
करिष्यामि जगच्छुद्धै र्यथाशक्त्युपचारतः ॥
अनुकम्पामुपादाय सशिष्यस्य च तन्मम
मण्डले सहिता सर्वे सान्निध्यं कर्तुमर्हथ ॥
ओँ आः हूँ वज्रधूपं निर्यातयामि वज्रधूपं प्रतीच्छ स्वाहा ॥

३. **निमन्त्रणा- जाकी ज्वना विनति याये**
अद्य मे सफलं जन्म सफलं जीवितं च मे
समये सर्वदेवानां भविताहं न शंसयः ॥
अवैवर्ती भविष्यामि बोधिचित्तैकचेतसा
तथागत कुलोत्पत्ति भव ममा ह्यस्यान्नसंशयः ॥
अग्रो मे दिवसो ह्यद्य यज्ञो मेद्य ह्यनुत्तरः
सन्निपातो भवेदद्य सर्वबुद्धनिमन्त्रणात् ॥
ओँ कुसुमाञ्जलिनाथ होः ॥

४. **जाकी छपुचः देपा ल्हातिं द्यःयान्त्यने तयाः जव ल्हातिं शंखं लः छतुलु तयेगु** (धाःमण्डल)
ओँ वज्रोदके हूं ॥ ओँ वज्रभूमौ सुरेखेसर्वतथागत अधिष्ठाना अधितिष्ठन्तु स्वाहा । ओँ वज्र सुवर्ण जलधारे स्वाहा ॥

५. सिन्ह तिकेगु

इदं ते परमं गन्धं पवित्रं घ्राणतर्पणम्
दादामि परमं भक्त्या प्रतिगृह्ण यथासुखम् ॥
सिन्दूरं सजलं शान्तं विचित्रं सुरसान्वितम्
निर्यातयाम्यहं प्रीत्या सर्वसिद्धिं प्रयच्छ मे ॥
ओँ वज्रगन्धे स्वाहा ॥
ओँ आः हूँ वज्रसिन्दूर तिलक भूषणे स्वाहा ॥

६. **जजंका क्वखायेकेगु**

ओँ वज्रवस्त्रालंकार पूजामेघ समुद्रस्फरण
यज्ञोपवीतं बोध्यंग दृढकवच वस्त्रवाससे स्वाहा ॥

७. **जाकिं पूजा याना स्वांछायेगु**

स्वस्ति वः कुरुतां बुद्धाः स्वस्ति देवाः सशक्रकाः
स्वस्ति सर्वाणि भूतानि सर्वकालं दिशन्तु वः ॥
बुद्धपुण्यानुभावेन देवतानां मतेन च
यो योर्थः समभिप्रेतः सर्वोर्थोद्य समृध्यताम् ॥
स्वस्ति वो द्विपदे भोन्तु स्वस्ति वोस्तु चतुष्पदे
स्वस्ति वो व्रजतां मार्गे स्वस्ति प्रत्यागतेषु च ॥
स्वस्तिं रात्रौ स्वस्ति दिवाः स्वस्ति मध्यदिने स्थिते
सर्वत्र स्वस्ति वो भोन्तु माचैषां पापमागमत् ॥
सर्वे सत्वाः सर्वे प्राणाः सर्वे भूताश्च केबलाः
सर्वे वै सुखिनः सन्तु सर्वे सन्तु निरामयाः ॥
सर्वे भद्राणि पश्यन्तु मा कश्चित् पापमागमत् ॥
यानीह भूतानि समागतानि स्थितानि भूमावथवान्तरिक्षे
कुर्वन्तु मैत्री सतत प्रजासु दिवा च रात्रौ च चरन्तु धर्मम् ॥
ओँ आः हूँ वज्रपुष्पं प्रतीच्छ स्वाहा ॥

८. होजा

ओं वज्र समयाचारं खाद्य भोज्यादिकं प्रभो महायान
षड्‌रस संयुक्तं वर्णगन्ध रसोपेत प्रतिगृन्ह यथासुखम ।

९. नैवेद्य

ओं नैवेद्य सर्व संयुक्त खाद्यभोज्य समन्वितम् ।
वर्णगन्धरसोपेतं प्रतिगृन्ह यथासुखम् ॥
ओं वज्र नैवेद्यं प्रतीच्छ स्वाहा ॥

१०. फल फूल छायेगु

ओं सर्ववित् आदर्शनफलाय स्वाहा ॥

११. पेय पदार्थ

क. **सादुदु छायेगु**

ओं सर्व बोधिचिन्तामृत जल धारे स्वाहा ॥

ख. **पेय पदार्थ (मद्य)**

ओं नमो भगवते वीरंवीरेश्वराय हूँ हूँ फट् स्वाहा ॥
ओं नमो महाकल्पाग्नि सन्निभाय हूँ हूँ फट् स्वाहा ॥
ओं नमो जटामकुटोत्कटाय हूँ हूँ फट् स्वाहा ॥
ओं नमो द्रंष्ट्राकरालोग्रभीषणमुखाय हूँ हूँ फट् स्वाहा ॥
ओं नमो सहस्रभुजभासुराय हूँ हूँ फट् स्वाहा ॥
ओं नमो परशुपाशत्रिशूलखट्वाङ्गधराय हूँ हूँ फट् स्वाहा ॥
ओं नमो व्याघ्रचर्म्माम्बरधराय हूँ हूँ फट् स्वाहा ॥
ओं नमो महाधूमान्धकारायवपुषाय हूँ हूँ फट् स्वाहा ॥

१२. मत बियेगु

नेत्राभिरामा बहुरत्नकोषा
नराधिपैरर्चित पादपद्माः
ज्ञानप्रदीपा हतमोहज्वाला
ये दीपमाला रचयन्ति तत्र ।
ओं आः वज्रदीपे ह्रीं प्रतीच्छ स्वाहा ॥

१३. तायें 'पूजा यायेगु

ये धर्मा हेतु प्रभवा हेतुस्तेषां तथागतो ह्यवदत्
तेषां च यो निरोध एवंवादी महाश्रमणः॥

१४. जाकी स्वां व लः तया पूजा यायेगु

ओं अकारो मुखसर्वधर्माणामाद्यनुत्पन्नत्वात्
ओं आः हूँ फट् स्वाहा॥

१५. दक्षिणा

मञ्जुश्रिये कुमार भूताय बोधिसत्वाय महासत्वाय
महाकारुणिकाय तण्डुल देवदक्षिणां सम्प्रढोषयाम्यहम्॥

६. **घण्टवादन याना रत्न मण्डल अर्पण यायेगु जाकी (स्वां लः तया मण्डलय् हायेकेगु)–**

चतुरत्न मयमेरु अष्टद्वीप शोभितं,
नाना रत्न समाकिरण तद्दनुत्तंर दायिने
गुरुभ्यो बुद्धः धर्मेभ्यः संघेभ्यश्च
निर्यातयामि भावेन सम्पूर्ण रत्न मण्डलम।

(गुरु मण्डलय् रत्न मण्डलया ज्या क्वःचाल)

७. **गुरु मण्डल : गुरु दर्शन**

गुरु दर्शन - जाकी ज्वनाः विन्ति याये वाक्य ब्वने क्वचायेवं आकाश पाखे पूजायाना छ्वये

ओं आः हूँ श्रीमत् वज्रसत्व गुरु वर चरण कमलाय्
सम्यक् ज्ञान भाष्कराय् नमोस्तुते हूँ नमो नमः
भगवत्यां त्वां नमस्यामि श्री गुरुनाथ प्रसिद्धये।

८. **शीलग्रहण (हानं जाकी ज्वना विन्ति याये)**

यस्य प्रसाद किरणै स्फरितात्मतत्व॥

Glossary

Ādi Buddha: This term refers to the primordial who exists before the generation of the saṃsāric universe, and is self-born (*svayaṃbhū*). Thus, it is another term for the formless and ineffable Dharmakāya (Dharma-body) in the Trikāya scheme. Chapter 4 of the *Guṇakāraṇḍavyūha* specifies that the world arises through the meditation of the Ādi Buddha. While ultimately one and contiguous with the cosmos, his creative and compassionate virtues are manifested and personified in the form of the five buddhas (*pañcabuddha*) on the Vajradhātu and Dharmadhātu maṇḍalas, who each have different forms and specialities corresponding with the elements of the world and the body.

Bhāvanā: *Bhāvanā* is a loanword from Sanskrit, from the Sanskrit root for the verb "to be", √bhū. It literally means to generate something, that is, to bring something into being. It is used to refer to meditation in Sanskrit yogic literature, since when one meditates one brings states of mind, visualizations, and other mental phenomena into being. It can refer to meditative visualization in Newar, and also to feelings and emotions that come into being. Often when discussing ritual Yagyaman Pati uses *bhāvanā* in a sense to mean both mental cultivation and creation of something, and it is left ambiguous as to whether a visualization is occurring or that something is simply created. It can also refer to the generation of oneself as a deity through meditative visualization and self-identification with that deity. The meaning of the word as meditation and/or imagination is reinforced by the Newar *bhāḥpāḥ*, which is directly derived from *bhāvanā* and refers to thought generally.

Dīkṣā: In a Newar Buddhist context, all tantric Buddhist authority to practice (ādhikāra) is bestowed upon the practitioner by the guru in an initiation. The term that Newar Buddhists translate to English is "*dekhā*", derived from Sanskrit *dīkṣā*. These *dīkṣās*, which always include a *kalaśābhiṣeka* (water pot consecration) are analogous to Tibetan *dbang* (empowerment, pronounced "wāng") rituals. The terminology, "*dīkṣā*", is curious given the Śaiva associations that term brings to mind, and at time of writing no scholarly research has been undertaken to explore the Newar Buddhist *dīkṣā* rites and their (apparent) peculiarity among Newars.

Paramparā: *Paramparā* is a word that has different but similar meanings depending on the language and context in which it is used. We translate it as both "lineage" and "tradition." Its dependence on context can be as specific as two different clauses in a single sentence. In both Newar and Nepali it most commonly refers to a tradition in the general sense, a set of cultural practices and norms that are passed down generationally. The word "*saṃskṛti*" has a similar valence of ambiguity, as it too may mean "tradition" in Newar or Nepali, but may also be translated as "culture" as context demands. In Sanskrit *paramparā* refers to a lineage in a strict sense, a practice and set of knowledge passed down individually from a guru to a disciple. But this could also be accurately translated as "tradition," depending on context. Yagyaman Pati uses both meanings of *paramparā* with the meaning directly related to the statement containing the word. He most commonly uses the more esoteric, Sanskrit meaning of *paramparā* as a tantric lineage passed from guru to disciple. However, there are some instances where the most appropriate translation of *paramparā* is tradition. For example, we translate "Tripitaka Paramparā" as "Tripitaka Tradition" since Śrāvakayānist forms of Buddhism do not place central importance on the guru as the transmitter of the tradition such that Vajrayāna does.

Prajñā: *Prajñā* is a technical term in Mahāyāna Buddhism that refers to liberative wisdom. A direct translation of the Sanskrit *prajñā* is "wisdom," but this English term fails to capture the meaning pregnant in *prajñā*. An entire corpus of sutras, the Perfection of Wisdom (*Prajñāpāramitā*) is dedicated to expounding the information one must understand to gain *prajñā*. There is no awakening without *prajñā*.

Pūjā: *Pūjā* is a word originally from Sanskrit that refers to any kind of ritualized worship, ranging in complexity from lighting a small butter lamp to multi-day rituals involving dozens of participants. *Pūjā* is the standard term in all South Asian religions for such ritual worship.

Ritual Client: This is a translation of Newar *jajmān* from the Sanskrit *yajamāna*. The *jajmān* (or *jajmāns*) is the patron of a ritual, the person for whom the ritual is being performed. The sponsor of the ritual, the *jajmān*(s) receives the merit that the ritual generates. In traditional Newar Buddhism *only* those born into the *vajrācārya* caste (*jāti*) may perform rituals on behalf of *jajmāns*.

Tīrtha: A *tīrtha* is a kind of sacred pilgrimage site in both Buddhism and Hinduism. The technical referent of the word *tīrtha* is where two rivers converge. There are plenty of examples of *tīrtha*s that are not river confluences, but in the Newar Buddhist context *tīrtha*s tend to be located at river confluences. Traditionally there is a set of 12 *tīrtha*s in the Kathmandu Valley. The exact sites of the set can vary. For example, there is a set of 12 *tīrtha*s connected to the goddess Vasundharā. There is another set of 12 *tīrtha*s delineated in the Buddhist Svayambhū Purāṇa. There is yet another set of 12 *tīrtha*s corresponding to four *stūpa*s, four Lokeśvara images and four *yoginī* images.

Vrat: *Vrat* is a word originally from the Sanskrit *vrata*, meaning vow. In the Newar Buddhist context, a *vrat* is a practice done occasionally that involves mandatory fasting. The *vrat* has two primary elements: the participant(s) vows to undertake a particular ritual practice according to a set procedure and the participant observes a fast during the duration of the *vrat*. Fasting is undertaken for the sake of ritual purity. Since all consumables are seen as ultimately polluting due to their being made of gross matter, the conclusion is that the best way to stay pure for the duration of a ritual is to abstain from eating or drinking (except medicine and sometimes water) from when a ritual participant wakes up on the day of the ritual *vrat* until the ritual is fully completed. At this point those fasting will break their fast with *prasāda* from the ritual, which is typically followed by a more substantial group meal.

Index

A

abhiṣeka xxi, 125, 161
ācārya / master 10–11, 35, 38, 41, 44, 49, 59–61, 65, 80–82, 95–96, 104, 172
ādhikārika / ritual authorization 29
Advayasiddhi xxxiv, 37, 40–41, 54, 65, 74
Advayavajra / Maitrīpā xxxiv, 23–24, 60–61, 176–180, 184
Advayavajrasaṃgraha 26, 60, 113, 177–178, 184
Agni /fire element 106, 146, 148
ajñāna / ignorance 5
Āḷāra Kālāma 28, 31, 33, 48
Amoghapāśa (maṇḍala) xxvi, 109
Amṛtakuṇḍalī 150, 166–167
Anaṅgayogī / Anaṅgavajra 72
Anuttara-yoga-tantra 31
Apabhraṃśa 52, 55
Aparagodāvarīya (continent) 131
Apte, Vaman Shivram 25
Ārolik 116
Āryadeva xxxiv, 41, 170
Asaṅga 89, 171
aṣṭamī vrat (var. poṣadha) xxxi
Aśvaghoṣa 12, 59
Avalokiteśvara xxi, 161
avidyā / delusion 5

B

bali bhāvanā (spirit offering) (pp. 42-151) 142
Bhadracārī
bharāṇḍo / *bhāro* 9
Bhattacarya, Benoytosh 37, 54
bhāvanā / generation 59, 122, 142, 156, 161, 165–167, 209–210
bhikṣu
Ānanda 21, 34
Upagupta 21
Jayaśrī 21
Śārīputra / Śārīputta / Upatissa 67–68
Mahākaśyāpa / Mahākassapa 36

Nāgasena 61
Maudgalyāyana 66, 68
Bhojmanpati Bajracharya xiv–xv, xvii
bodhicitta 104, 140, 178
bodhisattva vow xxi, 161, 167
"*buddho bhaveyaṃ jagato hitāya*" 138, 140, 178
praṇidhāna 8, 166
Bū Bāhāḥ 75
Buddha Maṇḍala 19, 101, 130
buddhakula 85–86
buddhaṃ śaraṇaṃ gacchāmi 16–17

cakra 105–107, 134
Cakrasaṃvara (maṇḍala) 101, 108
Caryāmelāpakapradīpa 41
caryānṛtya / tantric dance xix, xxii, xxiv–xxv
Chittadhar Hṛdaya xxxii
COVID-19 xxvi, xxx
cūḍā karma (var. *cūḍākarma*) xvii, 28–29, 156–157

D

darśan 28, 67–68, 165, 169, 176
David Snellgrove xxxv
Dharma xix–xx, xxiii–xxxv, 10, 13–14, 16–22, 27–28, 30, 34, 43, 45, 49, 53, 73, 77, 101, 105–106, 110, 113, 121, 123–124, 130, 136, 139–141, 178, 191, 209
Dharma Maṇḍala 19, 101, 130
Dharmadhātu Vāgīśvara 104, 109
Dharmakīrti 55, 69, 89
dharmaṃ śaraṇaṃ gacchāmi 18, 19
Dharmaśrīmitra 77, 104, 109
Dhīḥ xiii, 55, 69, 83, 97
dīkṣā/ *dekhā* xviii, xxii–xxiii, xxvi, 29, 86–88, 93–94, 103, 161, 210
Dohākoṣa 44
Ḍombī Heruka 43, 90
Durgatipariṣodha (maṇḍala) 109
Dveṣarati (*tārā*) 117

E

Eightfold Path 176
Elephant (Gem) 194, 198

F

Facebook xi, xxx
fire ritual / *hotra* xix
Five *pāramitā*s (dāna, śīla, kṣānti, vīrya, dhyāna, prajñā) 127–128
Five *tārā*s (Māmakī, Locanī, Padmīnī, Tārā, Prajñāpāramitā) 123

G

gambhīr / profound 30
Gaṇa Maṇḍala 42
Ganges River 15, 123
garbhin / gestation 30
Graha (maṇḍala) 109
Guhyasiddhi 38–40, 54, 76–77, 81, 84, 173, 183–184
Guhyādi-Aṣṭasiddhisaṃgraha 25, 54, 69, 84, 97, 183–184

Guñlā xiii
gurukula 85–86
Gurupañcāśikā 12
guthi 88–89

H

Hāḍābharaṇa (dohā song) 41, 50–52, 76
Hinduism 211
Horse (Gem) 194, 199

I

Indrabhūti xxxv, 13, 25, 37–38, 41, 43, 45, 54–55, 65, 68–69, 73, 76, 82, 90, 93
Īrṣyārati (*tārā*) 117

J

Jagaddarpaṇa (var. Darpaṇa) 59–60, 65, 95–96, 101, 104, 175–177, 184
jajmān / patron 182, 211
Jamal Bāhāḥ xvi, xxv–xxvi, xxxi
Jambudvīpa (continent) 53, 131, 199
jāt / caste xxxiii
Jinajik 116
Jñānasiddhi xxxiv, 13, 37–39, 41, 43, 45, 54–55, 65, 68–69, 77, 82
jungle 4, 6
Jvalitavajrānala 76

K

kalaśa (var. *kalaś*) / water jar viii, xxi, xxiv, 161
Kasthamandap / Kaṣṭhamaṇḍapa xiv, xxii, xxvii, xxvii–xxix, xxxi
Kriyāsaṃgraha 174–175, 177, 181
Kriyāsaṃgrahakārikā 177
Kriyāsamuccaya vi, xxxii–xxxiii, xxxv, xxxvii, 10, 24, 59–60, 65, 69, 88, 94–96, 101, 104, 119–120, 175–178, 180–181, 187–188

L

Lakṣmīṃkarā 37, 40–41, 43, 52, 65, 74, 90
Life cycle rites (pp. 156-159) 85
Līlāvajra xiv, xxxiv–xxxv, 41, 43, 46, 50–52, 74, 76, 90, 93–94, 97, 133, 172

M

Mahākāla (maṇḍala) 110
mahāsiddha xxxv, 133
Man (Gem) xix–xx, xxxii, 194, 199–200
Mañjuśrī 59, 77, 94, 104, 109, 195
Mañjuśrīnāmasaṃgītī (var. *Nāmasamgītī*) 52, 54, 104, 109
mha pūjā 74–75
Milindapāñha xxxiv, 61
Moharati (*tārā*) 117
mudrā 22, 119, 145, 173

N

Nāropā xxxiv
Newar rituals for clients 155, 163
nirvāṇa xxi, 12, 66, 142, 161
Nispannayogāvalī / Abhayākaragupta 101, 105, 174, 175

P

Padmanṛteśvara xxii
Padmāntaka 105, 117
Padmasaṃbhava 73
Padmavajra 37–40, 54, 76–77, 84, 90, 93, 171, 173
Pali Canon xii
Pañcarakṣā (maṇḍala) xx, 110, 178
pāpadeśanā (confession of sins) 166
paramparā / lineage v, xxxv, 85–89, 94, 97, 210–211
paubhāḥ 118–119
phalatantra 194
Piṇḍikā (maṇḍala) 110
Pradīpodyotana 119, 194
prajñā / wisdom xxxiii–xxxiv, 24, 52, 165, 211
Prajñā Devī 49–51
Prajñādhṛk 116
Prajñāntaka 105, 117
Prajñopāyaviniścayasiddhi / Anaṅgapāda 37, 76, 79–81
pratiṣṭhā (ritual installation) xxiv, xxviii
Pṛthvī / earth element 106, 143
Pūrṇimā / Full moon 13
purohita / preceptor xiv, xvii, xix, 162
Pūrvavideha (continent) 130, 132, 190, 198

R

Rāgarati (*tārā*) 117
Rājagṛha 32, 66
Ratnadhṛk 116
Ratna Maṇḍala vi, viii, xxxiii, xxxvii, 13, 110, 119, 122, 132, 135–136, 161, 165, 176, 183, 191, 193–195
Raviśrījñāna 52, 55

S

Sādhanamālā 54, 90, 97, 183–184
sagaṃ 75
sahaja 50, 52
Śākyamuni Buddha (var. Bhagavān Buddha; var. Gautama Buddha) xxxiv, 109
Saṃdhivyākaraṇa 103
Samgha xxiv, xxxiv, 13–14, 19–22, 45, 101, 117, 121, 124, 130, 136
Saṃgha Maṇḍala 19, 21, 101, 130
saṃghaṃ śaraṇaṃ gacchāmi 21
saṃyak-saṃbodhi / total awakening 12, 31, 50
Saptavidhānottara pūjā (var. *saptavidhānuttar*) 161
Sarnath (var. Sāranātha) 12, 48
Sarvārthasiddhi (var. Siddhartha Gautama) 47
śāstra / knowledge system 35, 94, 103

Shree Dhar Rana Rinpoche xxxi
Śikamū Bāhāḥ xiv, xxii
śikṣā 47, 57, 87
Śrīpuṣpaketu Rājā 126
stūpa xxiii–xxv
Sumeru 135–136, 143, 180, 189, 195–197, 202
sūtra
  Gaṇḍavyūha 16, 19, 123
  Daśabhūmika 19, 123
  Samādhirāja 19, 123
  Laṅkāvatāra 19, 123
  Saddharmapuṇḍarikā 19, 123
  Tathāgataguhya 19, 123
  Lalitavistara 19, 47, 123
  Prajñāpāramitā 8, 19, 123, 211
  Suvarṇaprabhāsa 19, 123
svabhāva / self-existent 30
Svayambhū mahācaitya xv–xvi, xxiii, xxv, 118, 158
Svayambhū Purāṇa 77, 212
syllable (semi-vowel)
  YAṂ 133, 143
  RAṂ 133, 143
  LAṂ 133, 143
  VAṂ 128, 133
  YĀ 132, 134, 200
  RĀ 132, 134, 200
  LĀ 132, 134, 201
  VĀ 132, 134, 201-202
  YA 128
  RA 128
  LA 128
  VA 128

T

tantra
  Guhyasamāja xxxv, 88–89, 97, 102–106, 110, 114–116, 120, 171, 194, 202
  Cakrasamvara 115, 118
  Hevajra 24, 171
  Kālacakra 105–106, 109
  Caṇḍamahāroṣaṇa 88
tantric song 43
Tārā (maṇḍala) 110
Tattvaratnāvalī 60–61
The Blue Annals xxxv, 94, 96–97, 104, 176
Theravāda xxi, xxvi, xxxi, xxxiv, 28, 32, 53
Three Jewels (var. Triple Gem) xxxiii, 139–140
Tibetans xxiii
Tilopā xxxiv, 91–92
Tipiṭaka 35, 53

U

Udraka Rāmaputra 28, 31, 33
upāya 18
Uṣṇiṣavijaya Maṇḍala 109
utkrānti 110
Uttarakuru (continent) 131, 133

V

vaidya xiv
Vaidya, Āśākājī 11
vajrācārya xii, xv, xix, xxi, xxiv, xxxiii–xxxiv, xxxvi, 10–12, 59–60, 89, 156–158, 160, 162, 163, 171, 182, 211

Vajradhara / *vajra*-holder 14, 22, 77–78, 94–95, 121, 136, 176
Vajradṛk 116
Vajragīti 44
Vajramayabhūmi 76
Vajrarati (*tārā*) 117
Vajrasattva xxxiv, 14, 22–25, 43, 122–124, 129, 136–137, 141, 151–153, 165, 170, 176, 181–183, 190, 196
Vajrāvali 174–175
Vajravarāhī (maṇḍala) 101, 108, 110, 115, 118
Varuṇa / water element 106, 145, 148, 196
Vasundharā (maṇḍala) 109, 212
Vāyu / wind element 106, 146, 148
vidyā / magical spell 15, 57
Vighnāntaka 105, 117
visarjana / dismissal xxxviii, 153, 167
Vyaktabhāvānugatatattvasiddhi 43, 55

W

Wayman, Alex 102, 110, 202
Woman (Gem) 194, 200

Y

Yamāntaka 105, 117
Yamuna River 43
ye dharmā hetu 67
Yoginī Cintā 43, 55, 65
Yogīśvara 44

Z

Zoom xxx